STUDIES IN PSALMS

BY

ROBERT R. TAYLOR, JR.

QUALITY PUBLICATIONS
P.O. BOX 7385
FT. WORTH, TX 76111
(800) 359-7708

ISBN: 0-89137-560-0

DEDICATION

This book is affectionately dedicated to Phil Davis who has just begun to preach during the 1980's. He is one of the brightest, best, and most talented of our younger preachers. He excells as a song director and is already an excellent writer. His earlier calling was in architecture. Now he has entered a higher and nobler calling as he seeks to build men and women, boys and girls into vessels of honor and service for the Master's Cause. The building he now does reaches not just up and out into this world but up, out, and into the very mansions of eternity. Phil is my son-in-law having married my beloved Rebecca on April 9, 1983. He currently preaches for the South Woodward congregation in Oklahoma City, Oklahoma.

FOREWORD

The beautiful book of Psalms has been called "The Songbook of the Bible." It is truly unique in that the psalms may be sung or read and neither method of contemplation detracts in the least from their overall beauty or vast value. Whether its precious psalms are sung, as the Israelite people were accustomed to doing, or read as we most likely are to do in their contemplation, they are beautiful to behold, profitable to peruse, comforting to consider, challenging in contents, thrilling to the spiritual taste buds, reinvigorating to those who rejoice and full of solace to the sorrowful. The Psalms have the unique ability to touch and tender every known chord of the human heart.

Sixteen previous volumes have come from my pen across the years. This seventeenth one has been a rewarding joy to spend the hundreds and hundreds of hours that have gone into the research behind this present volume and the actual composition of this literary endeavor. Adequate expressions escape me in conveying the fullness of gratitude to Benny Whitehead and Quality Publications for the invitation, unsolicited on my part and all that much more appreciated, to pen this book, STUDIES IN PSALMS. For the past two years it has been a work of faith and a labor of love.

Naturally, a limitation of pages had to be placed upon a book of this type. There was no way I could give an exposition of each chapter and verse as I have done in writing brief commentaries on about half the books of the New Testament. There are 150 chapters, 2,461 verses and 43,743 words in the Book of Psalms. Even two pages per chapter would have run well beyond the limitation of pages proposed by the publisher. Psalm 117, the shortest of all the psalms, would have been about the only one that two pages could have done a measure of justice to it. An entire volume could be written on just Psalm 119, the longest chapter in Psalms and also the longest in the Bible. If the Lord allows me enough time on earth, I hope to do a future volume on just Psalm 119. Therefore, some feasible plan had to be made. I decided to divide the work into two major divisions. The first major section of thirteen chapters deals with some great chapters in the book with a verse-by-verse exposition except for Psalm 119 where highlights are touched and many of its great verses are noted. The second major section of thirteen chapters deals with great topics suggested and elaborated upon within Psalms. The volume closes with some living lessons learned from this study. By deliberate design the book is divided into twenty-six chapters which will make for a six months' study for those who wish to use it in class work. With that view in mind a variety of questions concludes each chapter. The book has also been written for individual study also.

Many, many sources have been consulted freely for the composition of this volume. I am indebted to all of them. The Gospel Advocate Quarterlies by brother Guy N. Woods and the Annual Commentaries by a number of authors have been of inestimable aid as they have written on various of the psalms from time to time. Brother Hugo McCord's fine chapter in THE LIVING MESSAGES OF THE BOOKS OF THE OLD TESTAMENT dealing with the Book of Psalms was of great value. This was the second annual Spiritual Sword Lectureship.

A great debt of thanks is always due my faithful helpmeet, Irene, for her constant encouragement in ALL my writing endeavors. Likewise, I owe a continuing debt to a great congregation of God's people, the Ripley church of Christ in Ripley, Tennessee, and to its fine eldership composed of C. Fred Faulk and Everett Presson who allow me time to do such works as STUDIES IN PSALMS. They let me do the true and real work of an evangelist (2 Timothy 4:5) and this means I am not constantly bogged down with incidentals but can spend time in study, research, etc., for preaching, teaching, counseling, lecturing and writing. I know of NO congregation like them in this regard in ALL our brotherhood. Above all I am grateful to the Sublime Three for granting me health of mind, consecration of spirit and strength of body to begin and conclude the monumental task of penning STUDIES IN PSALMS.

It is my sincere hope and continuing prayer that this volume may do much good and no harm at all as long as it stays in print or is read. This has been the tone and tenor of its composition in every chapter, every page, every paragraph, every sentence, every word and even every syllable.

January 3, 1986   Robert R. Taylor, Jr.
Ripley, Tennessee

TABLE OF CONTENTS

CHAPTER ONE

PSALMS INTRODUCED AND OUTLINED

Psalms is perhaps the best loved and most frequently quoted book in the Old Testament. It is quoted more often in the New Testament than any of its thirty-eight literary colleagues in the first major section of God's Divine Library. With this chapter we begin a thrilling journey of STUDIES IN PSALMS. The first half of our study will center on great chapters in these precious psalms; the second half will cover thrilling themes from throughout the book. Introductory matters of crucial interest first focus before us.

THE TITLE OF THE BOOK

In the KJV it is simply and stately titled, "The Book of Psalms." Students of Holy Writ frequently refer to it as "The Psalms of David" due to his personal composition of so many of them and his ordering others to be penned.

Since the book initially was penned in the Hebrew language and we read its courageous contents in the beloved English language, it will be of interest to connect the book with both Hebrew and English. Ancient Hebrews entitled this beautiful book as *Tehillim*. This meant "Praises" and we can promptly relate to the accurate link between title and the scope of the Scriptural sentiments that both pervade and permeate this book. In English the title derives from the Greek title, *Psalmoi*. The meaning is "Psalms." Put the two stately sentiments together and one has "Psalms of Praise." Again and again we shall

1

focus literary attention upon the precious praises that inhere these stately songs of an ancient age. By way of earned tribute the Book of Psalms has been styled "The Songbook of the Bible."

THE AUTHORSHIP OF THE BOOK

The Holy Spirit is the heavenly author of all of them. But we now speak of the human penmen he employed in their composition. It would be an inexcusable mistake to present a surface sentiment and say that all one hundred and fifty of the Psalms are the work of the Shepherd King. He penned many of them. Some students have said sixty-eight, some seventy-three and some eighty-eight. It seems safe to say that he penned about half or more of the entire number. A number are attributed to him directly. Some are left with no attributed author either at the beginning or anywhere in the actual psalm. No doubt he penned a number of these left without names. Obviously, the entire work is of the Holy Spirit. God *originated* the truths set forth and the Holy Spirit *revealed* what is in the book. Paul affirms inspiration for all Scripture with one stately sweep of his prolific, powerful pen (2 Timothy 3:16). So does Peter in 2 Peter 1:21. With breathtaking beauty and stately simplicity David wrote, "The Spirit of the Lord spake by me, and his word was in my tongue" (2 Samuel 23:2).

Conservative Bible scholarship attributes some seventy-three to David, some twelve to Asaph, at least eight and perhaps as many as ten to the sons of Korah, one to Moses, two to Solomon, one to Ethan, one to Heman and almost fifty without an attributed human author. Though the inscriptions at the beginning of the various psalms are minus divine inspiration, yet they bear upon their bosom ancient age and reflect perhaps the first intense effort to delve deeply into the human authors employed by God's Spirit to pen this precious portion of the Heavenly Volume.

THE TIME ELEMENT OF THE PSALMS

In this aspect Psalms is unlike any other book of the Bible. Books like Genesis, some of the historical books of the Old Testament, John's Gospel record and 1 John cover many centuries in the sweep of their material and yet were all written in a relatively short time of actual composition. But Psalms was nearly a full millennium in its accumulating and ascending composition. Moses would have composed Psalm 90 nearly fifteen centuries before the birth of Jesus and the regal establishment of redemptive Christianity on earth. David and Solomon would have composed their respective parts either in the

2

eleventh or tenth centuries B.C. Psalms written during the Exile or shortly subsequent to such (Psalm 137 for instance) would have been penned in the sixth century B. C. Their resplendent perfection in running the entire gamut of all human experiences doubtless took time of long duration. We do know that the Holy Spirit so chose to compose the book from a position of literary longevity. Its earlier employed penmen died before later employed penmen were even born but death never laid claim to the guiding Spirit of Holiness who was behind the writing of every statement and syllable of the beautiful book. Its hoary age in actual composition adds immeasurably to the breathtaking beauty of this precious portion of Holy Writ.

ITS PROPER PLACE IN THE SACRED CANON

Psalms is *not* a New Testament book. This may surprise many people in view of the fact that many of the New Testaments now published have Psalms appended. But this is precisely what the book of Psalms is in such arrangements — an appendix or addition. Usually, it will be just subsequent to Revelation. No doubt this literary publishing arrangement has been done due to the striking popularity of Psalms and to give access to its great worshipful and praise content to those who purchase just a New Testament and not the entire Bible. But the New Testament is inclusive of only the twenty-seven books from Matthew through Revelation.

The book of Psalms was here long before a single syllable of the New Testament saw the light of literary day. Just subsequent to our Lord's baptism of John in Jordan as He stood upon the threshold of His personal ministry He met Satan in the Judaean Wilderness, on the temple pinnacle and upon the high mountain. In the second tempatation, as given by the inspired Matthew, Satan resorted to a Scriptural quotation. He gave it from Psalm 91:11,12. Obviously, he misused it and removed it from its overall context. Yet he could not have quoted from Psalms unless the book then existed in the permanency of writing. Yet at this time NO line of the New Testament had been penned and would not be for at least another fifteen to twenty years.

The Christ linked Psalms with the Mosaic Economy. To His aroused enemies in John 10:34-36 He declared, "Is it not written in your law, I said, Ye are gods? If he called them gods, unto whom the word of God came, and the scripture cannot be broken; Say ye of him, whom the Father hath sanctified, and sent into the world, Thou blasphemest; because I said, I am the Son of God?" Jesus here has His eye riveted on Psalm 82:6 which says, "I have said, Ye are gods; and all of you

3

are children of the most high." Note that Jesus quoted Psalms. Note further that He identified it as being in "your law." He was addressing the Jews. Hence, it is unequivocally the case that Psalms belongs to the Mosaic Covenant made with the descendants of Jacob (Deuteronomy 5:2-4) and is neither part nor parcel of the New Covenant. This is not to say that the book is minus all profit to us. Quite to the contrary, it is of intense importance to us but we are no more amenable to it as our binding law than we are to the Decalogue of Exodus 20 and Deuteronomy 5, the annual trips to Jerusalem for every male mentioned in Deuteronomy 16:16, animal sacrifices, temple worship in Jerusalem on Mount Moriah, the burning of incense, dependence upon a Levitical priesthood to officiate at God's altar of worship or a host of other mandates from Moses. We accept unreservedly the inspiration, the praise and worshipful content of Psalms, the predictive prophecies of the Messiah and all great lessons taught therein by precious principles. But this is far from affirming that we are now amenable to the Psalms or any of its thirty-eight literary colleagues which compose the Old Testament Canon.

Psalms belongs to the Old Testament in general and to the poetic section in particular. This is its proper placement in Holy Writ.

IMPROPER USAGE OF PSALMS

The book of Psalms is misused when people seek to appeal to it as an extra book of the New Testament. The foregoing section details why such is an abuse of Psalms.

Satan misused Psalms when he quoted from Psalm 91:11,12 in one of his temptations of the Lord. He ignored both the immediate and remote context. Jesus set both him and the record straight in Matthew 4:5-7.

The book of Psalms is misused by those who flock there in efforts to find Biblical proof for mechanical music in worship. The very fact they go to Psalms, an Old Testament book, is proof positive that ANY warrant for the foreign element or innovation in Christian worship is totally lacking in the New Testament. If authorized at all for Christian worship, proof of such must be forthcoming from New Testament law to which we are amenable and not to Old Testament law to which we are not amenable. It is my personal conviction that David introduced the mechanical instrument and that Jehovah tolerated such much as He did divorce, polygamy, their king, etc. Amos 6:5 voices God's attitude in a later prophet relative to what David had done.

Psalms is misued by Calvinists to uphold their total hereditary dogma. Sugarstick passages for them have been Psalms 51:5 and 58:3.

4

Psalm 51 is a confession of what David did as a man in the matter of Bath-sheba and Uriah, her innocent husband. He (David) was born to a mother who had sinned, into a world of sin and he sinned when accountable but not one moment earlier. Perverted Bibles on Psalm 51:5 have compounded the problem and not solved the matter at all of what David meant in this confession — a confession of a man perhaps fifty years of age at the time — and not of a child at conception or at birth. Psalm 58:3 has children *going* astray — not *born* astray. There is a tremendous difference in the two concepts. When they go astray they are speaking lies. This could not apply to children either at conception or at birth. Calvinists think they have found proof in Psalms for their once-saved-always-saved dogma. They will point to the passage of where even if a man falls, "he shall not be utterly cast down: for the Lord upholdeth him with his hand" (Psalm 37:24). But the previous verse exhibits quite clearly that the Psalmist depicts "a good man" (Psalm 37:23). He is the man whose steps "are ordered by the Lord: and he delighteth in his way" (37:23). There is NO proof for Calvinism in any of the Psalms.

Portions of this precious book have been used by materialists to prove "soul sleeping" or man's annihilation at death. They point to Psalm 6:5 which states, "For in death there is no remembrance of thee: in the grave who shall give thee thanks?" Another of their pet passages is, "O spare me, that I may recover strength, before I go hence, and be no more" (39:13). Materialists utterly fail to distinguish what dies in physical death and what continues to live. The body dies. This is what remembers nothing in the grave. The lifeless body in the grave is that which gives no thanks to God. But man has a spirit which can be committed to God its giver even as Psalm 31:5 stresses. Solomon, one of the writers of Psalms, stresses in Ecclesiastes 12:7 that at death a part of man (the body) returns to dust but the spirit returns to God its giver. Both Lazarus and the rich man in Luke 16 were conscious subsequent to death.

PROPER USAGE OF PSALMS

It is a proper usage of Psalms to use the book as did Jesus. In Luke 24:44 He referred to what had been written of Him by way of predictive prophecy in the law of Moses, in the prophets and in the psalms. Psalms, as used by Jesus and without doubt, refer to more of the poetic writings than just this one book but would surely include this precious product. In Psalms we have many, many precious, predictive prophecies relative to our marvelous Messiah. One planned chapter in

5

this volume will be devoted entirely to this attractive and admirable aspect of Psalms.

It is a correct usage of Psalms to breathe and breathe deeply the saintly spirit of worship and service to God as delineated so delightfully in this wonderful book. One's prayer life will be greatly enhanced by meditating on how the Psalmists approached God in their intense petitions and pronouncements of praise.

It is a proper usage of Psalms to have one's sensitive soul expanded by witnessing God's existence, God's greatness, God's patience, God's love, God's mercy and His compassion. It is a proper usage of Psalms to allow them to enhance the exalted and extolled manner in which we ought to hold God's word. Enhanced also will be our exalted view of the Messiah as He is protrayed in various of His attractive attributes in predictive Psalms of a Messianic nature.

It is a proper usage of Psalms to allow many of their precious pronouncements to form the very sentiments of the psalms, hymns and spiritual songs we sing in the unison of worship. It is a proper usage of Psalms to go there for strength in weakness, for comfort in sadness, for understanding in times of confusion and for greater faith in times of crippling disbelief. It is a proper usage of Psalms to witness how superior Christianity prepares and conditions us to have a better attitude toward our enemies, our persecutors and our troubles than did the psalmists who lived under a greatly inferior system during the Mosaic system than we do under Christ.

THE PSALMS IN STRUCTURAL FORM

Psalms is Hebrew poetry at its finest. They can be sung as originally was their primary purpose. They can be read as is most often our way of handling them. In Psalms we have precious parallelism, the most dominant, delightful characteristic of Hebrew poetry. In parallelism there is a definite link between the first and second lines. The second line may complement the first by repeating in slightly different words the same sentiment; it may sharply contrast the first or it may complete the thought that was begun in the first. Technically, these are synonymous, antithetic and synthetic forms of parallelism. In addition there are acrostic psalms using the letters of the Hebrew alphabet such as we have in Psalm 119.

The Psalms contain history, current conditions at the time of their composition and future events especially as relating to the Redeemer. They run the entire gamut of human experience in nearly all the checkered career of Israel from Moses to near the time of Nehemiah and Malachi with which inspired Old Testament history concludes.

INSPIRATION OF THE PSALMS

Peter affirms that the Holy Spirit spoke by David (Acts 1:16). David laid claim to inspiration in 2 Samuel 23:2. Jesus endorsed David as a writer who was inspired of the Lord (Matthew 22:43). Jesus placed Psalms in the same sacred and inspired categories of Old Testament books as He did the Law and the Prophets (Luke 24:44). No other Old Testament book is so frequently quoted in the New Testament as is the book of Psalms. Like all of its sixty-five literary kinsmen, Psalms is inspired of God. Writers of Psalms were moved (borne along) by the Holy Spirit in all their courageous compositions (2 Peter 1:21).

PSALMS OUTLINED

1. Psalms 1-41 — The works of David.

2. Psalms 42-72 — Composed by David, Solomon and others up to the general age of Jehoshaphat.

3. Psalms 73-89 — Psalms which depict the revival under King Hezekiah.

4. Psalms 90-106 — One psalm of Moses and the remainder from Isaiah to Josiah and to the time of the Captivity.

5. Psalms 107-150 — Written at various times in late Hebrew history and possibly collected shortly after the Captivity. They show a greatly rekindled interest in matters of deep spirituality.

POINTS TO PONDER

1. Psalms has its proper placement in the Old Testament — not the New Testament.

2. Psalms touches the chords of *every* emotion of the human heart.

3. Psalms enhances our worship concepts in general and our prayers in particular.

4. The greatness of our God is expressed so elegantly and eloquently in Psalms.

5. Great indeed would be our spiritual loss if Psalms had never been composed.

6. Psalms is a spiritual oasis to every soul that hungers and thirsts for God and His righteousness.

DISCUSSION QUESTIONS

1. Discuss matters relative to titles for this book.
2. What great claim is common among the precious passages of 2 Timothy 3:16; 2 Peter 1:21 and 2 Samuel 23:2?
3. List the various authors of Psalms and about how many each penned.
4. What value inheres in the inscriptions at the beginning of many of the Psalms?
5. Time-wise how is the book of Psalms different from all other Biblical books?
6. What value is seen in this lengthy time of literary composition?
7. Discuss in detail why Psalms is an Old — not New — Testament book.
8. Take John 10:34-36 and Psalm 82:6 and prove that Psalms is part and parcel of the Mosaic Economy and not part and parcel of the Christian Dispensation.
9. List and discuss the various misuses of Psalms and then the proper usage of Psalms.
10. Discuss the brief outline of Psalms and something about each of the five major sections.

MULTIPLE CHOICE: Underline correct answer

1. Psalms has been called: (A) "The Songbook of the Bible;" (B) "The Dark Ages of Hebrew History;" (C) "The Decalogue of the Bible;" (D) "The Book of Earthly Wisdom."
2. (A) David; (B) Solomon; (C) One of the sons of Korah; (D) Asaph; (E) Moses — is the generally conceded writer of Psalm 90.
3. (A) Satan; (B) Jesus Christ; (C) John the Baptist; (D) Matthew — misused Psalm 91:11,12 in the temptation atop the temple pinnacle in Matthew 4 and Luke 4.
4. "Soul sleeping" is: (A) taught in Psalms; (B) injurious error; (C) thoroughly rejected by all materialists; (D) a simple reference to the immortal souls who are asleep in the Lord.
5. Synonymous, antithetic and synthetic refer: (A) to Hebrew parallelism; (B) to three prominent errors taught in Psalms; (C) to various forms of Hebrew prose; (D) to the various types of writing materials used in producing the original Psalms.

SCRIPTURAL FILL-IN: Each blank requires only one word.

(1) "The _____ of the _____ spake by _____, and his _____ was in my _____."

8

(2) "I have _____, Ye are _____; and all of _____ are _____ of the _____ High."

(3) We read in Psalm 58:3, "The _____ are _____ from the _____: they go _____ as soon as they be _____, _____ lies."

(4) We read in Psalm 37:23,24, "The _____ of a _____ man are _____ by the _____: and he _____ in his _____. Though he _____, he shall not be _____ cast _____: for the _____ upholdeth him with his _____."

(5) In Matthew 22:43, Jesus said, "How _____ doth _____ in _____ _____ call him _____ saying,..."

TRUE OR FALSE: Put either a "T" or "F" in the blanks

_____1. Among Bible believers Psalms is the most ignored book in the Old Testament.

_____2. David personally penned all one hundred fifty of the Psalms.

_____3. The New Testament includes the twenty-eight books of Matthew through Psalms.

_____4. Since Psalms is not a New Testament book, then it is void of any and all profit.

_____5. Calvinists can truly find all their five basic religious foundations incorporated within Psalms.

THOUGHT QUESTIONS

1. Why is Psalms so universally loved and frequently quoted among Bible believers?

2. What confuses some people as touching whether Psalms belongs to the Old Testament or the New Testament section of Sacred Scripture?

3. What is basically wrong in seeking authorization for mechanical music in worship from Psalms?

4. Were mechanical instruments approved and delighted in by God or begun by David and simply tolerated by Jehovah? Give reasons for your answer.

5. Discuss the inspiration of Psalms.

CHAPTER TWO

PSALM 1: THE RIGHTEOUS AND WICKED IN MARKED CONTRAST

Though not directly called an introductory or preface psalm to the remainder of this beautiful book, yet the first one sustains that stately stance, that prominent position. It serves as a precious preface, a foundational foreword, an intense introduction. It establishes in tone and tenor what its one hundred forty-nine literary links develop with a precious preciseness and a dynamic development. It has been called "the threshold psalm." There is an old tradition to the effect that it was the last psalm to be penned. When the one hundred forty-nine compositions were collected and compiled, that one more was needed which would tersely state what all sought to develop, i.e., the blessedness of the righteous man and the sure sadness and ultimate gloom of the wicked man. This may or may not be true at all but every writer of books realizes that prefaces or introductions are frequently written last. This has been true of all books I have written and this one numbers my seventeenth volume over a twelve year period.

In noble notes of literary truth that march magnificently from syllable to syllable and statement to statement, this preface psalm presents a marked contrast between the choice, conduct and character of the righteous man and the choice, conduct and character of the wicked man.

THE BLESSED (RIGHTEOUS) MAN
NEGATIVELY DEPICTED

"Blessed is the man that walketh not in the counsel of the ungodly, nor standeth in the way of sinners, nor sitteth in the seat of the scornful" (1:1). This precious psalm begins with the same intense word of introduction as does the stately Sermon on the Mount, "Blessed." It is derived here from the Hebrew word *aishair* and properly means happy, blessed or fortunate is the man (any man, all men) who is so characterized. The word here is plural and thus means the "happinesses" or "blessednesses" of the man about to be delineated with such delight by the inspired pen of the psalmist. Real happiness or genuine blessedness is the foundational force of this expressive term. Man, as used here, is NOT the specific male as opposed to woman but is a general term inclusive of all — both men and women — both boys and girls — who abide by the marvelous manner of life about to be delineated.

Truth travels in trios here. We have counsel, way and seat; we have ungodly, sinners and scorners (scoffers — ASV); we have walking, standing and sitting. There is a graphic gradation herein enumerated. "Counsel" has reference to the evil plans, hidden purposes or secretive advice which are given out by the ungodly. "Way" portrays the well-known road that leads to a life of open and notorious sin. It is a definite direction of travel. "Seat" is the deliberate choice to settle down into a fixed mode of mischief, into a permanent realm of rebellion. "Ungodly" are those who are unrighteous; those who are wicked; those who reserve neither time nor place in their lives for the God of heaven. "Sinners" are those who miss the mark, who transgress law, pass beyond limits imposed or deliberately come short of duty's demands. The "scorners" or "scoffers" (ASV) are those who mock righteousness, scorn the salvation the Lord offers, disdain Deity and deride sacred truths. They are at the bottom of sinful men. "Walketh" means activity as one seeks to gain advice from the elements of evil. "Standeth" refers to a more deliberate or fixed position in the way of wickedness. "Sitteth" means that one has become part and parcel with the evil elements around him; he has finally and fully arrived; he finds his devilish delight in their cunning, corruptible company. This trio of verbs, Hebrew scholarship informs us, all fall into the perfect tense. Combined, they refer to settled actions, to fixed patterns of permanent behavior. Here are Satan's three steps of becoming a hardened sinner, an incorrigible criminal. (1) One *listens*

12

to evil counsel. (2) One *stands* to see the enticements of sin in full bloom. (3) One wholly *yields* by joining the evil and finding diabolical delight in the same. Alexander Pope once wrote,

> Vice is a monster of so frightful mein,
> As, to be hated, needs only to be seen;
> Yet seen too oft, familiar with her face,
> We first endure, then pity, then embrace.

This negative picture of the progression of sin is something the righteous man avoids as if it were the plague — a spiritual Bubonic Plague.

THE BLESSED (RIGHTEOUS) MAN
POSITIVELY PORTRAYED

"But his delight is in the law of the Lord; and in his law doth he meditate day and night" (1:2). "But" marks a strong contrast. The blessed or righteous man does not seek counsel from the devil's crowd. Quite to the contrary, he seeks it from the Lord's law. He goes to the original fountainhead of truth. He seeks it *delightfully*; he seeks it *regularly*; he seeks it *diligently*; he seeks it *studiously*; he seeks it *permanently*; he seeks it *consistently*; he seeks it *inwardly* or with the heart. He knows that the good man *outwardly* is first the good man *inwardly*. Speech and actions have their breeding grounds in the thought processes. An eminently correct observation has often been made, "You are not what you think you are; you are what you think!" Every great and good student of the Bible is a living personification of Psalm 1:2. This is the springboard of proficiency in Biblical knowledge and the workable wisdom despensed from the same.

"And he shall be like a tree planted by the rivers of water, that bringeth forth his fruit in his season; his leaf also shall not wither; and whatsoever he doeth shall prosper" (1:3). This is a marvelous figure of speech; it is a stately simile. The truly blessed and genuinely righteous man is likened to a tree. But it is not to just any type of tree to which he is likened. He is not like a tree that springs up spontaneously. He is like a *planted* tree. The tree is planted deliberately. Here is the idea of stability, purpose and design also set forth. He is not like a tree just planted anywhere. This tree is planted where it may receive the necessary moisture. It is a tree that is cultivated and cared for by the talented hand of a man with the proverbial "green thumb" i.e., one who is proficient in getting things to grow and grow well. This is a fruitful tree; it does not produce out of season but in season. This is

13

the realization and accomplishment of its reason for being. Its leaf is unwithering. Here is fadeless beauty; here is precious permanence. Whatever he does will ultimately end in genuine prosperity. The blessed (righteous) man is planted by the Lord. All his needs are met with amazing marvel. He does not betray the Lord's design in his being planted. He is successful as a fruitbearer (Cf. John 15:1-10). He is *consistent* in his fruitbearing and not spasmodic with an on and off or hot and cold type of approach to life and its challenges. Prosperity in the real sense of the term will be his. He will be spiritually prosperous; he will be physically prosperous. Set forth here is what a man's *choice* should be, what his *conduct* is to be and of what his separate *character* is to consist.

DELINEATION OF THE WICKED

"The ungodly are not so: but are like the chaff which the wind driveth away" (1:4). Quite literally, here the Hebrew reads, "Not thus (so) the wicked." The ungodly are those who live as though there were no God; they ignore His will and disdain His person; they are filled with iniquity and plan their lives and pursue their plans as though God had never spoken to man in the Bible. The ungodly (wicked — ASV) in verse four are the ones who have listened to the counsel of the ungodly; they stand in the way of sinners; they sit in the seat of scorners (scoffers — ASV). As such they are not like a tree planted by rivers of water; they are not fruit-bearing; theirs is not the unwithering leaf; theirs is not true, genuine prosperity. A sad — not happy — simile is used to portray them. They are like the worthless chaff with all the valuable grain stripped away. Grain growers of antiquity disposed of the worthless chaff by pitching both grain and chaff, while intermixed, into the air. The strong blowing wind would drive the chaff away while the valuable grain fell back to earth where it was then used for intended purposes. This is one of the most sharply drawn contrasts between righteous men and wicked individuals in all Holy Writ. The righteous man is like a planted tree that is well-watered, possesses an unwithering leaf, is ever a prolific fruit bearer and enjoys true prosperity. The wicked man is like the chaff, totally separated from valuable grain, which the wind blows away. John the Baptist likens the righteous to wheat saved in the heavenly garner and the wicked to chaff which faces the unquenchable fires of Eternal Gehenna (Matthew 3:12). It does not pay to be wicked when one sees the full portrait of unrighteousness as delineated here.

"Therefore the ungodly shall not stand in the judgment, nor sinners in the congregation of the righteous" (1:5). Here is a logical conclusion

14

deducted from the premises previously established by the inspired psalmist. What is meant that the wicked shall not stand in judgment? It surely does not mean that they will be excused from making an appearance there for all, both righteous and wicked, must there appear (Ecclesiastes 12:14; Psalm 96:13; 2 Corinthians 5:10; Romans 14:10,12). It simply means they will not be acquitted or justified in judgment. They will receive the condemnation reaped as a result of lives of unrighteousness and ungodliness. Such undesirables will be afforded no place in the congregation of the righteous. They will not be going to heaven. Here on earth our congregations are mixed with both good and bad, both the sincere and insincere, both the dedicated and the apathetic. Not so in heaven. Sinners there could never live. If taken, which they will NOT be, they would be total strangers in that sublime sphere. They would be clear out of their element. As one able student has well written, "Sooner could fish live upon a tree than a sinner in paradise"

A MARKED CONTRAST IN THE TWO DESTINIES

"For the Lord knoweth the way of the righteous: but the way of the ungodly shall perish" (1:6). In a true sense God knows the way of all men. However, here the psalmist has reference to the Lord's *approval* of the way of the righteous. He approves of their choices, their conduct and their character. He knows not the way of the wicked. He neither approves of their choices, their conduct, their character nor does He intend for them to populate the Palace of the Universe or the place of many mansions (John 14:1-3). The wicked may think they are really living it up but sinful pleasures are always seasonal in nature (Hebrews 11:25). Impoverished indeed will be their shriveled souls in judgment. Severe will be their everlasting lot in a never-ending hell. The contrast is as marked here as in Matthew 25:46 where the wicked go into everlasting punishment but the righteous into life eternal.

POINTS TO PONDER IN PSALM 1

1. Jehovah has joined real happiness with godliness.
2. He has linked eternal misery with wickedness.
3. Sin is progressive in its basic nature.
4. Whatever pleasure sin provides is found in this world only; not any will be found in yonder's world.
5. There is a sure and certain payday for ALL sinners.

15

DISCUSSION QUESTIONS

1. Why is Psalm 1 an adequate introduction to the book of Psalms?
2. What does this psalm actually present?
3. List, define and discuss the trio expressions in Psalm 1:1.
4. What is meant by the verbs being in present tense in Psalm 1:1?
5. What three steps are used in making hardened sinners and incorrigible criminals?
6. What descriptions are given of the righteous man's seeking proper counsel?
7. Discuss in detail the righteous man as he is likened to a tree and the wicked man as he is likened to chaff.
8. What three vastly important C's are set forth in Psalm 1:3?
9. Discuss the two destinies set forth in Psalm 1:6.
10. Read and discuss the Points to Ponder in Psalm 1.

MULTIPLE CHOICE: Underline correct answer

1. Psalm 1 begins with the same noble word as does: (A) Peter's sermon in Acts 2; (B) Stephen's discourse in Acts 7; (C) Paul's speech before Agrippa in Acts 26; (D) the Sermon on the Mount in Matthew, chapters 5, 6, and 7.
2. Chaff in Psalm 1:4 refers to: (A) righteous men; (B) wicked men; (C) just the refuse from grain and has no other significance; (D) a favorite sport practiced in times of antiquity.
3. (A) John the Baptist; (B) Stephen; (C) Philip the evangelist; (D) Andrew — referred to wheat and chaff in the New Testament as symbols of the righteous and the wicked.
4. Ecclesiastes 12:13,14; Psalm 96:13; 2 Corinthians 5:10 and Romans 14:10,12 are: (A) judgment day passages; (B) creation passages; (C) passages that give the gospel plan of salvation; (D) passages that give instructions relative to Christian worship.
5. Matthew 25:46 teaches that the wicked shall all be: (A) saved at last in heaven; (B) annihilated; (C) in purgatory for awhile and later removed to heaven for eternity; (D) cast into everlasting punishment.

SCRIPTURAL FILL-IN: Only one word for each blank is required.

(1) "_____ is the _____ that _____ not in the _____ of the _____, nor _____ in the _____ of _____, nor _____ in the _____ of the _____."

16

(2) *"But his* _____ *is in the* _____ *of the*
_____ *; and in his* _____ *doth he* _____
_____ *and* _____*."*

(3) *"And* _____ *shall be* _____ *a* _____
planted by the _____ *of* _____*, that* _____
forth his _____ *in his* _____*; his* _____
also shall not _____*; and whatsoever he* _____ *shall*
_____*."*

(4) *"The* _____ *are not so: but are like the* _____ *which*
the _____ *driveth* _____*."*

(5) *"Therefore the* _____ *shall not* _____ *in the*
_____*, nor* _____ *in the* _____ *of the*
_____*. For the* _____ *knoweth the* _____
of the _____*: but the* _____ *of the* _____
shall _____*."*

TRUE OR FALSE: Put either a "T" or "F" in the blanks

____1. *Psalm 1 has been called "the threshold psalm."*

____2. *"Blessed" in Psalm 1:1 means happy or fortunate is the man who chooses right over wrong.*

____3. *Psalm 1 applies only to men and not to women.*

____4. *"You are not what you think you are; you are what you think!" is an eminently true observation.*

____5. *Psalm 1:5 means that the wicked will not be required to make any appearance at judgment.*

THOUGHT QUESTIONS

1. *Why do you think a writer frequently pens his preface, introduction or foreword last?*

2. *Show from Psalm 1:1 that there is a definite progression of sin.*

3. *How do the words of Alexander Pope fit so well within the framework of Psalm 1:1?*

4. *Just how important are our thought processes to what we say and how we act in daily deeds?*

5. *Why will sinners not be present in the heavenly congregation of the eternally saved?*

Footnotes

₁ Guy N. Woods, ADULT GOSPEL QUARTERLY, Summer Quarter, 1972, p. 5.

CHAPTER THREE

PSALM 8: AN ELOQUENT EXHIBITION OF GOD'S GLORY

The book of Psalms is almost without peer in the Old Testament in declaring the glory, majesty and magnificence of Jehovah God—the Omnipotent One on high. The eighth, nineteenth and one hundred forty seventh psalms all do a marvelous job in portraying with power the greatness, goodness, glory and grandeur of our Heavenly Father on high. So do many others that could be listed and contemplated.

This psalm purports to be from the pen of David and there is no good ground for a denial of its Davidic authorship. The precise circumstances under which it was penned are somewhat difficult to determine. So many of the varied experiences David had confronted in his checkered career would easily fit the stately sentiments herein expressed.

The Bible used in the writing of this chapter sums up this stately section of Sacred Scripture by saying, "God's glory magnified by his words and by his astonishing love to man." This is a stately summary of its rich contents. The BEACON BIBLE COMMENTARY calls this chapter "The Paradox of Man Before God." Another writer, Edmond Jacob, has called Psalm 8 "Genesis 1 set to music" and as "the best commentary on Genesis 1." A rather unique feature relative to this psalm is seen in the fact that its opening and closing words are the same and stately are these repeated sentiments. These moving words are a translation of seven Hebrew words in the original.

The majesty of God and the measure of man form the two main concepts richly developed in this tremendous psalm.

19

THE MARVELOUS MAJESTY OF JEHOVAH GOD

"O Lord our Lord, how excellent is thy name in all the earth! who hast set thy glory above the heavens" (8:1). The Lord is Jehovah or the great "I Am" as He is addressed elsewhere within Holy Writ. He is *Adonai* which means master, Lord, ruler, owner or sovereign. He is greatly David's superior; David is greatly His inferior. This concept should be firmly fixed in mind in each of our prayerful or praise approaches to our lovely Lord on high. David praised God's name as being excellent. Name stands for the entire person. How excellent is Jehovah God or Adonai in all His amazing attributes and cardinal characteristics is David's sweet, stately sentiment. Israel's Sweet Singer not only acknowledges the eloquent excellence of that high and holy name in his own heart and upon his own lips but strongly desires there be a royal recognition of the excellence of God's name throughout earth. That excellency surely pervaded all the earth. David's desire was that all of God's footstool ring out in unique unison the excellence of Jehovah's noble name. In the Model or Disciples' Prayer of Matthew 6:9ff Jesus said so succinctly, "Hallowed be thy name." The Hebrew people lived under a law that warned them against taking the Lord's name in vain (Exodus 20:7; Deuteronomy 5:11) and, as here, inculcated the reverencing of God's name. God's glory has been set or established above the heavens. As glorious as clouds, sun, moon and stars are in the first and second heavens above and beyond all of us, the Psalmist recognizes that Jehovah's glory is exalted above the heavens. The glory of God's created wonders in the heavens above and beyond us pales into insignificance when made comparable to the glory of the Amazing Creator of all. How foolish for men to worship the objects of the sunlit and star-lit heavens and fail to worship Him who is the Maker of all we observe.

"Out of the mouths of babes and sucklings hast thou ordained strength because of thine enemies, that thou mightest still the enemy and the avenger" (8:2). God's glory is not restricted to what can be seen in the heavens above and the earth beneath generally but in particular what pours forth from the mouths of babes and children. Jesus knew this psalm to absolute perfection and He loved and deeply esteemed its treasured truths without human parallel. He seems to allude to this expressed sentiment in Matthew 11:2. as He speaks of what the Father has withheld "from the wise and p.udent, and hast revealed them unto babes." There is no doubt but what He has His eye riveted on this precious passage in the perfusive praise abundantly bestowed on Him during His triumphant entrance into Jerusalem just a few days prior to His ordeal on Execution Hill. The Bible says in Matthew 21:15,16,

And when the chief priests and scribes saw the wonderful things that he did, and the children crying in the temple, and saying, Hosanna to the Son of David; they were sore displeased, And said unto him, Hearest thou what these say? And Jesus saith unto them, Yea; have ye never read, Out of the mouth of babes and sucklings thou hast perfected praise?

Apparently, the Jewish leadership did not know the full intent of this precious psalm. The children of praise in this temple incident put to silence the error of the proud enemy and the antagonism of the ardent avenger. The earth, the starlit heavens and words of praise from babes and sucklings all combine to pronounce as great the marvels and majesty of Jehovah and Jesus His only begotten Son.

"When I consider thy heavens, the work of thy fingers, the moon and the stars, which thou hast ordained" (8:3). The stately sentiments of this valiant verse have constrained many close students of the eighth psalm to conclude that its composition was either at night or the end result of night time glimpses of starry glory and the thrill that such injected so intently into a reflective mind and impressed upon a meditative soul. Note that no mention is made of the sun. The moon and stars are specifically noted. David is the purported penman of this magnificent psalm. Being a shepherd lad in youth he no doubt had surveyed the moonlit and starlit constellations on numerous nights as he cast his youthful and deeply reverent eyes from his sheep below to the heavens above. With prompt reverence he sensed in his soul that all he saw belonged to God. They are HIS heavens. They are not the precise handiwork of humans; they are not the collections of Chance. They are the perfected handiwork of a Creator. They constitute the wondrous works of Jehovah's fingers. Fingers are richly suggestive of a skilled work that is done to total perfection. This marked with marvel what God had done with the high heavens that soared above a shepherd lad and now a shepherd monarch. Specifically, the reverent psalmist spoke of the moon and stars. These amazed him; they thrilled him; they turned his own mind to the Master Mind that had ordained, established or fixed them in their orbits of wondrous functions. How vastly different is the atheistic mind which can survey the very same heavens on a clear, starry night that David did thirty centuries ago and witness nothing but indefinite and evasive Chance as creator of it all!!

21

No wonder the psalmist will label the atheist as the fool just six chapters later and two pages removed in my beloved Bible (14:1). He repeats it in Psalm 53:1.

THE MARVELOUS MEASURE OF MAN

"What is man, that thou art mindful of him? and the son of man, that thou visitest him? For thou hast made him a little lower than the angels, and hast crowned him with glory and honour" (8:4,5). After the sweeping view he had of the marvels and majesty of Jehovah in the starlit night the Psalmist found amazement in the condescending fact that the power, glory and grandeur of this Almighty God took close cognizance of man on a tiny planet. He inquires as to what man is that the Almighty should be mindful of him and what of the son of man that Jehovah visits him with aid, help and the best of beautiful blessings. "What is man?" is asked here, Psalm 144:3 and in Hebrews 2:6. Hence, it is an important query of both testaments. The thrilling answer that the psalmist extends the query here in particular and what the whole Bible declares in general is to the eloquent effect that God is mindful of man and has visited him with manifold mercies. The psalmist, by inspiration, attractively answers his own query. (1) The Heavenly Creator has made man. Man is a precious product of creation; he is from the Sublime. In NO sense of the term is he the meaningless, purposeless product of aimless and mindless evolution at random work in an ancient age of antiquity. Man has a PURPOSEFUL maker—not an ACCIDENTAL maker. Man is NOT from the slime as silly, senseless and totally unproved organic evolution contends adamantly on a million infidelic battlefronts today. (2) God made him but little lower than angels or His created beings in the holy heavens above and beyond us. Redeemed man in heaven will be the equal of angels according to the ardent affirmation of Luke 20:36. What glory and grandeur to be a child of the resurrection in heaven on high at last. (3) God crowned man with glory. He made him in the image and likeness of God (Genesis 1:26,27). (4) God crowned him with honor. He raised him to a level unoccupied by fowl life, aquatic life or animal life on land. Man is unique; he is not an evolved animal as both atheistic and theistic evolution teach. Both are fatal and flagrant forms of gross, glaring and grievous falsehood. Deity conferred on humanity a gloriously high honor that sets man distinctly apart from ALL other forms of created life on earth. For just such reasons as the foregoing man should NEVER be labeled an animal. Such terminology is a senseless accomodation to the devilish, diabolical tenets of evolutionary teaching. Toward this type of spineless compromise I will neither be part nor parcel. May those be your words of courageous sentiment also.

"Thou madest him to have dominion over the works of thy hands; thou hast put all things under his feet: All sheep and oxen, yea, and the beasts of the field; The fowl of the air, and the fish of the sea, and whatsoever passeth through the paths of the seas" (8:6-8). To the quartet of points mentioned in comments on verses 4 and 5 we have several more of signal glory and high honor. (5) Man at the beginning was made to have dominion over the works of Jehovah's hands. Genesis 1:28 and 9:1-3 are informative and accurate commentaries upon these valiant verses in Psalm 8. (6) Closely akin to number 5 is the concept that God placed all things under man's feet. (7) Specifically, man's dominion extends over sheep, oxen, beasts of the field, fowl of the air and fish of the sea. Man is not as strong as oxen and land beasts such as lions, tigers, bears, horses, etc., and yet he controls them through his superior intelligence and the natural fear of man that the Almighty has placed into lower forms of earthly life (Cf. Genesis 9:2). It would seem that birds of the air and fish of the sea, places of habitation well beyond man's natural habitat, would be able either to fly or swim away from man's dominion. Not so!! His dominion extends to the air above and into the mighty deep as well. Had not sin entered in Genesis 3, man's dominion would no doubt have been far greater than it has been for him as a fallen creature.

The Hebrew writer in his second chapter looks back upon this very passage in Psalm 8, quotes it and then allows it to introduce a striking tribute to Jesus by writing with exacting and eloquent emphasis and ardent ascendancy,

> Thou hast put all things in subjection under his feet. For in that he put all in subjection under him, he left nothing that is not put under him. But now we see not yet all things put under him. But we see Jesus, who was made a little lower than the angels for the suffering of death, crowned with glory and honour; that he by the grace of God should taste death for every man (Hebrews 2:8,9).

God's majesty in a starlit sky or in the making of man is great. But far, Far, FAR greater is the Creator's sending of the Eternal Logos as His only begotten Son to redeem sinful humanity. The Hebrew penman had a far more lofty view of this from his vantage point than did the psalmist in an inferior dispensation. The Christ had already come, the atonement had already been made and Christianity was already a begun religion when the truthful treatise of Hebrews was penned.

Psalm 8:8 mentions "whatsoever passeth through the paths of the seas." This is of intriguing and quickening interest. Matthew Fontaine Maury lived from 1806 to 1873. While ill on one occasion he had his son read the Bible to him. The son read Psalm 8. Verse 8 caught the ill man's rapt attention. He declared that if the Bible spoke of paths of the sea, he would, upon getting well, discover them. He later found and charted these systems of sea travel involving an interaction between wind and water. He authored an informative book on oceanography. More than half a century ago C. L. Lewis wrote a book which he entitled, MATTHEW FONTAINE MAURY, PATHFINDER OF THE SEAS. The U.S. Naval Institute published it in 1927. Maury took God at His word and found it to be highly reliable. How came the ancient psalmist to know of these well-defined sea paths? He knew it by Inspiration.

CONCLUSION BY REPETITION

"O Lord our Lord, how excellent is thy name in all the earth!" (8:9). This served as the sublime introduction to this precious psalm; likewise it serves as the marvelous conclusion.

POINTS TO PONDER IN PSALM 8

1. This psalm is a real faith builder in the greatness, glory and grandeur of our God.
2. This psalm elevates the dignity of man.
3. The open eye and the open heart can find an abundance of evidences for the existence of God.
4. Atheism could never pen an exalted, extolled and lofty psalm such as the one we have contemplated in this chapter.
5. The more exalted God is in man's heart the more regard he will have for all of his fellowmen.

DISCUSSION QUESTIONS

1. *What is both an accurate and brief summary of Psalm 8?*
2. *What tributes have been beautifully bequeathed the eighth psalm?*
3. *What is unique relative to Psalm 8:1 and 8:9?*
4. *What emphasizes the glory of God in Psalm 8?*
5. *Discuss Psalm 8:2 and Matthew 21:15,16 as they relate to each other.*
6. *"What is man?" is found how frequently in the Bible and where all is it located?*
7. *List and discuss the points made relative to the vital query of "What is man?"*

8. *Relate Hebrews 2 to Psalm 8.*
9. *Discuss in detail Psalm 8:8 and Matthew Fontaine Maury.*
10. *Read and discuss the Points to Ponder.*

MULTIPLE CHOICE: Underline correct answer

1. Such psalms as the eighth, nineteenth and one hundred forty-seventh praise the power of: (A) Satan; (B) men; (C) demons; (D) idols; (E) God.
2. It seems very likely that: (A) David; (B) Solomon; (C) the sons of Korah; (D) Moses—penned Psalm 8.
3. Psalm 8 is an excellent commentary on: (A) Exodus 20; (B) Acts 2; (C) Revelation 20; (D) Genesis 1.
4. Adonai in Psalm 8 refers to: (A) idols; (B) demons; (C) Satan; (D) men; (E) the psalmist personally; (F) God Almighty.
5. "Hallowed be thy name" is an expression in the New Testament which was used by: (A) Satan as he tempted the Lord; (B) Jesus in the Model or Disciples' Prayer; (C) the enemies of Stephen in prayer just before they stoned the stalwart saint; (D) the enemies of Jesus in prayer as they milled atop Execution Hill on that fatal Friday.

SCRIPTURAL FILL-IN: Each blank requires only one word.

(1) "O _____ our _____, how _____ is thy _____ in _____ the _____! who hast _____ thy _____ above the _____."

(2) "Out of the _____ of _____ and _____ hast thou _____ strength because of thine _____, that thou _____ still the _____ and the _____."

(3) "When I _____ thy _____, the _____ of thy _____, the _____ and the _____, which thou hast _____; _____ is _____, that thou art _____ of him? and the _____ of _____, that thou _____ him?"

(4) "For _____ hast _____ him a little _____ than the _____, and hast _____ him with _____ and _____."

25

(5) "The _____ of the _____, and the _____
of the _____, and whatsoever _____ through the
_____ of the _____."

TRUE OR FALSE: Put Either A "T" Or "F" in the Blanks

____1. The book of Psalms does a par excellent job in emphasizing the glory, majesty and magnificence of God Almighty.

____2. David mentions sun, moon and stars in Psalm 8 as reflecting God's glory.

____3. Chance—not the Heavenly Creator—is responsible for moon, stars, man and all we observe in the marvelous universe.

____4. The book of Psalms considers the denier of God as "the fool."

____5. Far, FAR greater than God's glory reflected in the moonlit, starlit sky is His sending the Eternal Logos to earth for our redemption from sin and salvation at last in heaven on high.

THOUGHT QUESTIONS

1. Discuss David's lofty regard for Jehovah's name and how we should feel toward the same name of eloquent excellency.

2. How do Exodus 20:7 and Deuteronomy 5:11 relate to Psalm 8:1 and 8:9?

3. Why does it seem probable that Psalm 8 was either penned at night or as a result of night-time meditations?

4. What were the magnanimous feelings of David as his eyes surveyed a crystal starry sky scene of breathtaking beauty?

5. Contrast David and an atheist as each contemplates the bright, beautiful heavens above.

CHAPTER FOUR

PSALM 15: INSPIRATION'S PORTRAIT OF THE GOD-APPROVED MAN

The stature of this psalm is not determined by its length but by its solid, spiritual scope of eternal verities. It is neither long in verses nor in actual words. Yet it requires a lifetime to meet its courageous challenges, its stimulating stipulations, its lofty levels, its beautiful breadth of qualitative living.

Tremendous tributes by way of titles have been paid it by close students of the Bible. Keil-Delitzsch gave as title, "The Conditions of Access to God." G. Campbell Morgan called it "Jehovah's Friend Described." Spurgeon called it the question and answer psalm since both are incorporated therein. It has been called the "Gentleman's Psalm" since the hallmarks of a true gentleman or ideal person are delightfully delineated therein. "The Man God Approves" was the title selected for the GOSPEL ADVOCATE Bible Lesson on July 9, 1972. Another Quarterly study, January 8, 1984, called it "Truth and Integrity." The American Standard Version gives this precious psalm the title, "Description of a Citizen of Zion."

David is the human author of the epistle according to the introductory ascription. Of course the Holy Spirit is the heavenly author, the infallible guide of each word couched therein. Under what specific circumstances or geographical location David inscribed these moving, momentous words we are given no details either in the ascription that heads the psalm in our Bible or in the actual psalm itself.

The psalm easily divides into a trio of intently interesting areas of literary concern. (1) Two practical questions are raised in verse 1. (2)

27

Some eleven answers are given in verses 2-5. (3) A comforting conclusion is drawn in the latter portion of verse 5. Under these three basic parts we shall analyze the psalm and provide brief comments.

A DUET OF PRACTICAL QUESTIONS

"Lord, who shall abide in thy tabernacle? who shall dwell in thy holy hill?" (15:1). Lord in the KJV becomes Jehovah in the ASV. The God of heaven is the one addressed. Man is not equipped to give description of the person God approves for his earthly fellowship now and His heavenly fellowship in the sweet by and by. Only the Lord can do this!

In the first part of this Hebrew parallelism (a poetic balancing of lines synonymously, in contrast or by way of complement) we have *abide* and *tabernacle* in the first line or question and *dwell* and *holy hill* in the second line or question. Let it be kept firmly fixed in mind that this psalm was penned under the Mosaic Economy and from Hebrew imagery of the tabernacle and later the temple. "Abide" has as marginal reference here "sojourn" which is temporary in scope. "Dwell" has a permanency in mind for the intent querist. The tabernacle was a movable or portable tent of meeting designed for Israelites in their wandering or nomadic days. It was taken from place to place on the shoulders of priests or Levites. Sometime after they were situated in Canaan the city of Jerusalem became headquarters or the capital of the nation. Under David the city became theirs. Under Solomon, the Davidic successor, the permanent temple was built on Mt. Moriah. For centuries it was to be the place of the permanent sanctuary. Here at last there was permanency of worship in dwelling with their gracious, Heavenly Benefactor. The questions therefore raised by the sincere psalmist had to do with what manner of life was required for one to abide (sojourn) in the Lord's tabernacle and to dwell permanently with the Lord in His holy hill (the temple on Mt. Moriah). As applicable to us under the gospel dispensation the question would touch how are we to sojourn or abide with the Lord in the church on earth and then ultimately to dwell with Him permanently in heaven on high at last. The tabernacle was a type of the church and the temple a type of heaven as this psalm is made applicable and profitable for us. These two aspects are what Adam Clarke calls the church militant (here on earth) and the church triumphant (in heaven at last). Thus viewed this psalm becomes profit personified for each of us.

THE QUESTIONS ANSWERED

"He that walketh uprightly, and worketh righteousness, and speaketh the truth in his heart" (15:2). The three answers in this verse are positive in posture; the three in the subsequent verse will be negative in nature. To walk uprightly is to walk with the *right* side up—not the *wrong* side down. Walk is indicative of activity or our pilgrimage through life. The valiant adverb that modifies the verb "walketh" is "uprightly." This delineates the princely type of life one is required to live if the God-approved man he wishes to be. To walk uprightly is to deny ungodliness and worldly lusts and live soberly, righteously and godly in this present world (Titus 2:11,12). It means to doff, put off or mortify evil and to don or put on the good, true and right (Colossians 3:5-14). This is one of those plain and positive imperatives in the Bible that demands exercise therein more than an exegesis thereupon. The upright person seeks for spiritual maturity, for Scriptural completion in the beautiful basics of godly and righteous demeanor.

Positively required is one who works righteousness. Righteousness is "right-doing." Comprehensively involved in this kingly term is right THINKING, right SPEAKING and right ACTIONS or DEEDS. Motives and mission are unequivocally united in the heart and life of the righteous worker. Peter stated, "Of a truth I perceive that God is no respecter of persons: But in every nation he that feareth him, and worketh righteousness, is accepted with him" (Acts 10:34,35). John writes, "If ye know that he is righteous, ye know that every one that doeth righteousness is born (begotten—ASV) of him.... Little children, let no man deceive you: he that doeth righteousness is righteous, even as he is righteous" (1 John 2:29; 3:7). Righteousness is a key term used by our Lord in the Sermon on the Galilean Mount (Matthew 5:6,20; 6:33). In the Bible's longest chapter Israel's Sweet Singer affirmed with articulate attraction that "all thy commandments are righteousness" (Psalm 119:172). Righteousness exists first as an attitude of heart and then must express itself with eloquence and excellence in the action department. It cannot be borrowed; it is something we personally possess by doing God's will.

The marvelous man of whom God approves speaks truth in his heart. No sham or pretense forms a part of his character make-up. He is outwardly what he is inwardly. What appears on his lips is what the purity of his heart dictates. His soul thrives on sincerity; his personality prospers in purity. He speaks truth due to his lofty regard and deep appreciation for the pure, good and beautiful.

"He that backbiteth not with his tongue, nor doeth evil to his neighbor, nor taketh up a reproach against his neighbor" (15:3). This valiant verse depicts three noble negatives that beautifully belong to the God-approved man. He backbites NOT with his tongue. The literal Hebrew means, "He *foots not* upon his tongue." He refuses to kick about as a football the character of an absent person. This is what the backbiter, the gossiper and the slanderer major in on an ever-widening scale. Embedded in this term are knavishness, cowardice and brutality. The backbiter is of extremely low breeding; no real character adorns him. He is cowardly in that he fears to say to a person's face what he says to that person's back. He is brutal because he maliciously murders or massacres the character of those he disdains.

He does NO evil to his neighbor. The context demands that under consideration are such grevious iniquities as backbiting, gossip, slander, perjury, blasphemy, flattery on lips which is not felt in the heart at all, lying, false religions and their teaching, whispering, etc.

He refuses to take up (receive) a reproach against a neighbor and peddle it abroad. Some who hesitate to originate a piece of juicy gossip do not hesitate in the least in being its eager carriers as soon as a knavish person whispers it in their ever open ears. "Is it true?" and "will it do good to tell it if true?" are two questions we should constantly use as proper criteria or acceptable gauges relative to conversational items. The Golden Rule of Matthew 7:12 would do current society a world of needed good if universally heard and heeded. Unfortunately, that rule is neither heard nor heeded by today's masses. This is sad; it is immeasurably sad.

"In whose eyes a vile person is contemned; but he honoureth them that fear the Lord. He that sweareth to his own hurt, and changeth not" (15:4). The God-approved man has no fellowship with the unfruitful works of darkness (Ephesians 5:11). This certainly gets the drunkard, the immoral, the profane and all practitioners of iniquity regardless of how rich, famous or talented they may be. We must love the sinner but hate his deeds of disobedience. The God-approved man honors and respects the ones who fear God and love His will. These are the ones toward whom he extends fraternal and fervent fellowship.

His word is as good as a binding written document duly signed and properly notarized. He keeps his word even if a loss occurs. Obviously, this psalmist is not speaking about one who vows to do wrong. To carry out an evil vow only compounds the problem as in the case with Herod Antipas, Herodias, Salome and John the Baptist (Mark 6:16-28). Promises are sometimes made that the breaking or dishonoring of them would be more lucrative. This the God-approved man does not do. He keeps his word even at personal sacrifice. Gospel preachers who cancel meetings with small congregations where remuneration will be meager for last minute opportunities to preach in meetings for affluent churches where the take home check will be considerably fatter are verily guilty of the very principle inculcated here by the Psalmist.

"He that putteth not out his money to usury, nor taketh reward against the innocent" (15:5a). Usury here derives from a Hebrew term that means "to bite." It is "exorbitant interest: a higher rate of interest than reason would suggest or the law allow" (Guy N. Woods, THE SECOND COMING AND OTHER SERMONS, p. 159). Loan sharks, bloodsuckers and money lenders with no mercy and compassion all fall under the cutting sweep of this potent prohibition. Fair and humane interest on money loaned would be no more wrong than for a land owner to receive a certain percentage of the fruits or goods produced on rented land. The principle is precisely the same. The God-approved person is fair, merciful and compassionate in these important regards. He has to be. Neither God above nor conscience inside of him will allow for any other course pursued or prosecuted.

Those who take rewards against the innocent are up for sale to the highest bidder. They give bribes to obtain preferred treatment; they take them to pervert justice. The guilty are in their camp if there is a free flow of currency for perverted justice. The innocent man of poverty does not rate with the "For Sale" manipulators. The innocent man may only expect them to tell the truth if he can *pay* for such. If he has no money for such a rendered service, then he receives no help or aid from such heartless persons. This is a picture of glaring depravity. It but emphasizes how degraded men of that era were. God-approved men never, never stoop this low.

THE CONCLUSION STATED

"He that doeth these things shall never be moved" (15:5b). The God-approved man is a doer but not just a doer of anything or everything. He is a doer of *these things*. What things? The things delineated in this very precious psalm. Practice of these things distinguishes him from the doers of depravity. He is uncompromisingly loyal to these things. No one may move him away; he cannot be dislodged from such. He will not apostatize because doing these things will keep him safely removed from the apostate highway. Romans 8:35-39 serves as an excellent commentary of this concluding summary in Psalm 15.

POINTS TO PONDER IN PSALM 15

1. God—not man—determines the people of whom He currently approves and the ones ultimately approved to be taken to heaven for an eternity of ecstasy.

2. Acceptability in the Lord's church now paves the sure way for accessibility to heaven in the sweet by and by.

3. The bottom line of this entire chapter deals with both character (what God knows us to be) and reputation (what others think us to be).

4. Preachers, as observed earlier in this chapter, who cancel long promised gospel meetings with small, struggling congregations to hold one at the same times with affluent congregations where the pay will be greater fall under the strict condemnation of Psalm 15:4. If not, WHY NOT??

5. A religion based on faith only or apathy would not get to first base in seeking to be guided and gauged by this inclusive, active and industrious chapter of working charges.

DISCUSSION QUESTIONS

1. *What determines the stature of this psalm? Why not memorize it?*

2. *List and discuss some of the thrilling tributes that have been laid at the beautiful feet of Psalm 15.*

3. *Briefly analyze the psalm into its three prominent parts.*

4. *Analyze thoroughly Psalm 15:1 and explain its application in principle to us under the Christian Dispensation.*

5. *What three positive requirements are set forth in verse 2 and explain each one?*

6. *What three negatives are exhibited in verse 3 and explain what each means?*

7. *What two questions should be posed toward all we hear?*

8. *Discuss the prohibitions relative to usury here.*

9. *What conclusion is reached and discuss it?*

10. *Read and discuss the Points to Ponder.*

MULTIPLE CHOICE: Underline correct answer

1. *Psalm 15 has been called by the title of: (A) "The Shepherd Psalm;" (B) "The penitential psalm;" (C) "The Man God Approves;" (D) "The Babylonian Exile Song."*

2. *Psalms 15 was written by: (A) David; (B) Solomon; (C) Moses; (D) Asaph; (E) the sons of Korah.*

3. Solomon's temple was built on: *(A) Mount Moriah; (B) Mount Hermon; (C) Mount Meggido; (D) Mount Sinai; (E) Mount Tabor.*

4. Herod Antipas, Herodias and Salome were all: *(A) linked with a rash vow and its infamous execution; (B) members of a very godly family; (C) the best friends John the Baptist ever possessed; (D) defenders of truth and right.*

5. The tabernacle in the wilderness in general and the temple in Jerusalem in particular are associated in the Bible with: *(A) patriarchal people; (B) the Israelites under the Mosaic Economy; (C) the Christians under Christ; (D) Gentile pagans.*

SCRIPTURAL FILL-IN: Only one word is required in each blank.

(1) "_____, who shall _____ in thy _____?
who shall _____ in thy _____ _____?"

(2) "He that _____ _____, and _____
_____, and _____ the _____ in his
_____."

(3) "He that _____ not with his _____, nor
_____ _____ to his _____, nor
_____ up a _____ against his _____."

(4) "In whose _____ a _____ person is _____;
but he _____ them that _____ the _____.
He that _____ to his own _____ and _____
not."

(5) "He that _____ not out his _____ to
_____, nor _____ _____ against the
_____. He that _____ these _____ shall
_____ be _____."

TRUE OR FALSE: Put either a "T" or "F" in the blanks

____1. There is no Hebrew parallelism in the book of Psalms.

____2. The Lord's church paves the way for all accountable people therein and who are faithful to Christ to go ultimately to heaven in the sweet by and by.

____3. Righteousness is right-thinking, right-speaking and right-doing.

____4. All backbiters help the world to be a far better place in which to live.

____5. Bribe giving and bribe receiving are no longer a modern problem for human society and exist only as a memory of an ancient era of sinful ˀctions.

THOUGHT QUESTIONS

1. *Tell why the Lord is the only proper one to describe the man of whom He approves now and will bring home ultimately to heaven.*

2. *What is meant by the church militant and the church triumphant?*

3. *Explain why righteousness cannot be borrowed from another but must be personally possessed and practiced.*

4. *List and discuss all the sins you can think of that are linked with the unruly tongue.*

5. *How does the Golden Rule of Matthew 7:12 fit all eleven of the positive and negative requirements of the God-approved person?*

CHAPTER FIVE

PSALM 19: JEHOVAH'S TWO BOOKS OF NATURE AND REVELATION

This is a precious, powerful and priceless psalm. With marvel and majesty it exhibits the glory and grandeur of God in the realm of created wonders and in the even more exalted and extolled realm of revelation. The latter is an essential for man to come to wise and accurate conclusions relative to the former. In the GOSPEL ADVOCATE Adult Quarterly Lesson for July 16, 1972, the erudite Guy N. Woods wrote so sagely and succinctly.

> A look at creation impresses us with the fact of limitless, inexhaustible power in the universe. But, no one can determine by such observation, the character or attributes of God; indeed, whether there is one God or a million. When we have had revealed to us the one God *by the Bible,* nature declares his glory. Nature does not tell us how to be saved or enable us to go to heaven. The Scriptures are the sole source of such information (p. 15).

God has NEVER left humanity with just the book of nature; He knew such was insufficient. He has provided man with a word revelation of His will in Patriarchal, Mosaic and Christian Dispensations.

This psalm by David easily divides itself into three areas which will serve as segment headings. We cannot be sure just when the Sweet Singer penned it, where or under what circumstances. Great and permanent would have been our loss had he not penned it by the inspiration of God.

THE BOOK OF NATURE EXHIBITS JEHOVAH'S GLORY

> The heavens declare the glory of God; and the firmament sheweth his handywork. Day unto day uttereth speech, and night unto night sheweth knowledge. There is no speech nor language, where their voice is not heard. Their line is gone out through all the earth, and their words to the end of the world (19:1-4b).

Here we have more of the Psalmist's precious parallelism. The word "heavens" at first is eloquently equated with "firmament" that comes later; "firmament" in the first line equates with "handywork" in the second. Men speak of ten heavens or seven heavens. The Bible speaks of three (2 Corinthians 12:2-4). The two heavens above us and below the third heaven and which are composed of clouds, moon, sun and stars in the broad expanse or "vaulted arch of the sky" ardently declare with dynamic power Jehovah's resplendent glory. These are the heavens or the firmament created by Divine Fiat in the opening verses of Genesis 1, the Bible's great and wholly accurate chapter of creative activity and origins. It was all accomplished at God's word as Genesis 1 repeatedly affirms. The passage in Psalm 33:6-9 adds its repeated confirmation of this vital truth as do scores of other impressive passages within the Holy Writ. Without interruption or ambiguity they (the heavens) preach a constant sermon. The clouds, blue sky and the mighty monarch of the sky—the sun—do it by day; the moon and stars do it by night. They speak a message universally available to all. It is not with human voice or in an earthly language that they speak but somewhat like a master painting speaks the glory of its gifted artist or a beautiful building stresses the architectural, engineering and construction talents of planners and builders. They utter a speechless sermon (from a human appraisal) but how very attractively articulate it is to all discerning beholders and amazed spectators. Their line (their message of reflected glory) has gone throughout the world. Paul may have had his inspired eye riveted on this very passage when he delineated the wide sweep of the gospel (God's word revelation for the Christian age) in Romans 10:18.

> In them hath he set a tabernacle for the sun, Which is as a bridegroom coming out of his chamber, and rejoiceth as a strong man to run a race. His going forth is from the end of the heaven, and his circuit unto the ends of it: and there is nothing hid from the heat thereof (19:4c-6).

From a general description of the heavens as a whole the psalmist passes to a superb specific—the sun. A tabernacle is a tent and is suggestive of something temporary. Eternity is not the character of the sun. It was made or created by God in Genesis 1; both testaments proclaim its dissolution at the end of time (Psalm 102:25,26; Hebrews 1:10-12; 2 Peter 3:10-12). The Davidic analogy here is of a bridegroom's emerging from his chamber early in the morning and the intense imagery of the sun's rising (as it appeared to him and still does to us today although we know of the earth's revolving around it) in the morning for its long circuit across the long stretch of the vaulted sky—the bright, beautiful blue above us. Youth, vibrancy, joy, strength and resoluteness are all set forth in the accurate and attractive analogy. David changes the imagery from the bridegroom to a strong man ready for his race. Just as he will not cease running till the distant target or goal is reached the sun will run its course without failure or flagging. Relative to this intense imagery Spurgeon wrote, "No other creature yields such joy to the earth as her bridegroom the sun; and none, whether they be horse or eagle, can for an instance compare in swiftness with that heavenly champion." As man views the sun his long journey is from the distant east in the morning to the distant west late in the day. Nothing on earth is beyond its reach. Its wholesome rays of heat penetrate every particle of life on earth. No form of earthly life could exist without the sun. In its absence we would soon be a solid ball of ice.

THE BOOK OF REVELATION (THE BIBLE) EXHIBITS THE GLORY OF GOD

The law of the Lord is perfect, converting the soul; the testimony of the Lord is sure, making wise the simple. The statutes of the Lord are right, rejoicing the heart: the commandment of the Lord is pure, enlightening the eyes. The fear of the Lord is clean, enduring for ever: the judgments of the Lord are true and righteous altogether (19:7-9).

There are three vital areas here. (1) We have six *noble names* for God's word—law, testimony, statutes, commandment, fear and judgments (ordinances—ASV). *Law* here obviously refers to the law of Moses. It was the rule of action to which Israel in general and the psalmist in particular were all amenable. *Testimony* is that to which the God of truth has borne witness; this is a valiant voucher for its absolute accuracy in ALL its varied declarations. *Statutes* refer to the mandates of our Maker. A stately synonym would be *precepts* which is the accepted rendering in the ASV of 1901. These are rules to guide and govern God's people. A *commandment* is God's appointment, charge or rule for His people. His stately sovereignty gives it fullness of authority. *Fear,* by metonymy, is put for the effects it creates such as reverence, respect, awe, etc. *Judgments* (ordinances—ASV) are the sum of God's word and constitute God's revealed body of truth (Psalm 119:160).

(2) The second vital area in this trio of valiant verses deals with the nature, character or attributes of God's word. Attractively depicted they are: perfect, sure, right, pure, clean, true and righteous. What tremendous tributes to God's word these are! God's word is *perfect*; it is entire, complete and all-sufficient; the law of Moses accomplished what God intended it to do. It was NEVER intended to accomplish what God determined that Christianity would do and has done for nearly two thousand years now. They are sure because the simple are made wise thereby. They are *right* because they descend from right personified—Deity. Jehovah's commandment is *pure*; it contains no mixture of falsehood or error. It is "without wax"; it is what it seems to be. The fear of the Lord is *clean*; it is without any uncleanness, ugliness, contamination, deterioration or decay. God's judgments or ordinances are *true* and *righteous*. This is their basic and beautiful character. They are totally free from anything false. They are right; they are just; they are fair; they are equal.

(3) The third vital area touches the glorious effects of God's word. It *converts* the soul. It changes the man who obeys it. To the Israelite it led to God's favor when he obeyed it. It makes *wise* the simple. The simple here is not a mentally incompetent person but one who is teachable, humble, sincere and submissive. He desires salvation and views the knowledge of it as man's most wonderful wisdom. The stately statutes of Deity *rejoice*, gladden or make happy man's heart when he is submissive to them. Jehovah's commandments *enlighten* man's eyes; they make him an informed person; they instruct him in the proper way for his feet to tread. The fear of the Lord *endures* forever. It has permanency—not temporary—written across its beaming and beautiful countenance. They are *true* and *righteous* altogether. They are rewarding when kept as a wonderful whole. The psalmist breathed a beautiful spirit toward God's word in these three power-packed verses of devoted excellence.

"More to be desired are they than gold, yea, than much fine gold: sweeter also than honey and the honeycomb. Moreover by them is thy servant warned: and in keeping of them there is great reward" (19:10,11). Every faithful servant of God joins David in giving a similar appraisal to God's word. The words of God are far, far more valuable than gold, much fine gold or all earth's gold. Yet the masses of men prefer gold to God, silver to the Saviour, gadgets over the gospel, things over truth, hunting over holiness, fishing over the faith and Sunday comics over honoring Christ on His day each Sunday. This is sad; it is immeasurably, inexpressibly sad. Real riches are found in God; genuine wealth is found in Biblical wisdom. Yet how many currently believe it and act in harmony and active accord with such faith? Very few it strongly appears!! To the palate of a spiritually-minded man God's word is sweeter—far sweeter—than the purest of honey, than the very droppings from the honeycomb. David knew how sweet Palestinian bees made their honey. Far, far sweeter was God's word to his spiritual palate. God's word was his bread of life, his water of life, his everything so to speak. God's word points out the holes of error and the ditches of moral and religious sins into which we are liable to fall as we travel life's pathway. Happy is the man who can be and desires to be warned by God's word. The rewards touch felicity here and heavenly happiness at last.

PRECIOUS PETITIONS OF PRAYER

Who can understand his errors? cleanse thou me from secret faults. Keep back thy servant also from presumptuous sins; let them not have dominion over me: then shall I be upright, and I shall be innocent from the great transgression. Let the words of my mouth, and the meditation of my heart, be acceptable in thy sight, O Lord, my strength, and my redeemer (19:12-14).

No man is knowledgeable or wise to the degree that he can know all his faults, frailties, imperfections, sins, errors, weaknesses, etc. No man can always know just what is right in EVERY given moment or what prudent course he should pursue in EVERY choice. David was so characterized; so is each of us. It is a part of our being finite. Due to our lack of always understanding God's will we may sin many times without realizing it. How frequently must each of us say, "I just did not know!" With such recognition firmly engrained in his mind David prayed for a cleansing or clearing of his hidden faults, i.e., those of which he might not even be aware. All of us without exception have sins hidden from others and even our own sins go unrecognized per-

39

sonally from time to time. The devout David prayed for the Lord to keep him away from presumptuous sins. These are not sins of ignorance or isolated transgressions that belong to a moment of anger, passion or the like. Presumptuous sins are committed knowingly, daringly, arrogantly and with a high hand of intended rebellion against God. Perverted indeed is any personality who so engages; hardened indeed is any heart so characterized. King Saul committed such a sin in 1 Samuel 15 against Agag and the Amalekites who were devoted by God's justice to destruction. So did King Ahab in the battle of Ramoth in Gilead in 1 Kings 22. David knew well the stronghold that could be in a person's life. He knew it easily could be the master and take a person into abject serfdom. He prayed for delivery from such. This would free him from the great transgression or habitual sins and especially presumptuous sins.

The concluding petition of David in this precious psalm is a weighty wish and a dynamic desire to speak words of mouth and to experience meditations of mind that God would accept. Many men are more concerned about how their words appear to men than to God. "Public opinion is often greater than God's opinion" (Roy H. Lanier, Sr.). The Lord is the primary one to please. David portrayed the Lord as his strength (rock—ASV) and redeemer. The first envisions God as touching security, stability and firmness; the second delineates Him as deliverer. Often He had delivered Israel in general and David in particular. For all this David was profoundly grateful and ardently appreciative.

POINTS TO PONDER IN PSALM 19

1. He who can survey God's handiwork in heaven and on earth and write himself down as an adamant atheist is the worst fool of all human history barring none!!

2. When both are accurately understood there will never be a contradiction between God's book of Nature and His book of Revelation (the Bible).

3. David exalted and extolled the word of God in this chapter.

4. Those who always put down the Bible should go to school to David and allow this chapter to be a demanded part of the inspired curriculum.

5. Such prayers as Psalm 19:12-14 would go a long way to keep all of us very humble, very cautious relative to sin and very careful relative to the content of mind and words from the mouth.

DISCUSSION QUESTIONS

1. *What is the noble nature of this precious psalm?*
2. *Discuss brother Woods' statement made relative to this memorable psalm.*
3. *What parallelism do we have in Psalm 19:1?*
4. *What possible link may there be between Romans 10:18 and Psalm 19:4?*
5. *Discuss what the psalmist said of the sun in Psalm 19:4,5.*
6. *List and discuss the six noble names that we have of God's word as given in Psalm 19.*
7. *List and discuss the words which describe the nature, character and attributes of God's word.*
8. *List and discuss the words that touch the effects of God's word.*
9. *Read and discuss in detail Psalm 19:12-14.*
10. *Read and discuss the Points to Ponder.*

MULTIPLE-CHOICE: Underline correct answer

1. *By nature alone we can learn: (A) all about the attributes of God; (B) about how He has proposed to make men righteous; (C) absolutely nothing of God's glory; (D) much relative to God's glory when revelation is there to guide and govern our study of God's Book of Nature.*
2. *(A) David; (B) Solomon; (C) Moses; (D) Asaph; (E) The sons of Korah —wrote the nineteenth psalm.*
3. *The Bible speaks of: (A) ten heavens; (B) seven heavens; (C) three heavens; (D) one heaven; (E) no heaven at all.*
4. *Sins of presumption are: (A) sins of ignorance; (B) sins with which all men are born; (C) sins committed in moments of weakness; (D) sins committed deliberately, in deep rebellion and with a high hand against the God of heaven.*
5. *Saul and Ahab: (A) were two of the most obedient kings in all of the Old Testament; (B) were a father and son team who ruled conjointly on the Hebrew throne; (C) both served as high priests under the Levitical order; (D) were both guilty of sinning presumptuously.*

SCRIPTURAL FILL-IN: Each blank requires only one word.

(1) "The _____ declare the _____ of _____;
and the _____ sheweth his _____. _____
unto _____ uttereth _____, and _____
unto _____ sheweth _____."

41

(2) *"In them hath he* _____ *a* _____ *for the*
_____ *, Which is as a* _____ *coming out of his*
_____ *, and* _____ *as a* _____ *man to*
_____ *a* _____ *. His going* _____ *is from*
the _____ *of the* _____ *, and his* _____
unto the _____ *of it; and there is nothing* _____ *from*
the _____ *thereof."*

(3) *"The* _____ *of the* _____ *is* _____ *,*
_____ *the* _____ *: the* _____ *of the*
_____ *is* _____ *, making* _____ *the*
_____ *. The* _____ *of the* _____ *are*
_____ *,* _____ *the* _____ *: the*
_____ *of the* _____ *is* _____ *,*
_____ *the eyes. The* _____ *of the* _____ *is*
_____ *,* _____ *for ever: the* _____ *of the*
_____ *are* _____ *and* _____ *altogether."*

(4) *"* _____ *to be* _____ *are they than* _____ *,*
yea, than _____ *fine* _____ *:* _____ *also*
than _____ *and the* _____ *,* _____ *by them*
is thy _____ *warned: and in* _____ *of them there is*
_____ *reward."*

(5) *"* _____ *back thy* _____ *also from* _____
sins; let them not have _____ *over me: then shall I be*
_____ *, and I shall be* _____ *from the great*
_____ *. Let the* _____ *of my* _____ *, and the*
_____ *of my heart, be acceptable in thy* _____ *,*
O Lord, my _____ *, and my* _____ *."*

TRUE OR FALSE: Put either a "T" or "F" in the blanks

____1. *God has always expected man to learn Heaven's will by Natural Religion or what Nature teaches.*

____2. *Nature and revelation are in hopeless, hapless and helpless conflict and disarray.*

____3. *"Public opinion is often greater than God's opinion," a statement by Roy H. Lanier, Sr., is a valid observation of today's secular and even religious age.*

____4. *This chapter reveals the psalmist to have been an agnostic in philosophy.*

____5. *This chapter reveals the psalmist to have felt that God's word is of little value, teaches anything man wants it to teach and is a dead letter.*

THOUGHT QUESTIONS

1. *Describe the clouds, blue sky, sun, moon and stars as eloquent preachers with a constant message of God's glory and what way they declare their message.*

2. *How do such passages as Psalm 33:6-9; Psalm 19:1-6 and Genesis 1:1ff all complement each other?*

3. *How valuable and precious was God's word to David according to Psalm 19:10,11?*

4. *What do the masses of men prefer rather than spiritual riches?*

5. *From this chapter show what a study of nature and God's word together will do for one's faith.*

CHAPTER SIX

PSALM 23: JEHOVAH AS SHEPHERD AND HOST

This bright, blessed, beautiful and beaming psalm has been a precious part of the Bible's Songbook for some three thousand years. It has been read and revered by millions of Bible students. Great indeed would have been the world's loss if it had been neither penned nor preserved by God's providence. It presents a portrait of God that is almost without peer in the Old Testament. Perhaps his portrait as Father in the New Testament is somewhat superior. The late and lamented A. G. Freed, co-founder of Freed-Hardeman College in Henderson, Tennessee, was a great lover of this psalm. He called it "The Shepherd Hymn." Relative to it he wrote,

> For lofty sentiment, sublime thought, and striking imagery this psalm is unsurpassed. The authorized version of this song, given to us in the Golden Age of English Literature, will live as long as the English tongue is spoken" (SERMONS, CHAPEL TALKS, AND DEBATES, p. 129).

It was this precious psalm that brother Freed quoted and which brought tears to the eyes of his attending physicians as he faced serious surgery. From this surgery he did not recover. It sustained him nevertheless in death and it has done the same for millions both in life and in death. We tread sacred and solemn ground indeed in the treasured contemplation of these gifted words, these immortal gems of heavenly truths.

David was the human author; the Holy Spirit was the heavenly author. We know not what the precise circumstances were at the time of its composition. Jehovah is spoken of as shepherd and then as the generous host. The psalm is deeply personal. By actual count there are seventeen personal pronouns such as I, me, my and mine in just six verses.

JEHOVAH AS SHEPHERD

"The Lord is my shepherd; I shall not want" (23:1). By the Lord he has reference to Jehovah which is the actual rendering of the ASV of 1901. He is the Eternal One, the Self-Existing One, the Living One, the Great I Am and the Almighty One. He was David's maker; He was David's sustainer; He was David's confidence; He was David's hope. Note that David did not call Him the world's shepherd, Israel's shepherd or even his family's shepherd; He was David's shepherd. David held no monopoly on Him as shepherd, quite obviously, but he did possess a personal hold.

We are not surprised that David used this as the intense and inviting imagery. He came from a nation of shepherds. The Hebrew founding fathers, Abraham, Isaac and Jacob, had all been shepherds during their earthly pilgrimages. When Jacob's small family migrated into Egypt and representatives were brought before the king or Pharaoh they described their occupation by saying to the Egyptian monarch, "Thy servants are shepherds, both we, and also our fathers" (Genesis 47:3). David grew up as a shepherd lad. In fact he was summoned away from his sheep to be anointed as king by the aged seer—Samuel (1 Samuel 16:11). There had been a time when he had slain both a bear and a lion who attacked one of his lambs (1 Samuel 17:34-37). So linked with his days as a keeper of sheep he is frequently called "The Shepherd King." A later psalm says of David the shepherd who became David the king,

> He chose David also his servant, and took him from the sheepfolds: From following the ewes great with young he brought him to feed Jacob his people, and Israel his inheritance. So he fed them according to the integrity of his heart; and guided them by the skilfulness of his hands (Psalm 78:70-72).

Palestinian shepherds loved their sheep. They led them to places of grass and water by day and to the fold of safety and security at night. At times they would go before the sheep and make sure there were no poisonous weeds or hidden dangers in prospective pastures. They protected them against robbers and beasts of prey. No animal is more helpless than a sheep or lamb. How fitting that Jehovah cares for us for we are so very vulnerable to all types of seen and unseen dangers. All of this made the imagery of breathtaking beauty. What the Palestinian shepherds in general and David in particular had been to their sheep the Lord was a thousand fold more to them. He provides, feeds, waters, protects, guides, comforts, etc. He does all this with such boundless abundance that David in sweet assurance could say, "I shall not want." This is the kingly keynote of the whole psalm. If Jehovah is truly our shepherd, then we shall have no lack of any real need whether it be physical or spiritual in nature. A later psalm confidently confirms that "no good thing will he withhold from them that walk uprightly (Psalm 84:11). Jesus declared that His Heavenly Father gives "good things to them that ask him" (Matthew 7:11). James portrays the graciousness of the generous Father on high as the giver of every good and perfect gift (James 1:17).

"He maketh me to lie down in green pastures: he leadeth me beside the still waters" (23:2). Verse 1 is a general affirmation of the Great and Good Shepherd as the supplier of all needs both temporal and spiritual. Verses 2-4 provide the sublime specifics of the general generosity of the initial verse. "Green pastures" here does not refer to tough grass or grass ready for hay. The Hebrew term, *deshe*, literally refers to "pastures of green grass," to "the first shoots of vegetation from the earth—young herbage—tender grass—as clothing the meadows, and as delicate food for cattle" (Bible margin and Barnes). But note that the intense imagery is not of grazing animals but animals lying down. Sheep do not lie down when hungry; they do not lie down when fearful; they lie down when full and unafraid. This is a rich and meaningful portrait of Jehovah's human sheep who have all needs abundantly supplied and who feel no fear. Hebrews 13:5,6 urges us to be free of covetousness and feel content. Why? Because "he hath said, I will never leave thee, nor forsake thee. So that we may boldly say, The Lord is my helper, and I will not fear what man shall do unto me."

The Lord does not force; He does not coerce; He leads. He leads gently. Palestinian shepherds *led* their sheep; they went ahead; they did not drive them as is true in our land. Jesus alluded to this well-known attribute of the Palestinian shepherd in John 10:3,4. The Lord leads by the still waters. They are not stagnant waters; they are not poisonous waters; they are not swiftly flowing torrents; they are the waters of quietness; they are the waters of calmness; they are the waters of real refreshment. The Lord leads us into that which is good; He never leads us into places of danger and sin.

"He restoreth my soul: he leadeth me in the paths of righteousness for his name's sake" (23:3). Restoration of soul here seemingly does not refer to Jehovah's tender reception and merciful pardon extended to a returning prodigal though He does this as other verses so affirm. Here the thought is of a strengthening of the soul of one in the green pastures, one who is beside the still waters. Pulpit Commentary says that Jehovah "revives and reinvigorates it when it is exhausted and weary."

Barnes remarks, "It refers to the spirit when exhausted, weary, or sad; and the meaning is, that God quickens and vivifies the spirit when it is exhausted."

Spurgeon said, "When the soul grows sorrowful he revives it; when it is sinful he sanctifies it; when it is weak he strengthens it." God leads (guideth—ASV) into paths of peace, into the realm of righteousness. He does not drive as a dictator; He leads and guides as a Loving Shepherd. Righteousness is right-doing; it is the keeping of God's commands as is affirmed so ardently in Psalm 119:172. This He does for His name's sake. Our doing right as His people brings glory to Him while producing profit to us personally. Under Christianity He receives glory through the church. The church is composed of all who have obeyed His Son and are living the Christian life.

"Yea, though I walk through the valley of the shadow of death, I will fear no evil; for thou art with me; thy rod and thy staff they comfort me" (23:4). Neither sheep nor people *walk* when afraid; they then run and fright characterizes each step they make with rapidity. The psalmist portrays his *walking*—not running. Note that David does not say he walks in the valley of death though this is the surface connotation usually given this valiant verse. It was the valley of the SHADOW of death in which he walked. Shadows may strike fear in us but they are incapable of inflicting real physical harm. Dangers and death lurk there but no real harm will come if we walk hand in hand with the Heavenly Shepherd and with Deity as constant companion. Even physical death is but a release of God's sheep to come to the saints in Sheol and the holy in Hades or the patient in Paradise. David feared no evil. Why? The Lord was with him and that made the difference! Comfort was his lovely lot through it all due to the Lord's rod and staff. David did not deny the presence of evils to fear for dangers surrounded him. He had Jehovah's protection and that shielded him from any real harm. Though David was a finite man, this sort of confidence in God made him fearless and invulnerable in the face of any and all dangers. Rod and staff may not refer to two implements used by the shepherd but only to one implement that served dual purposes

—to care for and protect his sheep and to lean upon himself or for personal help.

JEHOVAH: THE GENEROUS HOST

"Thou preparest a table before me in the presence of mine enemies: thou anointest my head with oil; my cup runneth over" (23:5). The striking imagery changes from the role of the shepherd to the bountiful realm of a generous host. Jehovah is that heavenly, holy host. A table of beautiful bounties (food and drink) was prepared the psalmist. It was done in the very presence of the enemies. They were impotent in preventing Jehovah's *setting* of the table and David's *sitting* at the table of prepared bounties. Enemies do not prevail where God and man are in fervent fellowship and form a holy partnership. As Paul later would write in the New Testament, "If God be for us, who can be against us?...Nay, in all these things we are more than conquerers through him that loved us" (Romans 8:31,37). The generous host anointed the head of the invited and esteemed guest. This is an attractive allusion to a well-established Oriental custom of pouring perfumed oil upon the head of a guest. In Luke 7:46 Jesus rebuked Simon the Pharisee for a flagrant failure to provide such upon His entrance into the Pharisee's home. Obviously, this does not refer to a *literal* anointing of perfumed oil the Lord lavishes upon us but is a figurative expression richly suggestive of all the beautiful blessings the host provides. He is a gracious, warm and perfect host. The running over of the cup is generously suggestive of manifold mercies extended, of abundant blessings bestowed. Abundance there is; scarcity there is none. Jehovah's gigantic cup of blessings is brimmed full of good things and even overflows the top. These good things include air, water, food, health, vigor, vitality, a job, home and family, friends, protection, guidance and all spiritual blessings. "No human pencil can describe all that God pours into the lot of our life" (Guy N. Woods).

"Surely goodness and mercy shall follow me all the days of my life: and I will dwell in the house of the Lord for ever" (23:6). With full assurance and no particle of doubt David penned these weighty words of unbending, uncompromising confidence. Goodness refers to all the gifts and blessings beautifully bequeathed us by the God of all generosity (See James 1:17). Mercy is God's tenderhearted feeling toward His people. In a later psalm David prayed,

Withhold not thou thy tender mercies from me, O Lord: let thy lovingkindness and thy truth continually preserve me. For innumerable evils have compassed me about: mine iniquities have taken hold upon me, so that I am not able to look up; they are more than the hairs of mine head: therefore my heart faileth me (Psalm 40:11,12).

David was confident of these twin blessings as his prized possession all his days. He spoke of dwelling in the house of the Lord forever. The house of the Lord in his era was the tabernacle; the temple was built just subsequent to his death. Unlike Samuel, David, not of priestly descent from Levi's tribe, did not live in or about the tabernacle. It was a place of worship—not a residence for David and all God's people. Therefore it seems far more likely that he here expresses a sublime thought of that heavenly dwelling in the land of fadeless day and beyond the bright blue. Brother Guy N. Woods has sagely written,

Why not then conclude that David looked to the end of life and to the home ultimately awaiting all the faithful where association with Jehovah is unending, in the city whose builder and maker is God? (See Hebrews 11:8-10). (G. A. Adult Quarterly, July 23, 1972, p. 19).

These have been my sentiments relative to David's meaning here in verse 6.

POINTS TO PONDER IN PSALM 23

1. For breadth and beauty, for conciseness and comfort, this psalm is without peer among its one hundred and forty-nine literary colleagues—the other chapters in Psalms.

2. Some people know just the twenty-third psalm; others know both the psalm and its shepherd.

3. In all the annals of atheism there is nothing to compare with the precious beauty of this psalm.

4. The royal recipe for victorious living is found written in this psalm.

5. A reading ascendancy of this psalm is to read it three times. The first time give equal emphasis to each word. The second time accent each of the seventeen personal pronouns. The third and final time accent each reference to the Shepherd and the Host. Why not try it?

DISCUSSION QUESTIONS

1. *What tributes have been given Psalm 23?*
2. *What descriptions are given the Lord or Jehovah here?*
3. *How does Psalm 78:70-72 fit in with the shepherd imagery of Psalm 23?*
4. *Give and discuss the kingly keynote of Psalm 23.*
5. *Read and discuss verse 2.*
6. *To what does David refer by the Lord's restoring his soul?*
7. *Analyze verse 4.*
8. *Describe Jehovah as the perfect host.*
9. *Define goodness and mercy in verse 6.*
10. *Read and discuss the Points To Ponder in Psalm 23.*

MULTIPLE CHOICE: Underline correct answer

1. *Psalm 23 is about: (A) five thousand years old; (B) three thousand years old; (C) two thousand years old; (D) one thousand years old—as touching its literary age.*
2. *Brother A. G. Freed called Psalm 23: (A) "The Shepherd Hymn;" (B) "The Hymn of the Generous Host;" (C) "The Life and Death Psalm;" (D) "The Restoration Psalm."*
3. *By actual count there are: (A) no; (B) seven; (C) seventeen; (D) twenty-seven—personal pronouns in Psalm 23.*
4. *The three Hebrew founding fathers were: (A) Adam, Enoch and Noah; (B) Shem, Ham and Japheth; (C) Abraham, Isaac and Jacob; (D) Saul, David and Solomon.*
5. *Jacob's family told the inquiring Pharaoh relative to their occupation that they were: (A) farmers; (B) shepherds; (C) artisans; (D) merchants.*

SCRIPTURAL FILL-IN: Each blank calls for but one word.

(1) *"The _____ is my _____; _____ shall not _____. He _____ me to _____ down in _____ pastures: he _____ me _____ the still waters."*

(2) *"He _____ my _____: he _____ me in the _____ of _____ for his _____ sake."*

(3) *"_____, though _____ walk through the _____ of the _____ of _____, I will _____ no _____: for _____ art with*

_____; thy _____ and thy _____ they _____ me."

(4) "Thou _____ a _____ before _____ in the _____ of mine _____: thou _____ my _____ with _____; my _____ runneth _____."

(5) "Surely _____ and _____ shall _____ me all the _____ of my _____: and I will _____ in the _____ of the _____ for ever."

TRUE OR FALSE: Put either a "T" or "F" in the blanks

____1. *Palestinian shepherds drove* their sheep just as we do here in our country of America.

____2. Satan is the giver of all good and perfect gifts.

____3. One can be righteous whether he ever obeys God's commandments and engages in right-doing or not.

____4. Simon the Pharisee was a perfect host to the Lord while visiting in his home in Luke 7:36-50.

____5. David rejected the concept of the home of the soul for the next world.

THOUGHT QUESTIONS

1. *Why do you think this has become the most beloved psalm in the Bible?*

2. *What probable reasons led to David's use of the shepherd imagery in this psalm?*

3. *Discuss the Palestinian shepherds and then apply these principles to Jehovah as our Heavenly Shepherd.*

4. *Describe the Lord as a gentle leader.*

5. *Tell why you do or do not believe David refers to heaven in verse 6.*

CHAPTER SEVEN

PSALM 51: DAVID'S PRAYER OF PENITENCE

The inscription at the beginning is not inspired but seemingly sets forth the very posture of this psalm and the very stance of its sentiments of sorrow and contrition. It states, "A Psalm of David, when Nathan the prophet came unto him, after he had gone in to Bath-sheba." The background of the psalm is 1 Samuel, chapters 11 and 12. David had committed the crimson crime of adultery with Bath-sheba, a bathing beauty upon whom his eye of passion was riveted in a time of idleness. Soon David was faced with the plight of paternity outside his family. He walked Deceptive Lane to cover his crime and ultimately treaded Murder Trail by conspiring to have the innocent husband, Uriah the Hittite, slain by an Ammonite sword. David was still calloused and impenetent over this chapter of crime in his life until the noble Nathan confronted him with his courageous "Thou art the man" approach. Driven to the knee of sorrow, regrets and real penitence David penned this psalm of his penitential confession. Therein David pleads for pardon and for the granting of a new heart. In tribute one veteran student of this psalm wrote, "this psalm is the brightest gem in the whole book, and contains instructions so large, and doctrine so precious, that the tongue of angels could not do it justice to the full development" (Quoted by Guy N. Woods, G. A. Adult Quarterly, August 13, 1972, p. 31).

THE DAVIDIC PLEA FOR MERCY

"Have mercy upon me, O God, according to thy lovingkindness: According unto the multitude of thy tender mercies blot out my transgressions. Wash me throughly from mine iniquity, and cleanse me from my sin'' (51:1,2). Grace is God's giving us what we do not deserve; mercy is God's refusal to give us what we do deserve. David was guilty of sin. He threw himself upon the mercy of the Heavenly Court and the Judge of all the earth. He made no excuse; he offered no extenuating circumstances; he blamed no other for his sins. He was guilty and longed for Jehovah's mercies to be tendered to him. He knew God was characterized by the kindness of love and by mercies multiplied again and again and again. Look at the number of times he has been merciful to you, dear reader, and then multiply it by four billion plus and you witness the amazing multiplicity of Jehovah's marvelous mercy to just one generation of human kind to say nothing of all preceding generations. David penitently petitioned to have his transgressions blotted out, his iniquity washed and his sin-scarred soul cleansed. David described his wrong with three words and depicted desired pardon also by trio of vivid terms. Transgression means to cross over the line of right and invade the forbidden realm of wrong-doing. Iniquity means to deviate from the right and true. Sin means to miss the mark or to come short of the target that God has established for us. In his plea for pardon David prayerfully petitioned for his sin to be erased or wiped away from the register that Almighty God keeps. He petitioned to be washed over and over and over until all the soiling blemishes of sin were removed from him. Quite literally the words are ''multiply to wash me.'' He sought to be cleansed totally and entirely cleansed. It was not a cleansing of a soiled garment but of a soiled soul, of a sinful saint who had dishonored God, his nation, his family and himself. David was concerned with the removal of guilt— not of future consequences. This is the heart of genuine, true repentance.

THE DAVIDIC CONFESSION OF SIN

''For I acknowledge my transgressions: and my sin is ever before me. Against thee, thee only, have I sinned, and done this evil in thy sight: that thou mightest be justified when thou speakest and be clear when thou judgest'' (51:3,4). David had said to Nathan, ''I have sinned against the Lord'' (2 Samuel 12:13). He neither denied guilt nor sought to implicate others. He did not say, ''Look what another made me do.'' He knew he had done wrong in the passion incident, in the attempts to have hidden it for so long and in Uriah's cruel murder. It was his sin—not another's. It is his ever present problem. He cannot put it away. Like an object that refuses to move it is with him day and night. One may flee many things but his sins go with him wherever he goes. Though he had sinned against Bath-sheba, and she against him, against his family and nation and against one of his bravest men on the fighting fronts—Uriah the Hittite—yet all these were secondary to the primary one against whom his sin had been aimed, i.e., God. All sin is against God. To see how much graver it is against God than against man consider in the parable of the unforgiving servant that the ten thousand talents represent our sins against God and the one hundred pennies our sins against each other (Matthew 18:23-35). David does not eliminate the wrongs he had inflicted upon others; he simply magnifies the primary one he had shamed, dishonored and disappointed—his Heavenly Father on high. Adultery, though usually done in privacy with only the two participants present, yet, it, along with all sins, is done in Jehovah's sight. Nothing escapes the All-Seeing eye (Hebrews 4:13; 1 Peter 3:12). There is clear recognition here on David's part that Jehovah would be just in what He said and how He judged David relative to this matter. Deity—not David— was in the driver's seat in the full settlement of such. Like Abraham in Genesis 18:25 David knew that the Judge of all the earth would do right. He always has. He always will.

"Behold, I was shapen in iniquity; and in sin did my mother conceive me" (51:5). This is one of the most abused and misunderstood verses among the 2,461 verses that compose this Old Testament book. Proponents of total hereditary depravity, one of the five major tenets of theological Calvinism, adamantly assert that this verse is in their camp as sustaining proof. NOT SO!! They have NO verses at all in their camp! The Bible *nowhere* teaches that we are born in sin, that we have Adamic sin or original sin tainting our souls at birth. We are NOT born totally depraved. Jesus stressed that people must become like little children before kingdom of heaven citizenship can be theirs (Matthew 18:3). Surely the Lord is not saying we must become totally depraved to enter the kingdom. The proud and profane prince of Tyre was not always in sin. The Bible says of him, "Thou wast perfect in thy ways from the day that thou wast created, till iniquity was found in thee" (Ezekiel 28:15). In this verse David is not teaching that he was a sinner from conception or birth. Here are cogent reasons why he was not. (1) He was confessiong adultery, deception and murder when he was a man of perhaps fifty years of age; he was no adulterer, deceiver or murderer until he committed these crimson crimes. (2) He is not confessing that his parents sinned in his conception and birth. They were married and had several children older than David and therefore had the right to mate and procreate David. (3) Original sin will not fit such definitions of sin as,

The thought of foolishness is sin:...And he that doubteth is damned if he eat, because he eateth not of faith: for whatsoever is not of faith is sin...Therefore to him that knoweth to do good, and doeth it not, to him it is sin...sin is the transgression of the law...All unrighteousness is sin (Proverbs 24:9; Romans 14:23; James 4:17; 1 John 3:4; 5:17).

Each of these inspired definitions of sin requires PERSONAL participation before transgression occurs. (4) Sin is something we do; not something we inherit from parents *immediately* at conception and birth or from Adam *remotely*. (5) No judgment passage in either testament says that we shall give an account of Adamic sin. Quite to the contrary we shall give account of ourselves and deeds done in the body—ours and not Adam's (Romans 14:12; 2 Corinthians 5:10). (6) David was born to parents who knew sin and had sinned because all accountable sin as both testaments affirm (1 Kings 8:46; Romans 3:9,23). (7) He was born into a world where sin abounds and where all ultimately do sin. (8) He was born into a world where temptations to sin run strongly and to one of them—fleshly passion—he had surrendered in a moment of weakness. (9) One can be conceived in a potato patch and be born there nine months later but he will not be full of spuds until he eats potatoes. (10) Brother Guy N. Woods has well written on this verse, "One becomes guilty of personal transgression only on reaching accountability. This is when one's mental development is sufficiently mature to distinguish between right and wrong." Psalm 51:5 is not a total hereditary depravity passage by any stretch of the Calvinistic imagination or their self-appointed torture of scripture for which they are so well noted.

THE DAVIDIC PLEA FOR PARDON

Behold, thou desirest truth in the inward parts: and in the hidden part thou shalt make me to know wisdom. Purge me with hyssop, and I shall be clean: wash me, and I shall be whiter than snow. Make me to hear joy and gladness; that the bones which thou hast broken may rejoice. Hide thy face from my sins, and blot out all mine iniquities (51:6-9).

David recognized that God desired inward sincerity and not just an outward conformity to formal religious ordinances. Truth in the heart was the eloquent equivalent of knowledgeable wisdom. The hyssop was a plant with long stems and leaves. It was dipped in the blood of their sacrifices and sprinkled for purification. David longed for the purging, the cleansing that this Mosaic rite symbolized. Martin Luther rendered the thought in his German translation by saying, *"unsin me with hyssop!"* David desired to be washed and made whiter than the purest of snow. David had heard the voice of passion, the voice of deception, the voice of murder, the voice of a pained conscience subsequent to Nathan's parable in 2 Samuel 12:1ff and the voice of sorrow over his grievous sins. Now he longed to hear the voice of joy and gladness. There is no *real* joy and *lasting* gladness in sinful indulgences. They are strictly seasonal in nature as affirmed in Hebrews 11:25 and soon the pleasure gives way to pain and trouble. Pleasant at first, sin soon grows very bitter as harvest time approaches. David had been crushed by his sin as though his bones were broken. Restoration of divine favor would be to his relieved soul what crushed bones suddenly mended again would mean to a formerly injured body. David had tried to hide or cover his sins the wrong way. This but compounded his problems. Now he seeks to cover them by proper pardon at Jehovah's hands. Now he requests that the Lord hide and blot out his sins in the way that merciful pardon dictated.

THE DAVIDIC DESIRE FOR A NEW HEART

Create in me a clean heart, O God; and renew a right spirit within me. Cast me not away from thy presence; and take not thy holy spirit from me. Restore unto me the joy of thy salvation; and uphold me with thy free spirit (51:10-12).

David's heart had been soiled with sin; a wrong spirit dominated him in the hour of passion, in the days of deception that ensued and in his mission of murdering a good, brave and innocent man—military benefactor. Now David yearns for the Lord to give him a clean, purified heart, a spirit made right by precious pardon. Being cast away and the removal of the Holy Spirit mean the same. He longed for favor to be restored—not a forfeiture of the Lord's comforting presence. He longed for the joy of salvation and the Lord's upholding of him again. He had drunk deeply of the cup of sin. He pleaded for restoration—not rejection.

THE DAVIDIC DETERMINATION TO WARN OTHERS

Then will I teach transgressors thy ways; and sinners shall be converted unto thee. Deliver me from bloodguiltiness,

O God, thou God of my salvation: and my tongue shall sing aloud of thy righteousness. O Lord, open thou my lips; and my mouth shall shew forth thy praise (51:13-15).

With the rich treasure of restoration in his grasp David resolutely promised to take God's truth to others who were yet in the way of waywardness and traveling the trails of transgression. He prayed for deliverance from the blood of Uriah that had stained his once saintly hands. Upon reception of the same he would sing with gladness Jehovah's righteousness. He prayed for open lips with which to sound forth the praises of his Mighty and Merciful Maker on high.

THE DAVIDIC RECOGNITION THAT SACRIFICES ALONE ARE INSUFFICIENT

For thou desirest not sacrifice; else would I give it; thou delightest not in burnt offering. The sacrifices of God are a broken spirit: a broken and a contrite heart, O God, thou wilt not despise (51:16,17).

This is not a blanket rejection of animal sacrifice in God's process of pardoning mercies. It is a firm recognition that animal sacrifices only procure the desired blessings when coupled with one who is truly penitent, one with a broken spirit, one with a contrite heart. Both were required — not one minus the other — in God's plan of pardon. The High and Holy One who inhabits eternity condescends to dwell in the contrite and humble spirit. This is the soul He pardons; this is the heart He revives (Isaiah 57:15).

THE DAVIDIC CONCERN FOR ZION

Do good in thy good pleasure unto Zion: build thou the walls of Jerusalem. Then shalt thou be pleased with the sacrifices of righteousness, with burnt offering and whole burnt offering: then shall they offer bullocks upon thine altar (51:18,19).

Certain have thought this to be a psalm written either in or past the Babylonian Exile. But too much of it points to David to construe it at such a later time of Hebrew history. David's sin had been a slap at Zion's future prosperity since he was king. Now his concern rises for his beloved Zion. There may well have been wall building for extra fortification going on at this time. Verse 19 closes the psalm with David's recognition that the righteousness of the people and their sincere sacrifices would procure Jehovah's sure favor. Such would brighten and bless the lives of Zion's citizenship as well.

POINTS TO PONDER IN PSALM 51

1. That sin has a payday in deep regrets, loss of joy and a separation from God and all that is good is seen vividly in this chapter.
2. The only recourse for the sinner who desires pardon is to cast himself on God's mercy.
3. This chapter is a graphic reminder that pardon takes place in the mind of God — not the heart of the sinner.
4. To show his gratitude the pardoned sinner desires to turn others away from sin and toward God.
5. The walls of Spiritual Zion are weakened when we sin; they are strengthened when we repent and become stalwart saints again.

DISCUSSION QUESTIONS

1. *Discuss the inscription that heads this psalm.*
2. *Read and give a brief analysis of 2 Samuel, chapters 11 and 12.*
3. *What appropriate tribute was paid this psalm?*
4. *List and discuss the three terms David used for his wrong and the three words he used for the desired remission of this grievous wrong.*
5. *Describe David's confession of his sin in verses 3 and 4.*
6. *Read and discuss verse 5 and refute thoroughly the Calvinistic approach to it.*
7. *Discuss David's great desire for a new heart.*
8. *Discuss David's concern for Zion.*
9. *Why is Psalm 51 not an exile psalm?*
10. *Read and discuss the Points to Ponder in Psalm 51.*

MULTIPLE CHOICE: Underline correct answer

1. *David's crime of passion in 2 Samuel 11 was with (A) Bath-sheba; (B) Michal; (C) Abigail; (D) Maacah.*
2. *Her innocent husband was: (A) Abner; (B) Joab; (C) Ishbosheth; (D) Uriah the Hittite.*
3. *(A) Nathan; (B) Absalom; (C) King Saul; (D) Abner — once spoke the words, "Thou art the man," to King David.*

4. *(A) Abraham; (B) Abimelech; (C) Absalom; (D) Nimrod — in Genesis 18:25 declared that the Judge of all the earth would do right.*
5. *(A) Jehovah; (B) Satan; (C) The Pope; (D) Michael; (E) Gabriel — is the high and holy one who inhabits eternity and dwells in the heart of the humble and contrite.*

SCRIPTURAL FILL-IN: Only one word is required in each blank.

(1) "_____ me _____ from mine _____, and _____ me from my _____. For I _____ my _____: and my _____ is ever _____ me."

(2) "_____ thee, _____ only, have I _____, and _____ this _____ in thy _____: that _____ mightest be _____ when thou _____, and be _____ when thou _____."

(3) "_____, I was _____ in _____; and in _____ did my _____ conceive _____."

(4) "_____ me with _____, and I shall be _____: _____ me, and I shall be _____ than _____. _____ me to hear _____ and _____; that the _____ which thou hast _____ may _____. _____ thy _____ from my _____, and _____ out all mine _____."

(5) "The _____ of _____ are a _____ spirit: a broken and a contrite _____, O God, thou wilt not _____."

TRUE OR FALSE: Put either a "T" or "F" in the blanks

_____1. *David extended all sorts of excuses for his shameful conduct with Bath-sheba.*

_____2. *The removal of guilt — not consequences — is the very heart of genuine, true repentance.*

_____3. *David's prayer to be forgiven of bloodguiltiness has reference to all the Philistines he had killed in warfare with them.*

_____4. *David had no faith at all in animal sacrifices and felt they did no good at all.*

_____5. *David's heart is tender and his conscience is sensitive throughout Psalm 51.*

THOUGHT QUESTIONS

1. *Discuss grace and mercy as they relate to this psalm.*
2. *In what way may we be led to appreciate the multiplicity of Jehovah's mercy?*
3. *How will original or Adamic sin not fit a single Biblical definition of sin as given in some five scriptural passages?*
4. *Discuss in detail David's plea for pardon.*
5. *Discuss improper ways to cover sins and then the proper way to cover them.*

CHAPTER EIGHT

PSALM 90: A POETIC PRAYER OF MOSES

In actual material Moses, the man of God, penned about twenty-five percent of the Old Testament. He penned the Pentateuch or the five books of Genesis through Deuteronomy. The ninetieth psalm is his lone contribution to this precious poetic portion of Sacred Scripture. That Moses was of poetic ability is witnessed in the majestic Mosaic song of Deuteronomy 32. In this beautiful chapter near the end of Deuteronomy the magnanimous Moses presents a stately song that marvelously majors in the priceless, precious perfections of Jehovah.

Psalm 90 is a prayer. Two leading lines of thought compose it. They are: (1) the eternality of God; and (2) the frailty of man.

JEHOVAH'S ETERNALITY

"Lord, thou has been our dwelling place in all generations. Before the mountains were brought forth, or ever thou hadst formed the earth and the world, even from everlasting to everlasting, thou art God" (90:1,2). *Lord*, with which this psalm begins, is not the word for Jehovah but derives from the Hebrew word *Adonai* and is rendered "Lord" in both the KJV and the ASV. The term means one who rules or governs. Moses viewed the Lord as being their "dwelling place." Let it be recalled that Moses had known forty years of sojourning in the land of Midian as a wandering shepherd and then knew another forty years as a nomad up and down and from west to east in the barren wilderness. How precious to him therefore to know that in God he had a home wherein he could find refuge, peace, contentment, rest, strength and spiritual fellowship. A good home provides all these and they were all found in the lovely Lord of heaven. Not only Moses but all generations of the godly have found the same beautiful blessings in the Lord. What a delightful dwelling place He is to all lovers of truth and righteousness. He provides His people a temporary home here and an eternal home in heaven in the sweet by and by.

Being an eternal, infinite being God antedates the mountains. A glimpse of them gives indication of what has been here a long, long time. Yet there was a time when neither the earth nor the mountains had an existence. They were brought forth in the early morning of creation. Relative to their beginning Moses had written in Genesis 1. Prior to the creation of earth and all therein God had an existence — an eternal one. Even from everlasting (the eternity prior to time) to everlasting (the eternity that is subsequent to time) He is God. Such a concept soars far above our power to comprehend fully. By majestic and marvelous faith we can say, "We believe it because God said it and it is impossible for him to lie" (Hebrews 6:18; Titus 1:2). He is the First Cause though not caused by anything or anyone prior to Him. He has made all else we behold. Let him who reneges at this contemplate his only options which are the eternity of matter or that nothing somehow, somewhere and someway got busy one day and made something and look what we now have in the way of the universe and all therein and an amazing universe it is anyway it is beheld. Eternal Mind (God), Eternal Matter or something's coming from nothing are the three alternatives before intelligent men. A fourth alternative that some have suggested is hardly worth mentioning. It is a denial of all reality and that the universe is really just an illusion. It is a thousand, even a million times easier to accept what Moses penned here and in his sane, sensible, majestic and marvelous account in Genesis 1 than to accept Eternal Matter or that nothing made lifeless matter and lifeless matter somehow, somewhere and someway made all living organisms — both the simple and the deeply complex such as man.

MAN'S FRAILTY

"Thou turnest man to destruction; and sayest, Return, ye children of men. For a thousand years in thy sight are but as yesterday when it is past, and as a watch in the night" (90:3,4). In marked contrast with the eternality of God we have the frailty of humanity. By sin man was compelled to forfeit Eden and the tree of life. Because man has no access to this tree of life physical death is the common lot of all mankind. Only two of the past have escaped it — Enoch in Genesis 5 and Elijah in 2 Kings 2. No one will escape it in the future except those alive at Christ's advent the second time (See 1 Corinthians 15:50ff). "It is appointed unto men once to die, . . ." the Bible affirms in Hebrews 9:27. All men should set their houses in order for we all shall die and not live (Isaiah 38:1). Man's return to dust is not only an affirmation here but also in Genesis 3:19 and Ecclesiastes 12:7. Yet the same God who has decreed man's physical demise only has to speak specific words of power and the resurrection will occur. The children of men will be returned by resurrected bodies. Time is of great essence to man but not to God. Man is a creature of time; God transcends time. Just as we witness how quickly a yesterday has gone so is a thousand years with God. Such is as but a watch in the night to man. Hebrew watches in the Old Testament were of four hours' duration; Roman watches of the New Testament had narrowed a watch to three hours. The point is obvious. Life at its longest is short-lived. It is not much sooner begun than it ends. Man beats a rapid course of travel from the cradle to the cemetery.

> Thou carriest them away as with a flood; they are as a sleep: in the morning they are like grass which groweth up. In the morning it flourisheth, and groweth up; in the evening it is cut down, and withereth (90:5,6).

These are vivid comparisons. Brevity of life for all men is like a flood which can come so quickly and carry people to their destruction. It is no respecter of persons in that it is equally destructive to young and old, to rich and poor, to wise and ignorant and to the healthy and the infirm. Death is of like character. The next graphic comparison is that of sleep. How exceedingly short seems the time from when we pillow our heads for a night of sweet slumber and when we awake the next morning. Upon being asked how he slept one night a little boy once said, "I slept fast last night!" And indeed it seemed that way to him. Grass becomes the next vivid simile. It buds forth into the greenery of beauty in the morning only to brown into ugliness by sunset. The bright active child today is tomorrow's senior citizen facing his own soon-to-come sunset. So short is life that we speak of the life span of man by seasons. There is the springtime of youth, the summertime of prime adulthood, the autumn of advancing age, graying hair, stooped frames and finally the wintertime that brings death.

"For we are consumed by thine anger, and by thy wrath are we
 hast set our iniquities before thee, our secret sins in the

light of thy countenance" (90:7,8). Israel's Sweet Singer was keenly conscious of man's weaknesses, failures, frailties and follies. God's anger and wrath are not sinful in nature. They fall into what might be styled Jehovah's righteous indignation. Sin in Eden first caused God's anger and wrath to erupt into judicial indignation. Sins of humanity since have continued to prompt the crystal clear exhibition of God's anger and wrath. Sin has always extracted a high price from its willing practitioners.

Men have always had a tendency to hide their sins from God or at least attempt to do so and that is all it is — a futile attempt. All sins are known to God. Though secretly committed in dense and deep darkness yet they are seen clearly and completely by man's Maker. His is the All-seeing eye. Nothing escapes His minute scrutiny and ever apt attention (Hebrews 4:13; 1 Peter 3:12).

> For all our days are passed away in thy wrath: we spend our years as a tale that is told. The days of our years are threescore years and ten; and if by reason of strength they be fourscore years, yet is their strength labour and sorrow; for it is soon cut off, and we fly away. Who knoweth the power of thine anger? even according to thy fear, so is thy wrath (90:9-11).

Moses is not here saying that God is always angry with all humanity. The righteous are ever His deep delight and pure pleasure. But the righteous live on a sin-cursed earth and among sin-practicing people who defy God's law daily. Even the righteous suffer much due to the sins of others and ultimately must die physically. Wrath here may well represent the physical death that comes to all. Our years are spent so quickly. The ASV says, "We bring our years to an end as a sigh." Life is likened to a momentary breath and then disappears. Threescore and ten and fourscore refer respectively to seventy and eighty years of age at demise. This was life's average thirty-five centuries ago; it is still about life's average in our country. It is true that some live longer than this just as Moses, Aaron and Miriam who exceeded the average by one-half century in the very era this literary psalm was composed by Moses. Yet many died far short of this seventy to eighty mark just as is the case currently. Even an extension of life has its labors and sorrows as it is far more difficult to meet personal needs and sorrows seem to mount higher and higher the longer we stay on this mundane sphere known as earth. At best man is soon cut off; he dies. He flies away; his soul takes leave of his body just as in Rachel's case in Genesis 35:18. The body — not the immortal spirit or soul — is entombed; the spirit or soul goes to Sheol (Old Testament description of this intermediate sphere) or Hades (New Testament description of the same sphere) to await judgment on that final day. The wicked soul in the intermediate state will anguish in torments; the righteous soul will be comforted and contented in a realm of rest (Luke 16:19ff; 23:43; Revelation 6:9-11). Brother Guy N. Woods has sagely suggested, "How vastly important it is that we live through our allotment of time here in such fashion as to 'fly away' into the care and keeping of the Lord when the death angel comes" (G. A. Adult Quarterly, Summer, 1972, p. 43).

Finite man is incapable of comprehending or apprehending the incomparable power of God's righteous anger and His judicial wrath that have been aroused by man's foolishness and folly. Sin on man's part prompted the wrath of God. No mention is made of God's wrath until man rebelled against his marvelous Creator.

"So teach us to number our days, that we may apply our hearts unto wisdom" (90:12). This does not mean to determine the precise years of our pilgrimage on earth but make life count. Quality of life is vastly more important than quantity of life. We number our days when we glorify God, profit humanity and prepare adequately to go home to heaven in the sweet by and by. This and this only is the adequate application of the human heart in the ways of wisdom. To be wise means knowledge and practice of how to make a living and even more importantly how to make a life — a lovely life by Jehovah's stately standards.

PRECIOUS, PRAYERFUL PETITIONS IN CONCLUSION

Return, O Lord, how long? and let it repent thee concerning thy servants. O satisfy us early with thy mercy; that we may rejoice and be glad all our days. Make us glad according to the days wherein thou hast afflicted us, and the years wherein we have seen evil. Let thy work appear unto thy servants, and thy glory unto their children. And let the beauty of the Lord our God be upon us: and establish thou the work of our hands upon us; yea, the work of our hands establish thou it (90:13-17).

A succinct summary of these verses is: (1) a request for the Lord's return to and approval again subsequent to some visitation of His aroused wrath upon His servants; (2) their full spiritual satisfaction early in the morning somewhat like breakfast eaten and fresh air taken into the body upon arising from a night of sweet slumber; (3) a supreme wish to know gladsome joy the remnant of life; (4) to make

67

our period of joy as long as the past period of affliction and evil has been; (5) to manifest the wonders of thy work and exhibit the generosity of thy glory to us — thy servants — and to our children; (6) to let the royal and regal radiancy of thy spiritual beauty be our precious possession; and (7) to grant success to our efforts to serve thee and eloquently establish our works upon a firm and permanent basis.

What a tremendously prayerful psalm the Holy Spirit penned by Mosaic hands thirty-five centuries ago. Great would have been our loss had it never seen the literary light of day.

POINTS TO PONDER FROM PSALM 90

1. The Bible believer has Jehovah as the First Great Cause from which everything has sprung.

2. The Bible infidel has no one as the First Great Cause from which everything has sprung.

3. The average of life in our land is just about the same as Moses mentions some thirty-five centuries ago.

4. The egotistical man should look at God's greatness and his own littleness and his pride surely would vanish *promptly* and *permanently.*

5. Too many go through life and never learn to number the days or apply the heart to wisdom.

6. We should be a people eager to have the beauty of the Lord bequeathed us.

DISCUSSION QUESTIONS

1. *What two Bible chapters exhibit Moses as a writer of great poetic ability?*

2. *What are the two leading lines of thought developed in Psalm 90?*

3. *Discuss God as the infinite being who antedates the earth and its majestic mountains.*

4. *What options are open to the man who rejects God?*

5. *What is really much easier to believe and why?*

6. *Discuss time as man views it and as God views it.*

7. *Describe brevity of life and death in this chapter.*

8. *Describe the life span of man by use of the four seasons.*

9. *Where does the soul or spirit go at death?*

10. *List and discuss the points covered in Psalm 90:13-17.*

MULTIPLE CHOICE: Underline correct answer

1. *Moses penned: (A) none of the Bible; (B) all the Old Testament; (C) half of the New Testament books; (D) the Pentateuch and Psalm 90 which make up twenty percent of the whole Bible and twenty-five percent of the Old Testament.*

2. *Of all people of the past the only two men to have escaped the physical death penalty were: (A) Abraham and Jacob; (B) Job and David; (C) Noah and Isaiah; (D) Enoch and Elijah.*

3. *Hebrew people of the Old Testament divided the night watches into: (A) six; (B) two; (C) four; (D) three — hours' duration.*

4. *The Bible in Genesis 35:18 speaks of the death of: (A) Sarah; (B) Rebekah; (C) Leah; (D) Rachel — and how her soul took leave of her body or tabernacle of clay.*

5. *Sheol and Hades are names of: (A) Bible cities in Palestine; (B) countries where Israelites once lived before they inhabited Canaan; (C) two prominent men in Old Testament times; (D) the intermediate state where all souls go at death to await final judgment and ultimate destinies of eternity.*

SCRIPTURAL FILL-IN: Each blank requires only one word.

(1) "_____, thou hast been our _____ place in all _____. Before the _____ were brought forth, or ever that hadst _____ the earth and the _____, even from _____ to _____ thou art _____."

(2) "For _____ our _____ are _____ away in thy _____: we _____ our _____ as a _____ that is _____."

(3) "The _____ of our _____ are _____ years and _____; and if by _____ of _____ they be _____ years, yet is their _____ labor and _____; for it is soon _____ off, and we _____ away."

(4) "So _____ us to _____ our _____, that we may _____ our _____ unto _____."

(5) "And let the _____ of the _____ our God be upon us: and _____ thou the _____ of our _____ upon us; yea, the _____ of our _____ establish thou _____."

TRUE OR FALSE: Put either a "T" or "F" in the blanks

____1. Psalm 90 was written by an atheist.

____2. Psalm 90 teaches the eternality of matter and rejects the eternality of Mind (God).

____3. God is the First Great Cause and from Him everything has sprung.

____4. Physical death is the common lot of humanity because man has no access to the tree of life.

____5. Quality of life is more important in the long run than quantity of years.

THOUGHT QUESTIONS

1. Discuss the word "Lord" in Psalm 90:1.
2. Why would the stately sentiment of God as being "our dwelling place" be of such precious appeal to Moses?
3. Discuss God as being from everlasting to everlasting.
4. Discuss God's anger and wrath toward sin.
5. Why is it futile to try and hide our sins from God?

CHAPTER NINE

PSALM 119: GOD'S WORD DESCRIBED, EXALTED AND EXTOLLED (NO. 1)

Psalm 119 is one of the most brilliant, beautiful and breathtaking of all the precious psalms. It is unique in a marvelous multitude of ways. (1) It is the longest chapter in our current arrangement of the Bible — 176 verses. (2) It is divided into twenty-two equal divisions with eight verses in each section. (3) Each division is begun with a letter of the Hebrew alphabet such as Aleph, Beth, Gimel, Daleth, etc. Each verse in each of these divisions is begun with that alphabetical letter. The Hebrew alphabet was composed of twenty-two letters. (4) This chapter exalts and extolls the Bible. Almost every verse has something to say by way of thrilling tribute expressed relative to God's word. We do not overdraw the matter when we say that the Bible's longest chapter is a chapter about the Bible.

There is nothing in the Psalm to pinpoint its precise penman or the precise point of time for its courageous composition. David may well have been its human author; without quibble the Holy Spirit is the heavenly author. The sentiments are rather Davidic in their noble nature. Another devout disciple or pious person may have been its writer or compiler. We can point out some people who did not pen it. (1) It was not penned by an atheist or infidel. (2) It was not penned by a disciple of the devil. (3) It was not penned by a God-hater. (4) It was not penned by one who disdained right and held truth in contempt. (5) It was not penned by a prodigal who majored in fleshly lusts and the prompt fulfillment of the same. (6) It was not penned by one who believed the Bible is humanly derived. (7) It was not penned by one who counted the Bible as a dead document, as a non-living letter. (8) It was not written by one who thought a person can prove anything by the Bible. (9) It was not penned by one who believed the Bible had to be directly illuminated by the Holy Spirit before it is profitable or comprehensible on man's part. (10) It was not written by one who viewed the Bible as being of little value or worth. (11) It was not written by one who viewed the Bible as filled with myths, legends, contradictions, jarring disharmonies, unbelievable folklore, etc. (12) It was not written by one who viewed the Bible as obsolete, archaic or out-of-date for finite man.

Many years ago I heard the late and lamented J. Roy Vaughn, former news editor and later editor of the GOSPEL ADVOCATE, make mention of a memorization plan adopted by the brilliant Hall L. Calhoun. Brother Calhoun made it a point to memorize Psalm 119 at regular intervals. He did it for the mental exercise involved and the profit it would bequeath to his life. Brother Vaughn's mention of that lodged in my mind immediately. It was an idea whose time had come for me. For twenty-two days each year, I usually choose February for it is a less taxing month for me, I memorize Psalm 119. I take a division of eight verses per day. It is an enriching experience and I commend its adoption to every admirer of this precious psalm. It will be a rich adornment to you in character development. After one or two memorizations the remainder will simply be a refresher in its annual memorization.

Even with two chapters in this volume dedicated to this marvelous material there is no way every verse can be treated to the expository elaboration it richly deserves. An entire book could be devoted to this chapter and still not do it literary justice. I hope to do an entire book on this chapter sometime in the future. But currently it shall be my purpose to divide my comments into about ten topical studies as suggested by the contents of this unique chapter. Even then very brief will be comments made.

TEN COMPREHENSIVE WORDS EMPLOYED TO DESCRIBE GOD'S WORD

Numerous commentators have pointed out these terms which are: (1) testimonies; (2) commandments; (3) precepts; (4) word; (5) law; (6) ways; (7) truth; (8) judgments; (9) righteousness; and (10) statutes. Definitions will be given each of these ten terms and then an appropriate scripture from the chapter will be quoted where the stately term occurs. The quoted definitions are drawn from outstanding Biblical scholarship.

(1) Testimonies ("edoth, from ad") are defined as "beyond, farther, all along, to bear witness, or testimony." They are styled testimonies because "they are solemnly declared to the world." In the Aleph section the inspired writer wrote, "Blessed are they that keep his testimonies, and that seek him with the whole heart" (119:2).

(2) Commandments ("mitsvoth, from tasvah") mean "to command order, ordain." Jehovah's commandments are "given with authority and lodged with us as a trust." They pinpoint what should be done positively and what should not be done negatively. They provide the comprehensive boundaries of obedience, of submission to divine charges. In the Tau section we read, "My tongue shall speak of thy word: for all thy commandments are righteousness" (119:172).

(3) Precepts ("pikkudim, from pakad") are delineated in definition as "to take notice or care of a thing, to attend, have respect to, to appoint, to visit." They constitute God's rules which have been "prescribed to us." In the Mem section we read, "Through thy precepts I get understanding: therefore I hate every false way" (119:104).

(4) Word ("dabar") is defined as "to discourse, utter one's sentiments, speak consecutively and intelligently." Any and all pronouncements or declarations from Deity may be styled as God's word. In a real sense it is a favorite term among Biblical penmen to refer to the entire body of divine or inspired revelation. In the Lamed section we read, "For ever, O Lord, thy word is settled in heaven" (119:89).

(5) Law ("torah, from yarah") is defined as meaning to "direct, guide, teach, make straight, or even, to point forward." God's law is enacted by him who is the sovereign of the universe. Law shows us what is right and what is wrong. It encourages following the former and leaving off the latter. In the Tzaddi section we read, "Thy righteousness is an everlasting righteousness, and thy law is the truth" (119:142).

(6)Way ("derech") means "to proceed, go on, walk, tread." The ways of God point both to His providence over us and our obedient response to His prescribed manner of life. In the Daleth section we read, "I have chosen the way of truth: thy judgments have I laid before me" (119:30).

(7) Truth ("emunah, from aman") means "to make steady, constant, to settle, trust, believe." God's truth may be accepted in all confidence because He cannot lie (Hebrews 6:18; Titus 1:2). "The Bible said it; I believe it; that settles it!" is built on this very concept. In the Koph section we read, "Thou art near, O Lord; and all thy commandments are truth" (119:151).

(8) Judgments ("mishpatim, from shaphat") mean "to judge, determine, regulate, order, and discern." They are styled judgments because by them "we must both judge and be judged." They enable us to determine right over wrong and to act accordingly. In the Jod section we note, "I know, O Lord, that thy judgments are right, and that thou in faithfulness hast afflicted me" (119:75).

(9) Righteousness ("tsedakah, from tsadah") means "to do justice, to give full weight." Jehovah's righteousness "is all holy, just, and good, and

73

the rule and standard of righteousness." To be righteous we must give to God His due and to others their due likewise. In the Tau section we read, "My tongue shall speak of thy word: for all thy commandments are righteousness" (119:172).

(10) Statutes ("chukkim, from chak") mean "to mark, trace out, describe, and ordain." They are Jehovah's statutes "because they are fixed, and of perpetual obligation." In Deity's statutes to us we have marked out the way we should walk; we have traced for us the direction for our journey; we have described the manner of life to be lived; we have ordained for us the charges to be kept. In the Samech section we read, "Hold thou me up, and I shall be safe: and I will have respect unto thy statutes continually" (119:117).

All definitions and quotations by way of comment in this section have been taken from the scholarly and devotional commentaries by Adam Clarke and Matthew Henry.

"TRUE-HEARTED, WHOLE-HEARTED"

The title of this section of study is lifted from the name of a great Christian hymn. Frances R. Havergal penned the expressive words; George C. Stebbins provided the marvelous music. Psalm 119 is a clarion call for the true in heart and the whole in heart to serve God. A number of valiant verses in this courageous chapter mention wholeness of heart. Here is a quartet of them numbered and noted,

> (1) Blessed are they that keep his testimonies, and that seek him with the whole heart (119:2). (2) With my whole heart have I sought thee: O let me not wander from thy commandments (119:10). (3) Give me understanding, and I shall keep thy law; yea, I shall observe it with my whole heart (119:34) (4) The proud have forged a lie against me: but I will keep thy precepts with my whole heart (119:69).

These passages say nothing about the blood pump in the chest region of a person's body. This is the Biblical heart or the mind of man. The whole of man's heart consists of his intellect, his emotions, his will-power and his conscience. With the intellect we think, reason, understand, weigh evidence, come to valid and sound conclusions, etc. With the emotions we love, hate, trust, etc. With the will-power we choose, decide, execute a given action, etc. The conscience is man's "oughtness" mechanism. It approves when we do that we think is right; it disapproves when we do that we believe to be wrong. The conscience does not provide that standard of right or wrong; this is provided by God's word — the Bible. When the heart is saturated with God's truth that has been learned (intellect), that is now loved and trusted (emotions) and has been obeyed (will-power) then the tender, sensitive concience is in position to function in its "oughtness" manner. Pleasure is produced when we pursue the pure; pain is the end result when we revel in rebellion against God and His holy law.

Great is the Lord's need for dedicated disciples, for consecrated Christians who are "true-hearted, whole-hearted." Perusing and practicing the precious principles of this tremendous chapter can help produce such.

"HOW SHALL THE YOUNG SECURE THEIR HEARTS?"

This title also is lifted from a beautiful and beloved song that is a marvelous musical gem in helping youth be what Jehovah and Jesus intend. Isaacs Watts penned the words and the music is Beethoven's. There is little doubt but what Psalm 119 provided the beautiful background as touching Watts' expressed sentiments. Psalm 119:9-11 gives in essence this question and provides Inspiration's articulate answer in poetic preciousness. These opening three verses in the Beth section read,

> Wherewithal shall a young man cleanse his way? by taking heed thereto according to thy word. With my whole heart have I sought thee: O let me not wander from thy commandments. Thy word have I hid in mine heart, that I might not sin against thee.

The pivotal question of verse 9 is pressed deeply upon our minds. The fundamental, forthright answer is given in admirable, articulate fashion. The young man has his way cleansed by taking diligent heed to God's word. This has always been how heavenly pardon is received. Joseph in Genesis 39, Daniel in Daniel 1:8 and Jesus in Matthew 4 and Luke 4 kept their way clean by heeding God's word. They did not perform a miracle a day in Pat Boone fashion to keep the devil away. Jesus employed the "It is written" weapon to send the devil reeling in abject, humiliating defeat.

Then there is wholeness of heart dedication in seeking, finding and retaining Deity when once found. Isaiah 55:6; 2 Chronicles 15:2; Matthew 6:33 and Acts 17:27 are all great Biblical passages relative to humanity's seeking the God of heaven. Then we have the precious, prayerful petition aimed against our wandering (straying from) God's commandments.

Verse 11 portrays the greatest thing in the world (God's word) hidden in the greatest human vessel (man's heart) and with the greatest fruit as accruing (success in NOT sinning against God).

Here is Inspiration's sure formula for all (youth, older and all in-between) to secure our hearts. In NO other realm is there any semblance of spiritual safety and moral security.

THE STUDY OF GOD'S WORD

This entire Psalm emphasizes this greatly needed concept. The following quartet of verses does it so well. We number and note them,

> (1) Let the proud be ashamed; for they dealt perversely with me without a cause: but I will meditate in thy precepts (119:78) (2) O how love I thy law! it is my meditation all the day (119:97) (3) I have more understanding than all my teachers: for thy testimonies are my meditation (119:99). (4) Mine eyes prevent (anticipated — ASV) the night watches, that I might meditate in thy word (119:148).

These stately sentiments remind us of Psalm 1:2 which says, "But his delight is in the law of the Lord, and in his law doth he meditate day and night." Great love for God's word will make time for much meditation therein. Proper meditation therein leads to an understanding that Biblical ignoramuses will NEVER possess. There are not any more imperative duties devolving upon modern man than to hear and heed, to peruse and practice God's word.

COMMANDMENT KEEPING

Psalm 119:60 say it so tersely and so truthfully, "I made haste, and delayed not to keep thy commandments." Combined here we have a prompt positive — the making of haste; we have a noble negative injected — a refusal to delay. There is a precious priority that grows out of this haste, this delaying not — the keeping of God's commands. Should not all today be likeminded? How fine if people were prompt in gospel obedience— hearing, faith, repenting, confession and baptism (immersion) and not fill- ed with injurious indecision and perilous procrastination — perpetual thieves of souls. How fine if all were prompt in the living of the Christian life — worshipping, working, watching and waiting — and not filled with lukewarmness and procrastination.

The tone and tenor of Psalm 119 march to the triumphant tune of *learning, living,* and *loving* God's word. This chapter beautifully bequeathes to us these three lovely L's.

POINTS TO PONDER IN PSALM 119

1. God's word is precious to Him; it must be precious to man also.
2. The word of God is as much higher than man's word as the lofty heavens soar above mother earth.
3. God's word is neither dead nor dormant.

76

4. Quite to the contrary it is alive and active; it is powerful and penetrating.
5. How man feels about the Bible is a real index to his character.
6. There is far more true wisdom couched in Psalm 119 than can be found in entire libraries of just humanly produced works.

DISCUSSION QUESTIONS

1. Describe Psalm 119 and then list and discuss its uniqueness as a chapter.
2. List the ten terms for God's revelation that occur in this chapter.
3. Now define these various terms.
4. Now give a verse for each of these where the term is used in the verse cited.
5. Read and discuss Psalm 119:9-11.
6. Why are Joseph, Daniel and Jesus all mentioned in connection with Psalm 119?
7. Read and discuss the cited passages in other Biblical books that relate to seeking God.
8. What great lesson is taught in Psalm 1:2?
9. Discuss commandment keeping from Psalm 119.
10. What are the three lovely L's found in Psalm 119?
11. Read and discuss the Points to Ponder in Psalm 119.

MULTIPLE-CHOICE: Underline correct answer

1. Aleph, Beth, Gimel and Daleth are: (A) names of men who wrote Psalm 119; (B) great Bible cities wherein portions of the Psalms were written; (C) names of great, godly women in the Bible; (D) the opening four letters of the Hebrew alphabet and which head the first four divisions of Psalm 119.

2. The Hebrew alphabet had: (A) twenty-two letters; (B) twenty-six letters just as does ours; (C) twelve letters; (D) twenty-four letters which is the same as the Greek has.

3. Relative to the human author of Psalm 119 we can say that: (A) David is its definite author; (B) David is definitely ruled out as author; (C) we do not know the exact author; (D) Moses wrote it while he was in the wilderness.

4. Hall L. Calhoun: (A) greatly loved Psalm 119 and committed it to memory at regular intervals; (B) did not believe Psalm 119 belonged in the Bible; (C) thought Psalm 119 was a literary failure; (D) was largely indifferent to Psalm 119.

5. *Frances R. Havergal, George C. Stebbins, Isaac Watts and Beethoven are all mentioned in this chapter that deals with Psalm 119 because of: (A) two appropriate songs which are mentioned and they either composed or for which they provided music; (B) their dislike of Psalm 119; (C) commentaries they have written on Psalm 119; (D) the great sermons they frequently preached on Psalm 119.*

SCRIPTURAL FILL-IN: Only one word is required in each blank.

(1) *"My _____ shall _____ of thy _____: for all thy _____ are _____."*

(2) *"_____ thy _____ I get _____: therefore I _____ every _____ way."*

(3) *"For _____, O _____, thy _____ is _____ in _____."*

(4) *"Thy _____ have I _____ in mine _____, that I _____ not _____ against thee."*

(5) *"_____ how _____ I thy _____! it is my _____ all the _____."*

TRUE OR FALSE: Put either a "T" or "F" in the blanks

____1. *Psalm 119 could have been written by most any non-believer or irreligious person.*

____2. *The writer of Psalm 119 believed there is no law, no regulation and no rule for God's child — only grace.*

____3. *The Bible heart uniformly refers to the physical blood pump in the chest region of the human body.*

____4. *Conscience as a safe guide in religion receives much proof in Psalm 119.*

____5. *Great love for God's word will make time available for Biblical meditation.*

THOUGHT QUESTIONS

1. *List some of the people who did not write Psalm 119 and tell why.*
2. *Discuss wholeness of heart as set forth in Psalm 119.*
3. *Why is Bible Study such a neglected art in our day?*
4. *Why do you think so little of it is done by the rank and file followers of the Lord today?*
5. *Why is Biblical ignorance such a far-reaching sin in our day?*

CHAPTER TEN

PSALM 119: GOD'S WORD DESCRIBED, EXALTED AND EXTOLLED (NO. 2)

Psalm 119 has been called the "saints' alphabet." This is due to the twenty-two divisions which are begun respectively with letters of the Hebrew alphabet. With equal, eloquent appropriateness it might be styled "An Inspired Tribute To The Bible."

In the previous chapter attention was focused upon some precious preliminaries relative to the chapter. I listed, defined and exemplified with an appropriate scripture the ten terms employed to describe Jehovah's message to man. Then such segments of thought as whole-hearted religion, scriptural security for youth, the imperative need to study God's word and humanity's desperate need to hear and heed Jehovah's commandments were stressed. Of necessity comments on such a lengthy chapter have to be brief and very much to the point.

THE QUICKENING (LIVING) POWER OF GOD'S WORD

There are at least ten verses in this tremendous chapter that employ the concept of quickening. Five of them will be numbered, noted and comments relative to them will follow,

> (1) My soul cleaveth unto the dust: quicken thou me according to thy word (119:25). (2) Behold, I have longed after thy precepts: quicken me in thy righteousness (119:40). (3) I will never forget thy precepts: for with them thou hast quickened

me (119:93). (4) Plead my cause, and deliver me: quicken me according to thy word (119:154). (5) Great are thy tender mercies, O Lord: quicken me according to thy judgments (119:156).

Causing to live or "make me alive" is the major import of quickening in all these passages. Reference is to spiritual life for people who despise God's word possess physical life. Two agencies are involved in this living process — God and man. God wills for man to live spiritually when man wills to do God's bidding productive of such life. Israel's Sweet Singer was neither a "grace only" (with God only as active) or a "faith only" (with man only as active) advocate in this living process. The precious psalmist knew that God's word was powerful and penetrating; he knew that it was ardent and active; he knew that it was lovely and life-giving. The word of God was no dead letter to him. He knew better. So should all religionists today and especially those of the Calvinistic brand but alas, they do not!

THE MAJESTY OF LOVE IN PSALM 119

I have noted many marvelous verses in this unique chapter where love, or one of its delightful derivatives, is employed with eloquence. I choose six of these choice gems. Numbered and noted they read,

(1) And I will delight myself in thy commandments, which I have loved (119:47). (2) I hate vain thoughts: but thy law do I love (119:113). (3) Therefore I love thy commandments above gold; yea, above fine gold (119:127). (4) I hate and abhor lying: but thy law do I love (119:163). (5) Great peace have they which love thy law: and nothing shall offend them (119:165). (6) My soul hath kept thy testimonies; and I love them exceedingly (119:167).

Perhaps my comments could best be made by noting the comprehensive links of love. This is an area of comprehensive links of love. This is an area of comprehensive Biblical love that has escaped the attention of many people. Eight lovely links of love are worthy of emphatic mention. (1) Love is connected with delight in commandment keeping. (2) Love is connected with law — God's law. (3) Love is connected with great peace. (4) Love is connected with a shield that keeps one from being offended or turned away from God and truth. (5) Love is connected with a negative reaction — the hating of vain thoughts and lying. (6) Love is connected with a life of stedfastness, i.e., the continuous keeping of Jehovah's testimonies of truth. (7) Love is connected with a stately superlative — "I love them (God's testimonies) exceedingly.'' (8) Love of God's word is connected with vast wealth, i.e., of being more valuable than gold, yea, even of fine gold.

Religious people who lay claim to great love for God and ignore, disdain and disobey the word of this same God have not even begun to fathom what real love is all about. Love for God and love for His word cannot be severed; they are immutably linked and courageously connected.

GOD'S WORD IS RIGHT

We live in an age when multitudes distrust the Bible. To them the Bible is not a RIGHT book; they view it as a WRONG book. It is heart-warming to read the many ardent affirmations in this comprehensive chapter which stress the accuracy, rightness and correctness of God's word. Nine of these choice gems have been chosen. Numbered and noted they read,

(1) I know, O Lord, that thy judgments are right, and that thou in faithfulness hast afflicted me (119:75). (2) All thy commandments are faithful: they persecute me wrongfully; help thou me (119:86). (3) Righteous art thou, O Lord, and upright are thy judgments (119:137). (4) Thy testimonies that thou hast commanded are righteous and very faithful (119:138). (5) Thy righteousness is an everlasting righteousness, and thy law is the truth (119:142). (6) The righteousness of thy testimonies is everlasting: give me understanding, and I shall live (119:144). (7) Thou art near, O Lord; and all thy commandments are truth (119:151). (8) Thy word is true from the beginning: and every one of thy righteous judgments endureth for ever (119:160). (9) Seven times a day do I praise thee because of thy righteous judgments (119:164).

God's word is right in what it teaches us about creation. Deity — not Darwin—is authority relative to origins. Scripture—not Sagan—tells how all things came about to be. The Bible is right in its protrait of the Godhead — Father, Son and Holy Spirit. The Bible is right in what it declares relative to miracles and morals. The Bible is right in its predictive prophecies and their majestic, minute fulfillment. The Bible is right about how we ought to treat our fellowman. The Bible is right in all declarations relative to eternal destinies. Brother Marshall Keeble, the great black evangelist, had as one of his favorite expressions this short and stately sentiment, ''The Bible is right.'' This is one of the eloquent echoes heard from Psalm 119 again and again. An earlier psalm breathed this same beautiful statement of total trust by saying, ''For the word of the Lord is right; and all his works are done in truth'' (33:4)

There are no crippling doubts in these marvelous, majestic statements relative to the rightness of God's word. "The Bible said it; I believe it; that settles it!"

DEEP DELIGHT FOR GOD'S LAW

The precious psalmist in this choice chapter spoke with fervent frequency about the joy and delight he found in God's word. Seven selected passages depict that deep delight. Numbered and noted they read,

(1) Their heart is as fat as grease; but I delight in thy law (119:70). (2) Let thy tender mercies come unto me, that I may live: for thy law is my delight (119:77). (3) Unless thy law had been my delights, I should then have perished in mine affliction (119:92). (4) Thy testimonies have I taken as an heritage for ever: for they are the rejoicing of my heart (119:111). (5) Trouble and anguish have taken hold on me: yet thy commandments are my delights (119:143). (6) I rejoice at thy word, as one that findeth great spoil (119:162). (7) I have longed for thy salvation, O Lord; and thy law is my delight (119:174).

Were these stately sentiments to permeate every human heart the Bible would be the most universally studied subject ever contemplated by mankind. The Biblical message would be meditated upon day and night (1:2). Yet should not such an admirable attitude be universal? God delighted and rejoiced in the giving of this divine revelation. Why should not delight and joy be our prompt and permanent response in its regal reception?

REGAL REGARD FOR GOD'S WORD

Regal pertains to a king, something stately, something splendid. Surely this was the regard that the inspired scribe had for God's word as he contemplated it, described it, elevated it, exalted it, extolled it. These eight selected scriptures, numbered and noted, fully attest to that and read,

(1) The law of thy mouth is better unto me than thousands of gold and silver (119:72). (2) I am thine, save me; for I have sought thy precepts (119:94). (3) I have refrained my feet from every evil way, that I might keep thy word (119:101). (4) How sweet are thy words unto my taste! yea, sweeter than honey to my mouth (119:103)! (5) Thy testimonies are wonderful: therefore doth my soul keep them (119:129). (6) I opened my mouth, and panted: for I longed for thy commandments

(119:131). (7) Concerning thy testimonies, I have known of old that thou hast founded them for ever (119:152). (8) I have kept thy precepts and thy testimonies: for all my ways are before thee (119:168).

No enemy of God and His word could project such regal regard for sacred Scripture. Only a firm, faithful friend could do so and did so in this tremendous chapter. Of the person who possesses this type of attitude toward the Bible we can say that God's word is safe in his hands. He will view the Bible as a sacred trust committed into his care and keeping.

LOYALTY TO GOD'S WORD

A loving loyalty to the word of the Lord permeates this entire chapter of golden gems, of silver sentiments. Thirty passages in this remarkable chapter do it so excellently. Listing them for your *learning* them, *loving* them, *living* them and being so uncompromisingly *loyal* to them will be better than any comments I could make relative to them. Numbered and noted they read,

(1) Wherewithal shall a young man cleanse his way? by taking heed thereto according to thy word (119:9). (2) With my whole heart have I sought thee: O let me not wander from thy commandments (119:10). (3) Thy word have I hid in mine heart, that I might not sin against thee (119:11). (4) I will meditate in thy precepts, and have respect unto thy ways (119:15). (5) I will delight myself in thy statutes: I will not forget thy word (119:16). (6) Open thou mine eyes, that I may behold wondrous things out of thy law (119:18). (7) Thy testimonies also are my delight, and my counsellors (119:24). (8) I have chosen the way of truth: thy judgments have I laid before me (119:30). (9) I have stuck unto thy testimonies: O Lord, put me not to shame (119:31). (10) So shall I keep thy law continually for ever and ever (119:44). (11) I will speak of thy testimonies also before kings, and will not be ashamed (119:46). (12) I am a companion of all them that fear thee, and of them that keep thy precepts (119:63). (13) Before I was afflicted I went astray: but now have I kept thy word (119:67). (14) It is good for me that I have been afflicted; that I might learn thy statutes (119:71). (15) Let my heart be sound in thy statutes; that I be not ashamed (119:80). (16) They had almost consumed me upon earth; but I for-

sook not thy precepts (119:87). (17) For ever, O Lord, thy word is settled in heaven (119:89). (18) I have more understanding than all my teachers: for thy testmonies are my meditation (119:99). (19) I understand more than the ancients, because I keep thy precepts (119:100). (20) Through thy precepts I get understanding: therefore I hate every false way (119:104). (21) Thy word is a lamp unto my feet, and a light unto my path (119:105). (22) I have sworn, and I will perform it, that I will keep thy righteous judgments (119:106). (23) I have inclined mine heart to perform thy statutes alway, even unto the end (119:112). (24) Depart from me, ye evildoers: for I will keep the commandments of my God (119:115). (25) Therefore I esteem all thy precepts concerning all things to be right; and I hate every false way (119:128). (26) Thy testimonies are wonderful: therefore doth my soul keep them (119:129). (27) The entrance of thy words giveth light; it giveth understanding unto the simple (119:130). (28) Rivers of waters run down mine eyes, because they keep not thy law (119:136). (29) Princes have persecuted me without a cause: but my heart standeth in awe of thy word (119:161). (30) I have gone astray like a lost sheep; seek thy servant; for I do not forget thy commandments (119:176).

Should not this type of loyalty be emulated by all of us? What a lofty goal of loyalty is set for us in these precious pronouncments.

POINTS TO PONDER IN PSALM 119

1. To the psalmist nothing was of comparable value to the Bible.
2. The psalmist viewed God's word as his Jacob's Ladder that connected heaven and earth.
3. True knowledge is knowing God's will.
4. True wisdom is living God's will.
5. True joy is teaching God's will to others and observing their practicing such.
6. True satisfaction derives from being a staunch defender of God's word — the Holy Bible.

DISCUSSION QUESTIONS

1. *Read and discuss briefly the five verses given on God's quickening of mankind.*

2. Read and discuss briefly the six chosen verses that depict the marvelous majesty of love in Psalm 119.
3. How do the masses today feel toward the Bible?
4, Read and discuss briefly the nine verses given about the Bible's accuracy, rightness and correctness.
5. Read and discuss briefly the seven selected passages which depict the joy and delight the psalmist experienced in God's word.
6. Read and discuss briefly the eight selected passages in Psalm 119 that speak of the regal regard we should have for God's word.
7. Who could not have described the Bible in such lovely language and who could have done so?
8. Choose any ten of the passages that depict loyalty to God's word, then read and discuss them briefly.
9. Memorize any five passages suggested in our lesson today and be prepared to cite them to the class.
10. Discuss the Points to Ponder in Psalm 119.

MULTIPLE CHOICE: Underline correct answer

1. Psalm 119 has been aptly styled the: (A) "saints' alphabet;" (B) "creed of demons;" (C) "alphabet of scoffers;" (D) "devil's alphabet."
2. Jehovah God, according to Psalm 119, quickens people by: (A) the marvelous means of His word; (B) the direct impact and personal operation of the Holy Spirit upon the hearts of humanity; (C) unconditional salvation, i.e., with no conditions demanded on humanity's part; (D) faith only on humanity's part.
3. The precious psalmist in Psalm 119 considered God's word as: (A) a dead letter; (B) an unessential; (C) an indifferent matter; (D) powerful, penetrating, ardent, active, lovely and life-giving.
4. Relative to origins we should go to the authoritative source of: (A) Deity; (B) Darwin; (C) Satan; (D) Flew, Matson, Sagan and other leading atheistic evolutionists of our day.
5. "The Bible is right" was a favorite saying of: (A) Marshall Keeble; (B) Voltaire; (C) Robert Ingersoll; (D) Lenin and Stalin in Russia.

SCRIPTURAL FILL-IN: Only one word is required in each blank.

(1) "I have _____ unto thy _____: O _____, put _____ not to _____."

(2) "I will never _____ thy _____: for with _____ thou hast _____ me."

(3) "_____ I _____ thy _____ above
_____; yea, _____ fine _____."

(4) "For the _____ of the _____ is _____; and
_____ his _____ are _____ in
_____."

(5) "I _____ at thy _____, as _____ that
_____ great _____."

(6) "How _____ are thy _____ unto my
_____! yea, _____ than _____ to my
_____."

(7) "For _____, O _____, thy _____ is
_____ in _____."

TRUE OR FALSE: Put either a "T" or "F" in the blanks

_____1. "An Inspired Tribute To The Bible" is an appropriate designation of Psalm 119.

_____2. Love for God and love for His word cannot be severed because they are immutably linked.

_____3. Crippling doubts relative both to God and the Bible permeate Psalm 119.

_____4. The word regal is out of place as an accurate adjective in describing God's word.

_____5. The psalmist in Psalm 119 felt but little if any loyalty to the word of the Lord.

THOUGHT QUESTIONS

1. Show conclusively that the psalmist of this chapter was neither a "grace only" nor a "faith only" proponent.

2. What are the eight links of love set forth in this chapter and relate them to our living the Christian life today?

3. Explain quite fully the various ways that God's word is right.

4. What fruit would soon accrue universally if all people found deep delight and jubilant joy in Biblical meditation and then in Biblical obedience?

5. In whose hand will the word of the Lord be eminently safe?

CHAPTER ELEVEN

PSALM 122: A PSALM OF PRAYER, PEACE AND PROSPERITY

A greater grasp of the precious psalms, and this one in particular, would work wonders in our Christian worship both generally and specifically. These Sweet Singers of Ancient Israel, human penmen of the precious psalms, considered worship far more highly than simply an imposed or forced duty; it was a supreme privilege. Christians who have never climbed up to this blessed consideration could spend much time wisely and delightfully in the stimulating studies of the majestic motives and adorning attitudes that are royally reflected in "The Songbook Of The Bible," as Psalms is sometimes designated. Worthiness of worship, serenity in song, peace in praise and power in prayer fluently flow from the sacred sentiments of this devotional section of lovely literature — the precious psalms.

The specific study for this chapter, Psalm 122, is one of the most beautiful of all precious psalms. Truly one is treading heaven's borderland when he majestically meditates and restfully reflects upon its compact gems of golden truth. Gladness, worship, Jerusalem, the Lord's house, prayer and prosperity are key and kingly words observable in this penetrating passage of sacred scripture.

The gist of Psalm 122 is the joy felt of going to Jerusalem to worship, the exhilarating esteem in which Jerusalem was held by every faithful Israelite and the prayerful concern they were to feel for Jerusalem.

Psalm 122 takes on additional luster of a lovely nature when the student contemplates the beautiful section of Psalms in which it is centered. It is in that stately section of some fifteen psalms, 120-134, which are styled in the ascriptions in the KJV as the songs of degrees and in the ASV of 1901 as the songs of ascents. Many excellent students of the Psalms believe these were sung by the traveling Israelites on their way to Jerusalem for worship. Since Jerusalem was of higher altitude than most other sections of Palestine, they literally went *up* to the holy city. Hence, we can observe immediately how appropriate the ascription is, "The Song of Ascents." Though, for the most part, we *read* these psalms, the ancient Israelites *sang* them as well as read them. We know from other scriptures that they traveled to worship with a song on their lips. In Psalm 42:4 we note, "When I remember these things, I pour out my soul in me: for I had gone with the multitude, I went with them to the house of God, with the voice of joy and praise, with a multitude that kept holyday." A kindred sentiment is eloquently expressed by Isaiah, "Ye shall have a song, as in the night when a holy solemnity is kept; and gladness of heart, as when one goeth with a pipe to come into the mountain of the Lord, to the mighty One of Israel" (Isaiah 30:29).

The ascription attributes this psalm to David. Some think it is of later date and perhaps was written in view of the exiles as they returned from Babylon. Adam Clarke was of this latter view and suggested that the *hearts* of the captives had been in Jerusalem while their *feet* had been in Babylon. The Davidic authorship is preferred. Its sentiments fit him and there is nothing in the contents that forbids its being of Davidic composition. The student should keep firmly fixed in mind that the Holy Spirit is the real author of all these psalms as well as the other sixty-five books of the Bible — God's Divine Library.

THE GLADNESS, GREATNESS AND GLORY
OF WORSHIP

I was glad when they said unto me, Let us go into the house of the Lord. Our feet shall stand within thy gates, O Jerusalem. Jerusalem is builded as a city that is compact together: Whither the tribes go up, the tribes of the Lord, unto the testimony of Israel, to give thanks unto the name of the Lord. For there are set thrones of judgment, the thrones of the house of David (122:1-5).

What produces gladness within the human heart is quite an accurate index to the person's character, to his spiritual make-up. Some find gladness only in the lusts of the flesh, the lusts of the eyes and the pride or vainglory of life — the lower and baser appetites of depraved humanity (1 John 2:15-17). The penman of this blessed psalm found his gladness in the privilege of walking the way to worship in Jerusalem. Gladness, not sadness and not madness, was his instant response to the extended invitation to go to worship. Beauty, not boredom, reflected his real regard toward the prospect of journeying to the place of the central sanctuary and there rendering worship to the great and glorious God of his fathers, the very God who made him, sustained him, loved him. Intensity — not irksomeness — permeated his being as he contemplated worship in the Lord's house. The steps of travel that brought him near the anticipated goal of glorious worship were not reluctantly taken but eagerly treaded and rightly so!

Israelites who found neither gladness nor glory in setting foot inside Jerusalem were lacking in what made them a distinctive people. Jerusalem was more than their political capital. It was the center of their worship. It was the citadel of their existence as a nation. It served as the stately symbol of their unity. Jerusalem was not strung out over a wide area. Geography made sure of this. The city was surrounded by valleys on three of its sides. Of necessity the city was compactly erected. The physical lay-out of this compact city reminded the observant Hebrew worshippers of their compactness as a people. Likewise, Christians should be reminded of the Pauline portrait of the church. He wrote in Ephesians 4:16,

> From whom the whole body fitly joined together and compacted by that which every joint supplieth, according to the effectual working in the measure of every part, maketh increase of the body unto the edifying of itself in love.

Faithful pilgrimages to Jerusalem for the annual Passover, the Feast of Weeks (called Pentecost in the New Testament) and the Feast of Tabernacles strengthened and solidified the twelve tribes. The central worship in Jerusalem aided greatly in keeping them a unified and holy nation. Jerusalem was not *their* choice as the place of central worship; it was *Jehovah's* choice. They were happy to make God's choice their choice. Those who love and honor God and Christ today are happy to make Deity's choice relative to the church their choice. God, not man, is in the driver's seat in matters like this. In Jerusalem as choice center of worship in the tabernacle at first and later in the permanent temple on Mount Moriah for a full millennium was not of their invention but clearly and completely the Lord's choice. The ordinance that prompted their worshipful pilgrimages to Zion was of divine origin — not human choice. Here the sweetness of thanksgiving could be given acceptably in public worship. Here judgments of a right nature were dispensed by the king and his administrative assistants.

A lady of my acquaintance once said, "The elders of this congregation are trying to *church* us to death." Four hours of public worship each week were just too irksome and boring to her. In marked contrast consider the statement from a dedicated Christian man, also of my acquaintance, who said at the close of a gospel meeting, "One of the reasons I want to go to heaven is to worship God every day as we have done in this gospel meeting." In your judgment, which of the two had caught the gladness, the greatness and the golden glory of wonderful worship which permeated the sweet psalmist's attitude throughout this marvelous, majestic and moving chapter of Holy Writ?

A thorough conversion of the whole church today to the sparkling and stately sentiments of Psalm 122 would solve the poor response commonly characteristic of Bible Study on Sunday morning, Sunday evening worship, Mid-Week Bible Study and ALL the night services of gospel meetings. It is a crying shame the way twenty-five to fifty percent of our members treat regular worship assemblies. To say they treat such shabbily is really an understatement. Many of our members no more share David's sentiments in Psalm 122:1 or intend to obey the intense import of Hebrews 10:25 than an atheist's attitude is toward Genesis 1:1 or a "faith only" proponent's is relative to Mark 16:16 or James 2:24. Such members need to be *converted* to Christ. Such a conversion would inject new and deeply needed life into the whole program of congregational activities. How many of us can read this royal reflection of Psalm 122:1 and honestly declare, "That is my sentiment one hundred percent"? A person in the "Sunlight Age" of Christianity who cannot approach the love of worship as felt by one in the "Moonlight Age" of the Mosaic Economy still has much maturity to make in his future growth. And make it he *must* if heaven is ultimately to be his.

PRAYERFUL CONCERN FOR JERUSALEM

Pray for the peace of Jerusalem: they shall prosper that love thee. Peace be within thy walls, and prosperity within thy palaces. For my brethren and companions' sakes, I will now say, Peace be within thee. Because of the house of the Lord our God I will seek thy good (122:6-9).

Notice the attractive alliteration of P's in this passage. Such alliteration is also observable in the Hebrew text of verse 6 which but means that the Holy Spirit found beauty in alliteration just as many more modern writers have. Relative to the Hebrew text I have observed a quartet of times the Hebrew letter *shin* is employed in just a very few words. Prayer, peace and prosperity are key words in this quartet of verses. It is normal and natural to pray for the objects of intense love and deep personal regard. Jerusalem's peace was to be an intense object of prayerful concern in the pious hearts of Hebrew worshippers. Prayer, peace and prosperity have much more in common than their all beginning with the same alphabetical letter. Right prayers will lead to the harvest of proper peace. Proper peace in turn will lead to the harvest of soul prosperity — the supreme kind and the one most needed by current humanity. This desired peace will follow in the wake of real love. Real prosperity would evade those who withheld their love from Jerusalem. Prayers for a peaceful and prosperous Jerusalem would bequeath a beautiful blessing for all his Hebrew brethren and Israelite companions. Peace is desirable for the beautiful benefits which accrue to others and not just alone to the person who prays. For the sake of Jehovah's house he would seek the good of Jerusalem. It is significant to observe that the fall of Jerusalem to the Babylonians during sixth century Judah (586 B.C.) and the destruction of the first temple (the one erected by Solomon four centuries plus earlier) occurred together. It is again significant to observe that the collapse of the Herodian temple in the first century of our time era and Jerusalem's fall at the determined hands of the Romans in A.D. 70 occurred together. However, in the second case the temple had already ceased to be the Lord's house from Calvary onward and a greater temple had been erected for His people — the Lord's church. In fact on Tuesday of the Passion or Final Week the Lord referred to the temple on Mount Moriah as being "your house" and no longer as either His or the Father's house (Matthew 23:38).

The application from these precious principles in Psalms is one easily apparent to the serious student. God's people today should pray for the church. We should seek its peace. Real prosperity is available only for those who really and truly love the church. This is the only sphere where people today can find and enjoy peace. In the peace of spiritual Zion we will find our chief blessings. In the same sphere will our brethren and companions find theirs also. Peace built upon truth should be our daily prayer for God's church today. For the continued sake of the Lord's house we should seek her good patiently and persistently, fervently and fully.

POINTS TO PONDER IN PSALM 122

1. There are NO services of the church that any dedicated Christian will ever want to miss as long as the sentiment of Psalm 122:1 permeates his sincere soul.

2. People bored to death with worship here would be equally bored in heaven for worship is one of its dominant characteristics as a study of Revelation 4, 5 and 15 dynamically depicts.

3. The true worship of God was a cohesive element that bound pious hearts of all Israelites to each other and will do the same for Christians currently.

4. Worship and gratitude have a natural, mutual affinity.

5. For peace in this psalm the writer used the term Shalom — one of the richest of all Hebrew terms and an expression frequently heard in Jerusalem and Palestine by modern tourists.

6. Worthy worship and peaceful prayers should ever adorn our Christian pilgrimages.

DISCUSSION QUESTIONS

1. *How did the writers of these precious psalms consider worship?*

2. *What are some of the sacred sentiments that flow so fluently in the Psalms?*

3. *What are some of the key and kingly terms of Psalm 122?*

4. *Give a short gist of Psalm 122.*

5. *How do Psalm 42:4 and Isaiah 30:29 relate to the fifteen songs of ascents?*

6. *Discuss David as the probable writer of Psalm 122.*

7. *Discuss in detail how the psalmist in this chapter really felt about worship.*

8. *What would a thorough conversion to the stately sentiments of Psalm 122 do for today's average congregation?*

9. *Discuss in detail the section that deals with prayerful concern for Jerusalem.*

10. *Read and discuss the Points to Ponder for Psalm 122.*

MULTIPLE-CHOICE: Underline correct answer

1. *Psalms has been called the: (A) "Songbook of the Bible;" (B) "Book of Christian Liberty;" (C) "Book of Origins;" (D) "Book of Prophets, Kings and Priests."*

2. *The fifteen psalms of degrees (KJV) or ascents (ASV) are: (A) 1-15; (B) 50-64; (C) 136-150; (D) 120-134.*

3. *It is geographically accurate to describe a trip to Jerusalem as: (A) up to Jerusalem; (B) down to Jerusalem; (C) out to Jerusalem; (D) over to Jerusalem.*

4. *The three feasts of Passover, of Weeks and of Tabernacles were observed: (A) weekly; (B) monthly; (C) yearly; (D) just whenever the notion struck them — among the Israelites.*

5. *The years of 586 B.C. and 70 A.D. have in common: (A) the two great rebuildings of Jerusalem and her stately temples built respectively by Solomon and Herod the Great; (B) the two great destructions of Jerusalem and the fall of the two temples built respectively by Solomon and Herod; (C) the beginning and ending of the Mosaic Covenant: (D) the two most glorious years ever experienced by the physical descendants of Abraham, Isaac, and Jacob.*

SCRIPTURAL FILL-IN: Only one word is required in each blank.

(1) *"I was _____ when they _____ unto _____, Let _____ go into the _____ of the _____."*

(2) *"Our _____ shall _____ within thy _____, O _____. _____ is _____ as a _____ that is _____ together."*

(3) *"Whither the _____ go up, the _____ of the _____, unto the _____ of _____, to give _____ unto the _____ of the _____. For _____ are set _____ of _____, the _____ of the _____ of _____."*

(4) *"_____ for the _____ of _____: they shall _____ that _____ thee. _____ be within thy _____, and _____ within thy _____."*

(5) *"For my _____ and _____ sakes, I will now say, _____ be _____ thee. _____ of the _____ of the _____ our _____ I will _____ thy _____."*

TRUE OR FALSE: Put either a "T" or "F" in the blanks

_____1. *The psalms were never designed to be sung by worshippers of God.*

_____2. *The Holy Spirit is the real author of all sixty-six books in the Divine Library.*

_____3. *God — not Israel — chose Jerusalem as the place of central worship.*

_____4. Prayer, peace and prosperity have a natural, mutual affinity.

_____5. It is because they love the Lord and His church so much that people are so lukewarm about diligent and regular attendance at all worship periods.

THOUGHT QUESTIONS

1. Why would the singing of the songs of ascents on the way to Jerusalem help prepare the Israelites for more meaningful worship in the Holy City?

2. What is an accurate index to a person's heart and tell why?

3. Compare Jerusalem as a compact city and the compactness of the Lord's church.

4. Discuss the great contrast between "churching" people to death and desiring heaven as a place of daily worship just as a gospel meeting affords Christians.

5. Make an application of Psalm 122:6-9 to Christians today.

CHAPTER TWELVE

PSALM 139: THE ALL-KNOWING AND ALL-SEEING GOD

The ascription calls this a psalm of David and there appears no good reason to deny its Davidic composition. Where the renowned Hebrew bard was, at what time of life he penned it or under what literary circumstances it was composed are all undisclosed. It is an eloquent psalm and filled with a tremendous tribute to Jehovah God. He is the All-knowing one; He is the All-seeing one; He is the All-protecting one; he is the All-blessing one; he is the All-searching one; he is the All-leading one. No wonder the ardent admirers of this great psalm have called it "the crown of the psalms" and "one of the chief glories of the Psalter." The psalmist treads the mountain peaks of literary breadth, beauty and brilliance in its lofty composition. God was real to the psalmist. He was good, great and glorious. This psalm can help enhance Him in our eyes if we travel believingly through these valiant verses of sublime sentiments.

THE OMNISCIENCE OF JEHOVAH

O Lord, thou hast searched me, and known me. Thou knowest my downsitting and mine uprising, thou understandest my thought afar off. Thou compassest my path and my lying down, and art acquainted with all my ways (139:1-3).

Reverent and respectful is the address. There is none of this overt familiarity with God as though God were inferior to us or simply our equal as we frequently hear today. The inferior addresses the totally superior one in this psalm. Diligent had been the Lord's inspection and investigation of the psalmist; thoroughly genuine was his complete knowledge of the investigated man. What person knows the number of times he sits down or rises up in the course of a day's busy activity? Yet the All-knowing Jehovah knows. He knows such relative to the four billion plus people on earth currently. Though God is in heaven and man on earth yet the thoughts and meditations of man's heart are known by Jehovah as though Jehovah was near at hand. The psalmist recognized that he was sifted by God. The psalmist in all his travels was known thoroughly by the All-knowing and All-seeing God. The Almighty knew perfectly all his meditations when lying upon his bed. All the psalmist's ways were minutely monitored and resolutely recorded with an amazing thoroughness by the omniscient God.

> For there is not a word in my tongue, but, lo, O Lord, thou knowest it altogether. Thou hast beset me behind and before, and laid thine hand upon me. Such knowledge is too wonderful for me; it is high, I cannot attain unto it (139:4-6).

Not only is the Almighty aware of man's downsittings, uprisings, thoughts and ways at home and abroad but is deeply cognizant of man's full speech habits. No word escapes the ear that hears all and the mind that records all. God Almighty not only knows the words we speak but knows also the motives behind every oral message. This is absolutely staggering to contemplate!! His is a complete knowledge of the verbal department of every man on earth — all who have lived, who now live and who will ever live. David was sure the Lord knew him from beginning to end. God's hand was truly laid upon him. That holy hand could restrain; it also could bless and bless bountifully. Such knowledge in verse 6 refers to Jehovah's knowledge. It was too high, too holy and too comprehensive for the saintly psalmist to contemplate. It was beyond his tallest reach. Finite man has ever realized this when seeking to comprehend the wisdom of the infinite Jehovah. It is more vast than all human minds combined can fathom. It was beyond the psalmist's reach and it exceeds our reach today just as much if not more for he was inspired and we are not. Isaiah supplies this kindred sentiment, "For my thoughts are not your thoughts, neither are your ways my ways, saith the Lord. For as the heavens are higher than the earth, so are my ways higher than your ways, and my thoughts than your thoughts'' (Isaiah 55:8,9).

THE OMNIPRESENCE OF JEHOVAH

Whither shall I go from thy spirit? or whither shall I flee from thy presence? If I ascend up into heaven, thou art there: if I make my bed in hell (Sheol—ASV), behold, thou art there. If I take the wings of the morning, and dwell in the uttermost parts of the sea; Even there shall thy hand lead me, and thy right hand shall hold me (139:7-10).

Omnipresence refers to Jehovah's limitless presence. There is neither an eluding nor an evading of Him wherever we go or whatever we do. These verses sustain that proposition in marvelous fashion. His All-seeing eye surveys even the remotest ranges of His unique universe. Jonah found this to be the case when he sought to run away from God by heading toward Tarshish or the opposite direction of where he was charged to go. God's eye was on the wayward prophet as much when he was aboard a ship on the mighty Mediterranean Sea as when he was on land in Israel (Jonah 1). The inspired writer of Hebrews writes, "Neither is there any creature that is not manifest in his sight: but all things are naked and opened unto the eyes of him with whom we have to do" (Hebrews 4:13). There is no getting away from God's spirit; there is no fleeing His presence. Ascension into heaven is no escape from God for there He is. An entrance into Sheol (place of departed spirits between death and judgment and which is called Hades in the ASV New Testament) is no escape from God. He is there. The Hebrew here is very emphatic. The words in our English translation — behold, thou art there" — are literally, "Behold, thou!" The "wings of the morning" refer to the speed of light. Speeding as rapidly as light travels and dwelling in the uttermost parts of the seas (beyond the boundless oceans) would not put the psalmist out of God's eyesight. Even there God's hand would be present to guide; His arm of power would be there to protect.

If I say, Surely the darkness shall cover me; even the night shall be light about me. Yea, the darkness hideth not from thee; but the night shineth as the day: the darkness and the light are both alike to thee (139:11,12).

The darkest night earth has ever known will provide neither cover nor hiding place for the man who seeks to run away from God.

Darkness affects man's eyes and renders him almost helpless. Not so with God. Night to God is as bright as high noon on a clear, sunny day is to man and then some!! The All-Seeing Eye sees just as well at midnight when no moonlight is evident as it does at twelve noon when the mighty monarch of the sky—the sun—is in its brightest orb. Jeremiah observes, "Am I a God at hand, saith the Lord, and not a God afar off? Can any hide himself in secret places that I shall not see him, saith the Lord. Do not I fill heaven and earth? saith the Lord" (Jeremiah 23:23,24).

JEHOVAH: THE GREAT SEARCHER AND KNOWER

For thou hast possessed my reins: thou hast covered me in my mother's womb. I will praise thee; for I am fearfully and wonderfully made: marvellous are thy works; and that my soul knoweth right well. My substance was not hid from thee, when I was made in secret, and curiously wrought in the lowest parts of the earth (139:13-15).

The ASV of 1901 renders verse 13 in the following words, "For thou didst form my inward parts: Thou didst cover me in my mother's womb." Seemingly, the psalmist is suggesting that the Almighty Creator who made the inward parts of the complex human personality surely is in perfect position to know man perfectly. With great and grand precision God knitted "me together" in my mother's womb, the precious psalmist avers. Without quibble or doubt the psalmist knew perfectly that he was a human being while he was a fetus in his mother's womb. He was not just a part of the mother's bodily tissue analogous to tonsils or an appendix and which could be aborted at motherly discretion as millions now contend and which bears current legality in our morally abandoned and cruelly calloused era. Not only is abortion refuted in verse 13 but organic evolution and total hereditary depravity are refuted in verse 14. Praise or thanksgiving welled up within the psalmist's heart or mind as he contemplated his Creator, his marvelous Maker on high. He referred to himself as being fearfully and wonderfully made. This concept will not fit godless evolution which rejects complex man as a MADE creature. Genesis 1 and 2 have man *made*. So does the Christ in Matthew 19:4,5 and Mark 10:6. All the wonderful works of God were marvelous to David's inquiring mind. His soul knew this greatly and gratefully.

David's pre-natal state was not hidden from the eye of God Almighty. Man's eye could not see him in his mother's womb but God's eye surveyed him from conception onward. Note that David still emphasizes that he was made—not evolved. "Curiously wrought" translates a Hebrew expression that means literally "embroidered." Beautiful and precise had been God's handiwork in the intense interweaving of all that made him a unique unit of humanity. Beyond all successful doubt or debate to the contrary there is required a Maker for all this; evolution, which is minus a Maker, is left out in the cold here. This is where Godless, Christless and spiritless evolution—both the atheistic and theistic brands of it—belongs—out in the cold—way, Way, WAY out in the cold!! Relative to the marvels of the human body someone has written that Yours Is A Wonderful Body." It states:

If you are a person of average size, you perform in each day of 24 hours, the following functions:
1. Your heart beats 103,689 times.
2. Your breath (sic) 23,040 times.
3. You inhale 438 cubic feet of air.
4. You eat between 3 and 4 pounds of food and drink 3 quarts of liquid and perspire about 2 pints through your skin.
5. Your body maintains a steady temperature of 98.6 degrees under all weather conditions.
6. You generate 450 ft. tons of energy.
7. You speak 4800 words (men only), and move and use over 700 muscles, use 7,000,000 brain cells, and walk 7 miles (women only) in the home—not men, they ride.
And if you are a Christian this body, as described above, belongs to God (Romans 12:1,2). (Author unknown).

Verses 14, 15 also refute the Calvinistic folly of total hereditary depravity as previously indicated. Surely David did not thank God he was made totally depraved. Being fearfully and wonderfully made will not fit being made a vile and depraved sinner. Surely David would not classify God's works as marvellous if he were conceived in sin and born just as depraved as is the devil, just as sinful as is Satan. Did God embroider a precious object to be aborted to cover an immoral sin or destroy an unwanted baby by an insensitive mother and a non-caring father. Being fearfully and wonderfully made will not fit total hereditary depravity by any stretch of the imagination; it will not fit baby homicide in the name of abortion either.

"Thine eyes did see my substance, yet being unperfect; and in thy book all my members were written, which in continuance were fashioned, when as yet there was none of them" (139:16). From the time that conception occurred and even before the fetus began to take definite shape and form God saw David and knew exactly what he ultimately was to be. Surely, David did not consider his prenatal period as constituting an interval of no *human* existence for him. He was just as real and as human as a fetus as he was after birth. Abortion is dealt a well-deserved death knell in Psalm 139:12-16. Had David lived in our era he would not have been a Supreme Court judge who declared abortion to be legal in a landmark decision of total insensitivity for prenatal life in 1973. Over 1,550,000 babies are aborted annually in our nation. This is MURDER in MASS form!!

How precious also are thy thoughts unto me, O God! how great is the sum of them! If I should count them, they are more in number than the sand: when I awake, I am still with thee (139:17,18).

All of God's thoughts were precious to the psalmist. Especially, he seems mindful of all the masterful thoughts that went into the making of men. The sum total of such thoughts astounded David. Their sum greatly exceeded the innumerable sands that compose the seashore. When the psalmist was in forgetful slumber his God was neither sleeping nor slumbering. Upon awaking he found that his God was still very much with him. Man's sleep during a night works no change in the God who is ever the same, who changes not (Malachi 3:6). In another majestic psalm the psalmist expressed, "Behold, he that keepeth Israel shall neither slumber nor sleep" (121:4).

REFLECTED ATTITUDES TOWARD THE WICKED

Surely thou wilt slay the wicked, O God: depart from me therefore, ye bloody men. For they speak against thee wickedly, and thine enemies take thy name in vain. Do not I hate them, O Lord, that hate thee? and am not I grieved with those that rise up against thee? I hate them with perfect hatred: I count them mine enemies (139:19-22).

Seemingly, there is a change of thought here from a contemplation of how God viewed and knew the psalmist and the case of the wicked. And yet it may not be as abrupt as it would at first appear. If God knew David so perfectly, then God also knew perfectly the hearts of the wicked. David recognized tht God had every judicial right to punish all rebels against His government of earth. Since they were haters of God, enemies to His cause and executioners of men with much blood on their hands, David wanted nothing to do with them. Their presence was unwelcome with him. Their speech is filled with railing terms against God. In vain they take His name. Unlike Jesus they never say, "Hallowed be thy name" (Matthew 6:9). David hated those who hated Jehovah. This likely was not a sinful hatred but one of strong disapproval—one that felt deeply righteous indignation much as Jesus did in Mark 3:5. David was angry with what made them God's enemies, viz., sin. David hated them with perfect hatred. He extended no approval to their conduct; no sympathy welled up in his heart for any of their actions; he voiced no words of support for their infamous actions; he felt deep disapproval toward all the evil they practiced. Because they are at enmity with God they are at enmity with me also, David avers. Surely David will not be faulted for this!

THE PRAYER OF THE PIOUS PSALMIST

"Search me, O God, and know my heart: try me, and know my thoughts: And see if there be any wicked way in me, and lead me in the way everlasting" (139:23,24). Above everything the psalmist desired to be right with God. At all costs he desired to escape being on terms of enmity with God. Being an enemy of God he shunned as one would a deadly plague. He petitioned God's searching or examining of his innermost being. He desired the Almighty to know his heart. He would be tested; he would be known in thoughts and motives—the mainspring of human actions. He would have any and all wicked ways (ways of grief) *detected* and *deleted* from his life. He then petitions to be led "in the way everlasting." Relative to this way we may say: (1) there is such a way; (2) it is available to all of humanity; (3) it is clearly mapped out in great detail within Holy Writ. (4) salvation is found in it and in NO other; (5) it is in this way that God leads us; (6) man is unable to direct his own steps; (7) it is a way we must walk therein for simply knowing of it and talking of it are insufficient; (8) its destiny is heaven; and (9) flagrant failure to walk therein calls for destiny of eternal punishment.

POINTS TO PONDER IN PSALM 139

1. It is utterly foolish to try and hide any or all our sins from the All-Seeing Eye.
2. The psalmist had a remarkable grasp of God's greatness, goodness and graciousness.

3. Neither an organic evolutionist nor an ardent abortionist penned this great chapter.

4. Love and appreciation of Jehovah mean that His thoughts, words and ways are all precious to us.

5. The greater our love for God the less will be our desire to mix and mingle with His enemies.

6. Real spiritual growth is on our threshold when we can pray in all sincerity each petition of Psalm 139:23,24.

DISCUSSION QUESTIONS

1. *Give a gist of this psalm as touching the omni (all) characteristics of our great and glorious Jehovah.*

2. *What duet of tributes has been voiced toward this precious psalm?*

3. *Discuss the omniscience of God as set forth in Psalm 139:1-6.*

4. *Read, discuss and apply Isaiah 55:8,9 to Psalm 139:1-6.*

5. *Discuss the omnipresence of God as delineated in Psalm 139:7-12.*

6. *How does Hebrews 4:13 fit in with the theme of the omnipresence of Jehovah God?*

7. *How are both organic evolution and total hereditary depravity refuted by Psalm 139:14?*

8. *Read and discuss verse 16.*

9, *Discuss in detail the section that deals with reflected attitudes toward the wicked.*

10. *Read and discuss the prayer of the pious psalmist in verses 23,24.*

11. *Read and discuss the Points To Ponder In Psalm 139.*

MULTIPLE CHOICE: Underline correct answer

1. *There appears to be no good reason to deny the human authorship of this psalm to: (A) the sons of Korah; (B) Asaph; (C) Solomon; (D) Moses; (E) David.*

2. *(A) Jonah; (B) Samuel; (C) David; (D) Solomon—sought to flee God when he took shipping for Tarshish.*

3. *(A) Sheol; (B) Purgatory; (C) Limbo; (D) Gehenna—is the realm of departed spirits between death and judgment.*

4. *The expression "wings of the morning" has reference to: (A) a beautiful sunrise; (B) a task that one does with delight and speed early in the morning; (C) the speed with which light travels; (D) how quickly we pass our allotted days on God's green footstool.*

5. *(A) Jonah; (B) David; (C) Isaiah; (D) Jeremiah—wrote, "Am I a God at hand, saith the Lord, and not a God afar off? Can any hide himself in*

secret places that I shall not see him, saith the Lord? Do not I fill heaven and earth? saith the Lord."

SCRIPTURAL FILL-IN: Only one word is required in each blank.

(1) "O _____, thou hast _____ me, and _____ me. Thou _____ my _____ and mine _____, thou _____ my _____ afar off. Thou _____ my _____ and my _____ down, and art _____ with _____ my _____."

(2) "_____ shall I _____ from thy _____? or whither shall I _____ from thy _____? If I _____ up into _____, thou art there: if I make my _____ in _____ (_____—ASV), behold, thou art _____. If I _____ the _____ of the _____, and _____ in the _____ parts of the _____; Even there shall thy hand _____ me, and thy _____ hand shall _____ me."

(3) "I will _____ thee; for I am _____ and _____ made: _____ are thy _____; and that my _____ knoweth _____ well."

(4) "_____, he that keepeth _____ shall neither _____ nor _____."

(5) "_____ me, O _____, and _____ my _____: _____ me, and _____ my _____: And _____ if there be any _____ way in _____, and _____ me in the way _____."

TRUE OR FALSE: Put either a "T" or "F" in the blanks

___1. *David was greatly impressed with the total knowledge and wisdom possessed by God.*

___2. *Had David lived today he would have been a charter member of every drive to make abortion popular and acceptable in any and all circumstances.*

___3. *David, the Sweet Singer of Israel, was an avid advocate of godless evolution as touching his origin and the origin of all other men.*

_____4. *"Curiously wrought" in David's language in this chapter fits right in with the evolutionary development of life.*

_____5. *The thoughts of God were precious indeed to David.*

THOUGHT QUESTIONS

1. In what ways can a study of Psalm 139 be of spiritual profit to us?
2. In approaching God discuss such terms as "overt familiarity," "inferior" and "superior."
3. Just how thorough is God's knowledge of us?
4. Why is it the nth degree of folly to think that darkness will cover a crime from Jehovah's All-Seeing Eye?
5. Refute thoroughly the acceptability of abortion by an ardent appeal to Psalm 139:13-16.

CHAPTER THIRTEEN

PSALM 148: A PRECIOUS PSALM OF PRAISE

The psalms constitute inspired poetry and were composed by pious Hebrew or Israelite penmen to be sung in their worship periods. Praise of God is intensely interwoven throughout this unique book which has been aptly appraised as "The Songbook Of The Bible." The last five chapters in this beautiful book abound in pronouncements of praise to Deity. Each of these psalms (146-150) begins and ends on the same noble note, the same marvelous melody—"Praise ye the Lord" (146:1,10; 147:1,20; 148:1,14; 149:1,9; 150:1,6). Quite accurately this stately section might be called "The Hallelujah Psalms."

Tremendous tributes have been paid this precious psalm. Adam Clarke wrote relative to it that "as a hymn of praise, this is the most sublime in the whole book." Another has called it "the joy song of creation." One of our greatest and most beloved hymns, "Hallelujah, Praise Jehovah," is based so beautifully upon it. It is a psalm of praise from the opening syllable to the closing one.

Neither the ascription nor the contents tell us who wrote it, when it was composed or under what circumstances it was penned. The penman must have been a pious worshipper of God who was jealous that God's praise be not slow in coming from any and all his creation—from both inanimate and animate.

A STATELY SUMMONS FOR CELESTIAL PRAISE TO BE GIVEN GOD

"Praise ye the Lord. Praise ye the Lord from the heavens: praise him in the heights. Praise ye him, all his angels: praise ye him, all his hosts" (148:1,2). Praise or hallelujah is summoned by Israel's Sweet Singer. It is to be directed to a proper and deserving source, viz., the Lord. The summons for extended praise is first general and then becomes specific. This psalmist begins with the heavens or the location nearest Deity's residing place and proceeds to the specific outreaches of both heaven and earth. All created beings in heaven are included in this ascription of praise and honor. In verse 1 we have Hebrew parallelism which is the most dominant characteristic of Israelite poetry. God is to be praised from the heavens; He is to be praised in the heights—a slight change of terminology but no basic difference is to be made between the terms. God is to be praised in the most lofty ranges of His creative work.

Verse 2 is specific. It, too, contains Hebrew parallelism by employing angels in the first line and hosts in the second. Some commentators seek to make a distinction between angels as somewhat higher and hosts as somewhat lower ranks with the former as messengers and the latter as doers of the message. But the Bible Doctrine of Angels has all his angelic beings as doers. Note this delightful description of His angelic beings who are styled both angels and hosts. David wrote in Psalm 103:20,21,

> Bless the Lord, ye his angels, that excel in strength (mighty in strength—margin), that do his commandments, hearkening unto the voice of his word. Bless ye the Lord, all ye his hosts: ye ministers of his, that do his pleasure.

Whether styled angels or hosts they all delight to do the Father's will. This is the very background of Jesus' remarkable petition in the Model Prayer when He stated, "Thy will be done in earth, as it is in heaven" (Matthew 6:10). Angelic beings or the powerful hosts in the third heaven (2 Corinthians 12:1-4) do God's will joyfully, reverently, completely and promptly. Praise from the lips is most meaningful when it comes from hearts that are devoted to doing God's will. Praise is hollow if there are no obedient dispositions to back it up and give it true meaning and proper direction.

"Praise ye him, sun and moon: praise him, all ye stars of light. Praise him, ye heavens of heavens, and ye waters that be above the heavens" (148:3,4). From animate (living) beings in the heavens the pious psalmist passes to inanimate (non-living) objects in what might be called the second and first heavens. The sun, moon and stars composed the second heaven and these are summoned to join the heavenly chorus with their message of praise. The waters that be above the heavens could well be the clouds. These are situated in the first

106

heaven. The sun is the mighty monarch of the sky. Its fiery domination of our solar system, its rays of warmth and light and its life-giving powers all combine to form eloquent evidence of God's glory in the formation of it on Day Number 4 of creative week. The moon is God's faithful witness (Psalm 89:37) and preaches a constant sermon that the hand that made me is divine. The stars of light are so distant from tiny earth that measurements are made in light years—distance light travels in a year's time. Yet from their far off orbits in outer space we can observe the sparkles of light they emit and send through billions of miles of amazing space.

Praise is summoned from the "heavens of heavens." Quite literally, these are the "heavens beyond the heavens" or what is far, far beyond our own solar system. Who has not looked up at the silvery clouds, the beautiful sky and at night the starry hosts and witnessed the stately sermon they proclaimed of the greatness of their Maker? Surely, the more astute must have wondered of the great beauties that lie even beyond what his naked eye can observe on a clear day or night. An earlier psalm expressed this breathtakingly beautiful sentiment, "Who layeth the beams of his chambers in the waters: who maketh the clouds his chariot: who walketh upon the wings of the wind:..." (104:3). That *all* the heavens, both seen and unseen by human eyes, reflect the glory of God is a stately sentiment found repeatedly throughout this book of Psalms (19:1; 50:6; 89:5; 97:6).

"Let them praise the name of the Lord: for he commanded, and they were created. He hath also stablished them for ever and ever: he hath made a decree which shall not pass" (148:5,6). This stately passage joins scores of other Biblical expressions which stress   God's creative work in the beginning. Genesis 1 forms a marvelous major in this department. This is the very beginning of the Bible. Psalms is near the middle of the Bible. Both here and elsewhere creation is affirmed in crystal clear certainty. An earlier psalm affirms with total confidence, "By the word of the Lord were the heavens made; and all the host of them by the breath of his mouth...For he spake, and it was done; he commanded, and it stood fast" (33:6,9). Revelation is the final part of Holy Writ and creation is affirmed therein also (Revelation 4:11). Not only is Deity creator but sustainer as well. The Godhead establishes, sustains and upholds what has been made. The New Testament teaches that it is by the Christ as creator that all things consist (Colossians 1:17). He, quite literally, holds all things together. Hebrews 1:3 affirms that He upholds "all things by the word of his power." Their being made forever and the decree that says they shall never pass are to be understood in connection with how long He intends the heavens and earth to last. Hebrews 1 has them ultimately folded up as a garment and 2 Peter 3:10-14 has the present earth and heavens to be dissolved or destroyed at Christ's second coming. For ever and ever sometimes has a limitation of duration as with incense burning and the Levitical priesthood (See Exodus 28:43; 30:8).

A STATELY SUMMONS FOR TERRESTRIAL PRAISE TO BE GIVEN GOD

Praise the Lord from the earth, ye dragons, and all deeps: Fire, and hail; snow, and vapour; stormy wind fulfilling his word: Mountains, and all hills; fruitful trees, and all cedars: Beasts, and all cattle; creeping things, and flying fowl (148:7-10).

The psalmist passes with ease from his stately summons for all heaven to ascribe praise to God and calls upon earth and sea to join the ascending chorus. The earth is called God's footstool and is a part of His great handiwork that lends praise to its marvelous Maker on high. This marvelous passage begins with life in the sea. The dragons (sea-monsters—ASV) would refer to the largest of marine life such as whales, sharks and porpoises (dolphins belong to this group also). Included would be all forms of life in the great deeps. By "deeps" the writer evidently refers to the deepest parts of the great seas and the mighty oceans. David wrote in an earlier psalm, "Thy righteousness is like the great mountains; thy judgments are a great deep; O Lord, thou preservest man and beast (36:6).

In verse 8 we have fire and hail paired. Quite likely, the fire, since it is paired with hail, refers to lightnings. Both are mighty exhibitions of Jehovah's power and the praise this eloquently exhibited power rightly demands. Snow and vapor are next paired. That no two snowflakes have ever been found with the same precise design intensely illustrates the majesty of our great, glorious God above. The vapor would doubtless be the fine mist that frequently accompanies the falling snow. No reader who lives in a cold climate and often braves the driving snow in winter has to be told relative to this mist; he has faced it time and time again. The snow and vapor attest to God's greatness. The stormy wind that fulfills His word bears its *blowing* testimony to the greatness of the Godhead on high.

Mountains and hills are paired in verse 9. The former would be of higher elevation; the latter would be of lower elevation. Those who have viewed the Smokies, the Appalachian range, the Rockies, the Alps or the mountains mentioned in Bible Lands, as has the writer of these notes, have frequently thrilled to the marvel and majesty of rugged mountainous terrain and the towering peaks as they reach for the vaulted blue sky that beautifully hovers above them. The mountains, hills and all valuable minerals, ores, etc., therein are the precisesly planned products of God's creative genius at work and designed so perfectly for man's needs.

Fruitful trees and cedars are next paired. The former would refer to trees that bear fruits such as the apple, the orange, the pear, the fig, the date, etc. The latter trees, represented by the tall and stately cedar, provide building material that proves to be such a beautiful blessing to man. Brother Guy N. Woods has well written relative to Psalm 148:9, "All are mute evidence of God, and thus praise him for his mighty and wonderful works" (GOSPEL ADULT QUARTERLY, September 24, 1972, p. 62).

Beasts and cattle are paired in verse 10 as well as creeping things and flying fowl or "birds of wing" as the margin states. Beasts would probably refer to wild animals while cattle would be inclusive of that vast group of animals that man has domesticated for his own uses. These would be inclusive of animals vital to man in farming, ranching, etc. Creeping things would be inclusive of all reptiles. Life in the air would be comprehended by the "flying fowl."

In this terse section we have the two stately divisions of created realities—non-living objects and living creatures—summoned to extend praise to God. A car proclaims the deserved praise of its designers and makers. A beautiful and beneficial building does the same for its architects and its builders or carpenters. God's green footstool does the same for Him whether we contemplate the non-living or the living creatures who are minus human reason and human rationale. All of this was created by God's limitless power and omniscient wisdom. All combined presents a continuous sermon of a one liner that is truly lovely—"The hand that made us is divine." Even stormy winds and flashing lightning, seemingly so *disordered,* are all the *ordered* parts of God's universe that exhibit His greatness and glory.

A STATELY SUMMONS FOR UNIVERSAL HUMAN PRAISE TO BE GIVEN GOD

"Kings of the earth, and all people; princes, and all judges of the earth: Both young men, and maidens; old men, and children" (148:11,12). Kings, princes and judges would embrace rulers from the top levels of governmental authority to the lower levels. "All people" would be inclusive of the rest of humanity. Young men and maidens (virgins—ASV) would be inclusive of those in the early morning of their lives, in the springtime or the early pilgrimage. Youth with the bloom of early life stamped upon their energetic countenances should remember God. Solomon so taught in a classic passage filled with preciousness (Ecclesiastes 12:1). Paul does the same in a New Testament Classic—1 Timothy 4:12. "Old men" would be inclusive of those in their advanced years, their sunset years as it were. Surely those closest to death should be persistent in the praise they extend the Heavenly Maker on high. "Children" are those youngest in life. By pairing "children" and "old men" the psalmist apparently and appropriately includes the beginning and the end of life.

WHY JEHOVAH IS EMINENTLY WORTHY OF PRAISE

Let them praise the name of the Lord: for his name alone is excellent; his glory is above the earth and heaven. He also exalteth the horn of his people, the praise of all his saints; even of the children of Israel, a people near unto him. Praise ye the Lord (148:13,14).

These worthy words serve as a stately climax to the entire psalm which has majored in praise for Jehovah. To praise the Lord's name is to praise His person. The name here, as is frequently the case in Holy Writ, stands for the whole person. His name transcends all names. Excellency is its attractive alias. Because of His power, wisdom and goodness His glory transcends both heaven and earth. He has lifted up the horn of his people. Upon them He has bestowed peace, prosperity and power. Because God has lifted up His people to such exalted, elevated levels His saints find additional cause to extend Him their profound praise. In the psalmist's age the children of Israel, the physcal descendants of faithful Abraham, were His people. They were a people near and dear to Him. Now Spiritual Israel, all Christians, constitute the people of God. They are His saints. They are near and dear to Him also. No nation is His people today who hate His Son, reject the New Testament as God's word for this dispensation and despise the Lord's blood-bought institution—the church of the Lord Jesus Christ. That is the apt description of infidelic Jews in our day.

As the psalm began so it ends—"Praise ye the Lord." Not many in our world today are really praising Him in the precise way He has outlined within Holy Writ. How sad; how immeasurably and inexpressibly sad!

POINTS TO PONDER ABOUT PSALM 148

1. Psalm 148 establishes the eternality of Mind (God) and refutes the eternality of matter (the non-living).
2. Psalm 148 establishes creation and refutes organic evolution.
3. Psalm 148 establishes that God is separate from His creation and hence refutes pantheism which calls all nature God.
4. Psalm 148 refutes Deism by proving that God is keenly and lovingly interested in His created universe.
5. Psalm 148 refutes Humanism which makes man his own god.
6. Psalm 148 refutes all idolatry for all created objects are summoned to praise God—not to be objects of idolatrous adoration themselves.

DISCUSSION QUESTIONS

1. *What is unique about how each of the five final psalms begins and ends and how does this fit the design of this section of psalms?*
2. *What tributes have been given Psalm 148?*
3. *Discuss the celestial praise the psalmist desired that God should receive.*
4. *What great truth is taught in the beginning of the Bible, near its middle and in the final book of Revelation?*
5. *Read, discuss and tie in Psalm 19:1; 50:6; 89:5 and 97:6 with Psalm · 148:1-6.*
6. *How is "for ever and ever" sometimes used in the Bible and give two examples to show that it does not always imply or demand an exacting eternity in meaning?*
7. *Discuss in detail the section that deals with terrestrial praise that God should receive.*
8. *Who of the human family should praise God and why?*
9. *Read and discuss Psalm 148:13,14.*
10. *Read and discuss Points to Ponder on Psalm 148.*

MULTIPLE CHOICE: Underline correct answer

1. *Psalms has been called: (A) "The Songbook of the Bible;" (B) The Book of the Law;" (C) "The Book of Origins;" (D) "The Book of Israelite Conquests;" (E) "The Book of Conversions."*
2. *The five final psalms (146-150) might be styled accurately as: (A) "the psalms of ascent;" (B) " the psalms of sorrow;" (C) "the Hallelujah psalms;" (D) "the psalms of Asaph."*
3. *Parallelism is the most dominant characteristic of: (A) Hebrew law; (B) Hebrew history; (C) Hebrew prose; (D) Hebrew poetry.*

4. "*Thy will be done in earth, as it is in heaven*" *is a Biblical statement and was uttered by: (A) Job; (B) Moses; (C) Abraham; (D) Jesus Christ; (E) David.*

5. *According to Psalm 89:37 God's faithful witness is: (A) man; (B) woman; (C) the moon; (D) the sun.*

SCRIPTURAL FILL-IN: Only one word is required in each blank.

(1) "_____ ye the _____. Praise ye the _____ from the _____: _____ him in the _____."

(2) "_____ ye him, _____ and moon: praise him, all ye _____ of _____."

(3) "Let them _____ the _____ of the _____: for he _____, and they were _____. He hath also _____ them for _____ and _____: he hath made a _____ which shall not _____."

(4) "By the _____ of the _____ were the _____ made; and all the _____ of them by the _____ of his _____...For he _____, and it was _____; he _____, and it _____ fast."

(5) "Let them _____ the _____ of the _____: for his _____ alone is _____: his _____ is above the _____ and _____. He also _____ the _____ of his _____, the _____ of all his _____; even of the _____ of _____, a _____ near unto him. _____ ye the _____."

TRUE OR FALSE: Put either a "T" or "F" in the blanks

____1. *The Psalms were composed by pious Hebrew penmen and designed originally to be sung.*

____2. *We can be positive about the author of Psalm 148, when he wrote it and under what particular circumstances.*

____3. *Creation of the universe by God is never stressed in the Bible from beginning to end.*

____4. *Mountains and hills are impressive monuments to the greatness of God as creator and sustainer.*

____5. *Non-living things can never lend any praise to the greatness of God.*

THOUGHT QUESTIONS

1. *Have a class discussion of some things which can be known about angels.*

2. *Discuss God as both creator and sustainer of our marvelous universe.*

3. *How do Colossians 1:17 and Hebrews 1:3 fit in so marvelously with Psalm 148:5,6?*

4. *How does such a small thing like a snowflake lend praise to God's greatness?*

5. *In what ways do both inanimate and animate objects praise God's greatness?*

6. *Who were and who are now God's people?*

7. *Who cannot be God's people today and why?*

CHAPTER FOURTEEN

THE BREADTH AND BEAUTY OF PSALMS

The first half of this volume of twenty-six chapters was devoted to some of the great chapters in Psalms. The last half will be devoted to some of the great themes embedded so eloquently and excellently in this precious product of sublime worth and wonder. It seems appropriate that we begin this second and last segment of our study with some golden glimpses of the breadth and beauty of Psalms.

THE BREADTH AND BEAUTY OF OUR GOD

David recognized both Jehovah's breadth and beauty when he wrote,

> One thing have I desired of the Lord, that will I seek after; that I may dwell in the house of the Lord all the days of my life, to behold the beauty of the Lord, and to inquire in his temple. For in the time of trouble he shall hide me in his pavilion: in the secret of his tabernacle shall he hide me: he shall set me up upon a rock (27:4,5).

With great intensity of desire David sought to be where the Lord was, to dwell with Him, to drink deeply of His spiritual beauty, to seek instruction in His house and to receive the Lord's protection in time of trouble.

Another psalmist expressed, "Whom have I in heaven but thee? and there is none upon earth that I desire beside thee" (73:25). Priority of God in heaven and upon earth permeates this stately sentiment.

There is the breadth and beauty of assurance that God is. "Be still, and know that I am God: I will be exalted among the heathen, I will be exalted in the earth" (46:10). Restless man needs to be still long enough to come to a knowledge of God's existence and of His greatness.

There is the breadth and beauty of Him as helper, aid and protector. We read,

> From the end of the earth will I cry unto thee, when my heart is overwhelmed: lead me to the rock that is higher than I. For thou hast been a shelter for me, and a strong tower from the enemy (61:2,3).

Finite and frail man needs just such a sure help as is Jehovah God.

There is the breadth and beauty of His name and glory. "And blessed be his glorious name for ever: and let the whole earth be filled with his glory; Amen, and Amen" (72:19). The holy man in whose heart God's name is revered and who glorifies his maker desires for all the world to experience that glory. The double Amen—So be it— sparkles with emphasis.

There is the breadth and beauty of His leadership. "Give ear, O Shepherd of Israel, thou that leadest Joseph like a flock; thou that dwellest between the cherubims, shine forth" (80:1). Israel was led by the Heavenly Shepherd. That Shepherd dwelt between the cherubims (mercy seat on top of the ark of the covenant) in their very house of worship in the Holy of Holies. The psalmist pleads for a manifestation of God's light around them.

There is the breadth and beauty of Jehovah's uniqueness. "For who in the heaven can be compared unto the Lord? who among the sons of the mighty can be likened unto the Lord?" (89:6). No one in heaven above or on earth below is comparable to God. All are greatly His inferiors; He is greatly their superior.

There is the breadth and beauty of His creative and sustaining power. "I will lift up mine eyes unto the hills, from whence cometh my help. My help cometh from the Lord, which made heaven and earth" (121:1,2). The God who made heaven and earth and sustains them would be powerful in helping the psalmist in trouble. So also with us we might add.

THE BREADTH AND BEAUTY OF HEAVEN

In a delightful duet of passages the psalmist expressed, "Thou wilt shew me the path of life; in thy presence is fulness of joy; at thy right hand there are pleasures for evermore...Surely goodness and mercy shall follow me all the days of my life: and I will dwell in the house of the Lord forever'' (16:11; 23:6). Learn here that heaven is a place of life—eternal or everlasting life. Eternal *life* is never associated with eternal Gehenna though its pathetic population will be there forever. There is a quality associated with eternal life forever separated from hell and its pathetic population. Heaven will be eternal life with quality; hell will be eternal death or separation minus all quality. Heaven is fulness of joy. The very personification of joy therein will be enjoyed. At Jehovah's right hand there are pleasures without end and far above apt appraisal. Heaven is a place of eternal security. Citizenship in God's house on high is not temporary; it is eternal in its stately sweep of tenure.

To the psalmist there was a breadth and beauty about heaven that greatly quickened his intense desire to go there. What about you, dear reader? Are you piloting your immortal soul toward that upper and better realm? If not, WHY NOT??

THE BREADTH AND BEAUTY OF JEHOVAH'S ADMIRABLE ATTRIBUTES

Jehovah God is faithful as keeper and protector. We read in Psalm 17:8, "Keep me as the apple of the eye, hide me under the shadow of thy wings." The apple of the eye would be an object of precious value. This is how important the psalmist desired to be in God's sight. The shadow of God's wings reflects the protection that a fowl gives its offspring. The fowl becomes a buttress against any approaching danger. To His people God is that invincible buttress, the immovable shield, the all-powerful protector. What a great, golden and glorious glimpse of our God!

Two of the most majestic verses in the entire book of Psalms set forth the character of our great God on high. "Justice and judgment are the habitation of thy throne: mercy and truth shall go before thy face...Honour and majesty are before him: strength and beauty are in his sanctuary'' (89:14; 96:6). Total justice and right judgments form the foundation of God's throne. Abraham was positive the judge of the earth would do right (Genesis 18:25). Where there is the face of Deity there mercy and truth will be in the forefront. Where God is, honor and majesty of necessity must be present. Strength and real beauty are ever His attractive attributes.

The Lord is lavish in His liberality to us. He is basically and beautifully the generous giver. "The heaven, even the heavens, are the Lord's: but the earth hath he given to the children of men'' (115:16). He retains possession of the Palace of the Universe where He resides but gives man His footstool. Understood here is man's stewardship. What a generous gift and yet its recipients so infrequently look up and say "Thanks unto thee!" The psalmist knew God far outgave him. Hence, he inquired, "What shall I render unto the Lord for all his benefits toward me?" (116:12). The blessings He bestows are vast and comprehensive. The psalmist expressed it so well in Psalm 146:7-9,

> Which executeth judgment for the oppressed: which giveth food to the hungry. The Lord looseth the prisoners: The Lord openeth the eyes of the blind: the Lord raiseth them that are bowed down: the Lord loveth the righteous. The Lord preserveth the strangers; he relieveth the fatherless and widow: but the way of the wicked he turneth upside down.

The counterpart of this in the New Testament would be Acts 10:38 wherein Peter stated of Jesus and Luke penned these words of wisdom and weight, "How God anointed Jesus of Nazareth with the Holy Ghost and with power: who went about doing good, and healing all that were oppressed of the devil; for God was with him." The goodness of Deity is above finite appraisal and human comprehension. Let us be grateful we can be its rich recipients regardless of how little we comprehend it.

THE BREADTH AND BEAUTY OF RIGHTEOUSNESS

In both testaments righteousness is a key, kingly term. Defined so correctly as right-doing it comprehends right motives, right thoughts, right speech and right deeds. The book of Psalms is a Divine Primer on righteousness. It depicts the God of righteousness. It was penned by men of piety, of deep righteousness. It exalts righteousness as the only worthwhile manner of life. Here are a few selected passages that speak of righteousness. "For the Lord knoweth the way of the righteous: but the way of the ungodly shall perish" (1:6.) Jehovah approves of the righteous. They are heaven-bound in the next world. He does not approve of the ungodly. They shall perish. Hell—not heaven—is on their future horizon. "If the foundations be destroyed, what can the righteous do?" (11:3). Moral and spiritual foundations all around us are faltering, failing and falling. Yet the righteous still have God as a rock, the Bible as anchor, the church as a spiritual haven, Christ as surety of redemption, prayer as our power and heaven as ultimate hope. Faltering foundations make more necessary than ever our remaining loyal to the Lord.

In the sincerity of his soul David framed the prayerful petition, "Let integrity and uprightness preserve me; for I wait on thee"

(25:21). The opposites, dishonesty and unrighteousness, have no preserving powers. They lead to perishing—not preservation!

Righteousness has a kingly kinship of companions. Its kindred list of holy allies is partially portrayed in a breathtakingly beautiful verse, "Mercy and truth are met together; righteousness and peace have kissed each other" (85:10). The subsequent verse portrays righteousness as looking "down from heaven" (85:11).

Righteousness is a seed that must be sown before its rich harvest is seen in human lives. James says in the New Testament, "And the fruit of righteousness is sown in peace of them that make peace" (James 3:18). Books like Psalms that major in sowing the desperately needed seeds of righteousness play a vital part in every harvest of righteous men, women, boys and girls.

Many Biblical passages encourage righteousness and portray it without the actual usage of the exacting word. These two passages do that very thing. "Blessed is every one that feareth the Lord; that walketh in his ways... I stretch forth my hands unto thee: my soul thirsteth after thee, as a thirsty land" (128:1; 143:6). No man can be righteous unless he fears God, walks in His prescribed ways and greatly thirsts after God. One of the beautiful beatitudes connects hunger and thirst with righteousness. The Saviour in the Sermon on the Mount declared "Blessed are they which do hunger and thirst after righteousness: for they shall be filled" (Matthew 5:6).

The Bible in general and the book of Psalms in particular breathe forth the breadth and beauty of regal righteousness. Righteousness enables us to walk with the King of kings and the Lord of lords.

THE BREADTH AND BEAUTY OF JEHOVAH'S MERCY

Mercy or one of its sympathetic derivatives occurs, according to my count, about one hundred and thirty times in the book of Psalms. Space will allow for only one or two passages to be presented. One selection that sparkles with breadth and beauty is Psalm 103:11,12 wherein we read,

> For as the heaven is high above the earth (according to the height of the heaven—margin), so great is his mercy toward them that fear him. As far as the east is from the west, so far hath he removed our transgressions from us.

By a rich contemplation of high heaven over lowly earth the psalmist is able to focus our minds on the transcending greatness of God's marvelous mercy on those who fear Him and hold His name in awe and reverence. This stately duet of verses links God's mercy and God's pardon. The former makes possible the reality of the latter. Why use east and west as directions instead of north and south? There may be a perfectly good reason. One on earth may only go so far north and then he will begin to travel south. But one may travel east or west indefinitely! Just that far has God removed the transgressions from His people who hear and heed His will. There is no sweeter verse in Holy Writ touching pardon than this one.

Psalm 136 is a marvelous message on mercy. It is a very unique chapter. There are twenty-six verses and twenty-six times the eloquent expression, "For his mercy endureth for ever," occurs. These six words in our KJV rendering end each verse. The ASV of 1901 has lovingkindness in all these eloquent endings rather than mercy. Mercy is lovingkindness and lovingkindness is mercy. The Hebrew word the psalmist used in this chapter is *chesed* and is defined by Hebrew scholarship as "Kindness, lovingkindness." The student is urged to read this beautiful chapter and drink deeply of its breadth of God's majestic mercy as extended to His people.

THE BREADTH AND BEAUTY OF BEING GOD'S PEOPLE

Physical Israel constituted Jehovah's people in the time of the psalmist; Spritiual Israel (composed *only* of Christians) is God's people now (Romans 2:28,29; Galatians 6:16). Israel's Sweet Singer wrote about the blessedness of being Jehovah's people in these weighty words, "Blessed is the nation whose God is the Lord; and the people whom he hath chosen for his own inheritance" (33:12). To His people He gave a banner. We read, "Thou hast given a banner to them that fear thee, that it may be displayed because of the truth" (60:4). A banner was a standard, flag, sign, signal or ensign. The great Christian hymn, "There's a Royal Banner," is the stately sentiment of this valiant verse set to a moving song of music. Our royal banner is the Great Commission of King Jesus and His blood-bought church. What an ensign fair we have the privilege to lift high and keep it exalted.

THE BREADTH AND BEAUTY OF BROTHERLY UNITY

Psalm 133 majors in this tremendous theme. (1) Brotherly unity is good; (2) it is pleasant; (3) it, to use a stately simile, is like the precious ointment on Aaron's head, beard and garments; (4) it, to use another stately simile, is like Hermon's dew and the dew that descended upon the mountains of Zion; (5) it is connected with the location where "the Lord commanded the blessing, even life for evermore" (133:3).

Great passages on unity for God's people under Christ are Mark 3:24,25; John 17:20-23; 1 Corinthians 1:10-13; Ephesians 4:3-6; Philippians 1:27. It would be well for the studious reader to peruse with care and profit all these and drink deeply of their spirit. The unity for which Jesus prayed and for which Paul pled is nearly lost in the religiously divided climate of today.

POINTS TO PONDER ON THE BREADTH AND BEAUTY OF PSALMS

1. Breadth and beauty of character is determined by the nature of the God we worship and serve—Jehovah or idols.
2. Breadth and beauty of character is determined by a righteous heart that is filled with mercy.
3. Breadth and beauty of character is determined by the direction of our destiny, viz., heaven or hell.
4. Breadth and beauty of character is determined by what we put into our mind, allow to fall from our lips and exhibit in daily deeds.
5. Breadth and beauty of character is developed by a slow, tedious process but its possession exceeds in value all of earth's gold.
6. Much time spent in perusing and practicing God's Book is the only way to develop breadth and beauty of character.

DISCUSSION QUESTIONS

1. *What is the proposed gist of the final half of this volume of STUDIES IN PSALMS?*
2. *What did David say relative to the beauty of the Lord in Psalm 27:4,5?*
3. *Discuss the various aspects of the breadth and beauty of our great God on high.*
4. *Discuss in some detail the various attributes suggested about our great, holy and glorious God on high.*
5. *Tie in Psalm 146:7-9 and Acts 10:38 as great passages that depict Deity's unparalleled goodness to man.*
6. *Describe in some detail what is said about the breadth and beauty of righteousness.*
7. *Discuss in some detail the breadth and beauty of Jehovah's mercy.*
8. *List and discuss the two Israels of God in the Old and New Testaments.*
9. *Read and discuss briefly the unique psalm on brotherly unity—Psalm 133.*

10. Read and discuss the New Testament passages which are cited relative to unity.

11. Read and discuss the Points to Ponder on The Breadth And Beauty of Psalms.

MULTIPLE CHOICE: Underline correct answer

1. Relative to the existence of God David took the position of: (A) an agnostic; (B) an atheist; (C) a half-way theist who THOUGHT there MIGHT be a God in heaven; (D) a firm, full-fledged theist who KNEW beyond doubt that God exists and rewards those who seek and serve Him with fidelity.

2. In Israelite worship in the Old Testament God's presence was: (A) at the brazen altar in the court area of the tabernacle; (B) at the laver of washing in the open court area; (C) in the Holy Place where the golden candlestick, table of showbread and altar of incense were housed; (D) between the cherubims on the mercy seat on the ark of the covenant in the holy of Holies in their house (tabernacle or temple) of worship.

3. Eternal life as an actuality is: (A) nothing but a figment of man's imagination; (B) available right now in this life; (C) associated with hell or Gehenna; (D) lovingly linked with heaven and heaven only.

4. In Genesis 18:25: (A) Abraham; (B) Lot; (C) Satan; (D) Abimelech—expressed total confidence that the Judge of the earth will do right.

5. "And the fruit of righteousness is sown in peace of them that make peace" was penned by (A) David in one of his psalms; (B) James in the New Testament; (C) Moses in the Pentateuch; (D) Isaiah in one of his great Messianic predictive prophecies.

6. Psalm 136 is a unique chapter which deals with God's' (A) mercy; (B) refusal to pardon; (C) final judgment of the wicked; (D) total disinterest in his human creation.

SCRIPTURAL FILL-IN: Each blank requires only one word.

(1) "Be _____, and _____ that I am _____: I will be _____ among the _____, I will be _____ in the _____."

(2) "I will _____ up mine _____ unto the _____, from whence _____ my _____. My _____ cometh from the _____, which made _____ and _____."

122

(3) "_____ and _____ are the _____ of thy
_____: _____ and _____ shall
_____ before thy _____."

(4) "_____ and _____ are met _____;
_____ and _____ have _____ each other."

(5) For as the _____ is _____ above the _____,
so _____ is his _____ toward them that
_____ him. As far as the _____ is from the
_____, so _____ hath he _____ our
_____ from us."

TRUE OR FALSE: Put either a "T" or "F" in the blanks

____1. Nobody in the Old Testament knew anything about heaven or eternal life therein since this is strictly a doctrine of the New Testament.

____2. The Psalms set forth Jehovah as a giving God and one totally lavish in His lovely liberality.

____3. The Book of Psalms is a beautiful and delightful Primer on righteousness.

____4. The banner of Christians under Christ is the Great Commission of King Jesus and His blood-bought church.

____5. Mercy and lovingkindness may be used as synonymous or interchangeable terms in the Bible.

THOUGHT QUESTIONS

1. Give proof from this chapter that no writer of the Psalms was either an atheist or an evolutionist.

2. How would the writers of the Psalms, were they here now, surely react to the modern error that truth is unattainable and that no one can really know anything for a surety?

3. How do we know that the various psalmists (writers of this book) knew of heaven and hoped to go there ultimately?

4. Why is eternal life never associated with that realm known as hell or everlasting punishment and damnation?

5. Do somewhat of an in depth study of the marvelous message embedded in Psalm 116:12.

6. Why should there be a great hunger and thirst in man for righteousness?

CHAPTER FIFTEEN

A PORTRAIT OF OUR GOD IN PSALMS

It is no exaggeration to affirm that the various psalmists were totally God-centered. He was the precious pivot of their motive and mission, their attitude and action, their love and life. God was not hazy in their thinking. He was not some remote power who was totally disinterested in the world. He was as near to them as prayer. He was as real as the earth on which they stood, the air they breathed, the food they ate and the water that slaked their thirst. They KNEW He existed. There was no leap-in-the-dark in their system of firm, unbending and uncompromising faith. They registered neither agnosticism nor atheism anywhere in Psalms in the depiction of their faith, in the delineation of their hope. We may also possess a similar sentiment; yea, we MUST!!

What is God like? The psalmists knew. Some of His admirable attributes will now be presented in the actual words of these Spirit-guided penmen. Several passages will be given consecutively that describe each selected attribute and then brief comments will follow. The last section of this chapter will be an attractive array of scriptures which will be given minus any human comment at all. These will be divine comments and they are preferred any day to human comments. There is a place for human comments but it is always secondary to divinely derived comments. Of that we may be sure!

THE GREATNESS OF OUR GOD

"How Great Thou Art" and "O Mighty God" are great hymns today that Christians love to sing in unison. They breathe forth sentiments of God's greatness abounding in the Psalms. Here are an even dozen passages of power and pathos in portraying Jehovah's genuine greatness. Numbered and noted they are:

(1) The Lord is King for ever and ever: the heathen are perished out of his land (10:16). (2) The voice of the Lord is powerful; the voice of the Lord is full of majesty (29:4). (3) Great is the Lord, and greatly to be praised in the city of our God, in the mountain of his holiness (48:1). (4) The earth shook, the heavens also dropped at the presence of God...the God of Israel (68:8). (5) He divided the sea, and caused them to pass through; and he made the waters to stand as an heap (78:13). (6) O Lord God of hosts, who is a strong Lord like unto thee? or to thy faithfulness round about thee? (89:8). (7) O Lord, how great are thy works! and thy thoughts are very deep (92:5). (8) For the Lord is a great God, and a great King above all gods (95:3). (9) Bless the Lord, O my soul. O Lord my God, thou art very great; thou art clothed with honour and majesty (104:1). (10) The works of the Lord are great, sought out of all them that have pleasure therein (111:2) (11) The Lord is high above all nations, and his glory above the heavens (113:4) (12) Great is the Lord, and greatly to be praised; and his greatness is unsearchable (145:3).

These pertinent passages stress the: (1) greatness of His kingship; (2) inability of pagans to withstand His judgments; (3) full authority of His spoken word; (4) majesty of His person; (5) greatness of God in His immaculate character of holiness; (6) greatness of His presence at Sinai when the law was given initially; (7) greatness of His power over waters such as the Red Sea at the time of Israel's deliverance from bondage; (8) greatness of His faithfulness; (9) greatness of His works; (10) depth of His thoughts; (11) absolute supremacy of His sovereign sway over all lifeless gods created by human hands; (12) greatness of His honor; (13) greatness of His works in which good men derive profitable pleasure; (14) greatness of His glory above nations on earth and the very heavens He created; and (15) various ways in which His multi-greatness is beyond finite minds to search out and comprehend with any degree of fullness. Truly, how great and mighty our God is.

THE GOODNESS OF OUR GOD

There is only one letter's difference between God and good. God is good in the ULTIMATE and ABSOLUTE sense; man is good only in a RELATIVE sense. The following ten passages stress His genuine, absolute goodness. Numbered and noted they read,

(1) For thou art not a God that hath pleasure in wickedness: neither shall evil dwell with thee (5:4). (2) For the righteous Lord loveth righteousness; his countenance doth behold the upright (11:7). (3) Good and upright is the Lord: therefore will he teach sinners in the way (25:8). (4) Oh how great is thy goodness, which thou hast laid up for them that fear thee; which thou hast wrought for them that trust in thee before the sons of men (31:19)! (5) Blessed be the Lord, who daily loadeth us with benefits, even the God of our salvation (68:19). (6) Truly God is good to Israel, even to such as are of a clean heart (73:1). (7) For the Lord God is a sun and shield: the Lord will give grace and glory: no good thing will he withhold from them that walk uprightly (84:11). (8) For thou, Lord, art good, and ready to forgive; and plenteous in mercy unto all them that call upon thee (86:5). (9) For the Lord is good; his mercy is everlasting; and his truth endureth to all generations (100:5). (10) The Lord is righteous in all his ways, and holy in all his works (145:17).

Positive goodness in Jehovah means He can have NO pleasure in the wicked or corrupt. Evil is diametrically opposed to His goodness. This is why the wicked and evil are incompatible with God; it is why they feel so very uncomfortable in His presence. God's goodness is seen in: (1) His delight of righteousness; (2) His approval of the upright; (3) His great desire to teach sinners the way of truth they should tread; (4) the rich rewards He has stored up for practitioners of good; (5) the material benefits He gives daily; (6) the salvation He graciously tenders; (7) the bountiful benedictions and beautiful blessings He bestows upon the clean of heart; (8) the sun and shield He is to His people; (9) His unwillingness to deprive His people of any really good thing; (10) the merciful, plenteous pardon He confers so graciously; (1)) the etenal truth of which He has made us the rich, regal recipients; and (12) the righteous and holy character of all His works. The psalmists were great and godly believers in the inherent goodness of Jehovah God. This book has a beautiful and basic lesson for us as touching belief in God's goodness. In fact, to believe the book of Psalms is to believe in the gracious, genuine and golden goodness of Jehovah God. Psalms is a great book to dissolve anyone's doubts as touching whether God is good. HE IS!!

THE MERCY OF GOD

August Jehovah is a God of marvelous mercy. Mercy is a key, kingly term in Psalms. Mercy and compassion permeate the book. Here are seven stately passages that depict our Merciful Maker on high. Numbered and noted they are,

(1) Thy mercy, O Lord, is in the heavens: and thy faithfulness reacheth unto the clouds (36:5). (2) For thy mercy is great unto the heavens, and thy truth unto the clouds (57:10). (3) But thou, O Lord, art a God full of compassion, and gracious, longsuffering, and plenteous in mercy and truth (86:15). (4) But the mercy of the Lord is from everlasting to everlasting upon them that fear him, and his righteousness unto children's children (103:17). (5) Gracious is the Lord, and righteous; yea, our God is merciful (116:5). (6) If thou, Lord, shouldest mark iniquities, O Lord, who shall stand? But there is forgiveness with thee, that thou mayest be feared (130:3,4). (7) Let Israel hope in the Lord: for with the Lord there is mercy, and with him is plenteous redemption. And he shall redeem Israel from all his iniquities (130:7,8).

God's mercy is: (1) far-reaching; (2) plenteous; (3) always based on truth; (4) eternal in its noble nature; (5) gracious in its beautiful bearing; (6) pardoning in its power; and (7) redemptive in its persistent purpose. How grateful we all should be that God deals with us mercifully and not strictly according to straight justice minus mercy. No accountable, intelligent creature is willing to cry out, "Lord, just give me what I DESERVE!" In reality we deserve hell as punishment for our sins; in His mercy He offers heaven if we hear and heed His holy will. Thanks be unto God for such marvelous mercy!

THE WRATH OF GOD

The greatness, goodness and mercy of God are all emphasized topics in current religious talk circles. No so with his wrath. This is an unemphasized topic of our day. Yet the Bible has more to say relative to His wrath than about His goodness according to excellent Bible scholarship. Paul joins the goodness and severity of God in the same passage (Romans 11:22). The following five passages speak of Jehovah's severity or wrath in Psalms. Numbered and noted they are,

(1) The ungodly are not so: but are like the chaff which the wind driveth away. Therefore the ungodly shall not stand in the judgment, nor sinners in the congregation of the righteous. For the Lord knoweth the way of the righteous: but the way of the ungodly shall perish (1:4-6). (2) The wicked shall be turned into hell (Sheol—ASV), and all the nations that forget God (9:17).

(3) For the Lord loveth judgment, and forsaketh not his saints; they are preserved for ever: but the seed of the wicked shall be cut off (37:28). (4) Before the Lord: for he cometh, for he cometh to judge the earth: he shall judge the world with righteousness, and the people with his truth (96:13). (5) The Lord is righteous: he hath cut asunder the cords of the wicked (129:4).

The wrath of God calls for: (1) the ultimate perishing of the wicked; (2) the punishment of the wicked by God subsequent to death; (3) the cutting off of the wicked; (4) the judgment of all with truth as the courageous criterion, the uncompromising standard; and (5) the cutting asunder the chords of the wicked. God's wrath calls for a payday for sin. He is not the doting, indulgent grandfatherly image that so many have Him pictured to be. Such is NOT one of His attributes at all!

THE RICHES OF OUR GOD

God is maker of all; He is sustainer of all; these make Him owner of all. The whole Bible reiterates these self-evident truths again and again. The book of Psalms does as the following quartet of precious passages attests. Numbered and noted they read,

(1) The earth is the Lord's, and the fulness thereof; the world, and they that dwell therein (24:1). (2) For every beast of the forest is mine, and the cattle upon a thousand hills. I know all the fowls of the mountains; and the wild beasts of the field are mine. If I were hungry, I would not tell thee: for the world is mine, and the fulness thereof (50:10-12). (3) Our help is in the name of the Lord, who made heaven and earth (124:8). (4) Which made heaven, and earth, the sea, and all that therein is: which keepeth truth for ever:... (146:6).

By rights of creation and sustaining powers Jehovah is owner of ALL that has been made. Technically, man owns nothing; he is but a temporary tenant. We should view our world as one which belongs to God. It is not ours to pollute and abuse; it is ours to cultivate with care and use with prudence.

JEHOVAH: MAN'S IMPERATIVE NEED

Jehovah has made man and man will never find peace, happiness, contentment, real satisfaction and true meaning in life until he finds such in God. With Him life is *fine;* minus Him it is a *fit.* These six passages underscore man's essential need and desire for God. Numbered and noted they read,

> (1) As for me, I will behold thy face in righteousness: I shall be satisfied, when I awake, with thy likeness (17:15). (2) The Lord is my rock, and my fortress, and my deliverer; my God, my strength, in whom I will trust; my buckler, and the horn of my salvation, and my high tower (18:2). (3) The Lord is my light and my salvation; whom shall I fear? the Lord is the strength of my life; of whom shall I be afraid? (27:1). (4) The Lord is my strength and my shield; my heart trusted in him, and I am helped: therefore my heart greatly rejoiceth; and with my song will I praise him (28:7). (5) As the hart panteth after the water brooks, so panteth my soul after thee, O God. My soul thirsteth for God, for the living God: when shall I come and appear before God? (42:1,2). (6) God is our refuge and strength, a very present help in trouble (46:1).

We need God as shield and saviour; we need God as guide and governor; we need God as informer and intercessor; we need God as refuge and redeemer; we need God to satisfy the deepest essentials in our personality make-up—communion with our Maker, Sustainer, Saviour and ultimately as Judge. In political conventions loud cries fill the air about our needing this man or that man for the next four years in the Oval Office in Washington. As a gospel preacher I wish I could have the ear of America and tell our people that we need God; we need Christ; we need the Bible; we need the gospel; we need the church. These are the pressing needs of priority for this or any generation, for our country and all countries of the world.

A PORTRAIT OF JEHOVAH IN BOOK, CHAPTER AND VERSE CITATIONS

Numbered and noted these twenty-five precious passages read,

> (1) But thou, O Lord, art a shield for me; my glory, and the lifter up of mine head (3:3). (2) The Lord also will be a refuge for the oppressed, a refuge in times of trouble (9:9). (3) The Lord is in his holy temple, the Lord's throne is in heaven: his eyes behold, his eyelids try, the children of men (11:4). (4) For thou art my rock and my fortress; therefore for thy name's sake lead me, and guide me (31:3). (5) Our soul waiteth for the Lord: he is our help

and our shield (33:20). (6) The Lord is nigh unto them that are of a broken heart; and saveth such as be of a contrite spirit (34:18). (7) Many, O Lord my God, are thy wonderful works which thou hast done, and thy thoughts which are to us-ward; they cannot be reckoned up in order unto thee: if I would declare and speak of them, they are more than can be numbered (40:5). (8) Blessed be the Lord God of Israel from everlasting, and to everlasting. Amen, and Amen (41:13). (9) For God is the King of all the earth: sing ye praises with understanding. God reigneth over the heathen: God sitteth upon the throne of his holiness (47:7,8). (10) We have thought of thy lovingkindness, O God, in the midst of thy temple (48:9). (11) For this God is our God for ever and ever: he will be our guide even unto death (48:14). (12) Behold, God is mine helper: the Lord is with them that uphold my soul (54:4). (13) Because of his strength will I wait upon thee: for God is my defense (59:9). (14) O God, thou art my God; early will I seek thee: my soul thirsteth for thee, my flesh longeth for thee in a dry and thirsty land, where no water is; To see thy power and thy glory, so as I have seen thee in the sanctuary. Because thy lovingkindness is better than life, my lips shall praise thee. Thus will I bless thee while I live: I will lift up my hands in thy name. My soul shall be satisfied as with marrow and fatness; and my mouth shall praise thee with joyful lips:... (63:1-5). (15) That men may know that thou, whose name alone is JEHOVAH, art the most high over all the earth (83:18). (16) For thou art great, and doest wondrous things: thou art God alone (86:10). (17) O turn unto me, and have mercy upon me; give thy strength unto thy servant, and save the son of thine handmaid (86:16). (18) The Lord reigneth, he is clothed with majesty; the Lord is clothed with strength, wherewith he hath girded himself: the world also is stablished, that it cannot be moved. Thy throne is established of old: thou art from everlasting...The Lord on high is mightier than the noise of many waters, yea than the mighty waves of the sea (93:1,2,4). (19) The Lord reigneth; let the earth rejoice; let the multitude of isles be glad thereof. Clouds and darkness are round about him: righteousness and judgment are the habitation of his throne (97:1,2). (20) O Lord, how manifold are thy works! in wisdom hast thou made them all: the earth is full of thy riches (104:24). (21) He will bless them that fear the Lord, both small and great (115:13). (22) Behold, he that keepeth Israel shall neither slumber nor sleep. The Lord is thy keeper: the Lord is thy shade upon thy right hand...The Lord shall preserve thee from all evil: he shall preserve thy soul. The Lord shall preserve thy going out and thy coming in from this time forth, and even for evermore (121:4,5,7,8). (23) Unto thee lift I up mine eyes, O thou that dwellest in the heavens (123:1). (24) The Lord hath done great things for us; whereof we are glad (126:3). (25) Let every thing that hath breath praise the Lord. Praise ye the Lord (150:6).

POINTS TO PONDER ABOUT JEHOVAH'S PORTRAIT IN PSALMS

1. Our God is great in the POWER He wields.
2. Our God is great in the GOODNESS He confers.
3. Our God is great in the MERCY He bestows.
4. Our God is great in the PARDON He bequeathes.
5. Our God is great in the PROTECTION He provides.
6. Our God is great in the GUIDANCE He supplies.

DISCUSSION QUESTIONS

1. *What absolutely controlling and all-engrossing attitude characterized all the psalmists or writers of this great Biblical book?*
2. *Read and discuss briefly the twelve selected passages in Psalms which depict the greatness of our God.*
3. *Read and discuss briefly the ten selected passages in Psalms which depict the gracious goodness of our glorious God.*
4. *Read and discuss briefly the seven stated passages that delineate the marvelous mercy of Jehovah God.*
5. *Read and discuss briefly the five selected passages that portray Jehovah's wrath.*
6. *Read and discuss briefly the quartet of passages in Psalms about the riches of God.*
7. *Read and discuss briefly the six passages that underscore man's essential need and desire for God.*
8. *What are the real needs of modern America?*
9. *What great thoughts did you glean about Jehovah's portrait from the twenty-five book, chapter and verse citations given in the final section of this chapter?*
10. *Read and discuss the Points to Ponder.*

MULTIPLE CHOICE: Underline correct answer

1. *"How Great Thou Art"* and *"O Mighty God"* are: (A) atheistic; (B) agnostic; (C) irreverent; (D) God-honoring and truth-defending—in their lyrical lines.

2. The law under which the psalmists lived was given by: (A) Abraham in Ur; (B) Noah after he left the ark; (C) Moses at Sinai; (D) Christ on a Galilean Mountain just prior to His ascension.

3. Relative to God's wrath the Bible says: (A) more than about His goodness; (B) nothing; (C) but very little and that very apologetically; (D) that any amount of wrath would be incompatible with His love, kindness, mercy and compassion.

4. In Romans 11:22: (A) Matthew; (B) Luke; (C) Paul; (D) Jude—joined the goodness and severity of God.

5. Modern man: (A) no longer needs God; (B) is self-sufficient; (C) has learned there is really no God behind all things; (D) needs God just as all other generations have needed Him.

SCRIPTURAL FILL-IN: Only one word is required in each blank.

(1) "_____ is the _____, and _____ to be _____; and his _____ is _____."

(2) "For the Lord _____ is a _____ and _____: the _____ will give _____ and _____; no _____ thing will he _____ from them that _____ uprightly."

(3) "But thou, O _____, art a _____ full of _____, and _____, _____, and _____ in _____ and _____."

(4) "The _____ are not _____: but are like the _____ which the _____ driveth away. Therefore the _____ shall not _____ in the _____, nor _____ in the _____ of the _____. For the _____ knoweth the _____ of the _____: but the way of the _____ shall _____."

(5) "The _____ is the _____, and the _____ thereof; the _____, and they that _____ therein."

(6) "_____ is our _____ and _____, a very _____ help in _____."

TRUE OR FALSE: Put either a "T" or "F" in the blanks

____1.   It is impossible to know that God exists and therefore we have to take the popular leap-of-faith in seeking God.

____2.   God is infinite while man, His creature, is finite.

____3.   Psalms is a great and glorious treatise on God's goodness.

____4.   The various writers of Psalms were really unsure about God's existence and whether He is a rewarder of those who seek Him.

____5.   The very last verse of Psalms is a call for all His living creation to give Him proper praise.

THOUGHT QUESTIONS

1.   Why should we be far more interested in divine communications than human comments on what the Bible says?

2.   Discuss the two uses of goodness in the Bible.

3.   Read Psalm 42:1,2 and Matthew 5:6 and relate how they fit each other so marvellously.

4.   Why is there really no incompatibility between the goodness of God and His judicial wrath?

5.   Tell why a chapter like this can be a real faith-building exercise relative to our varied relationships wtih Jehovah God.

CHAPTER SIXTEEN

MESSIANIC PROPHECIES IN THE PSALMS

Jesus both recognized and recorded the fact that the Psalms spoke of Him. In one of His post-resurrection appearances He said to His dedicated disciples, "These are the words which I spake unto you, while I was yet with you, that all things must be fulfilled, which were written the the law of Moses, and in the prophets, and in the psalms, concerning me" (Luke 24:44). The thrust of this chapter will exhibit the Marvelous Messiah as the grand and striking object of many of the most precious psalms.

PREDICTIVE PROPHECIES ABOUT HIS DEITY

The second psalm states, "The kings of the earth set themselves, and the rulers take counsel together, against the Lord, and against his anointed, saying,... (2:2). The Lord here is Jehovah; the Anointed is Christ. Messiah in Hebrew and Christ in Greek mean Anointed in English. Acts 4:26 establishes clearly the Messianic intent of Psalm 2:2. Psalm 2:7 states, "I will declare the decree: the Lord hath said unto me, Thou art my Son; this day have I begotten thee." Hebrews 1:5 refers to this very passage and adds further proof of its Messianic intent. The second psalm ends with this intensely interesting charge, "Kiss the Son, lest he be angry, and ye perish from the way, when his wrath is kindled but a little. Blessed are all they that put their trust in him" (2:12). The Son is the Messiah or the same one contemplated in 2:7. To kiss refers to the homage, adoration and worship which is His rightful due. The anger refers to the displeasure of the Son if His Messiahship is rejected. Such a rejection leads to perishing. His wrath will be kindled against all who reject Him as Redeemer and spurn Him as Saviour. But blessed indeed will be those who place their trust in Him as Deity and as Saviour.

Israel's Sweet Singer writes so eloquently and excellently,

> Thy throne, O God, is for ever and ever: the sceptre of thy kingdom is a right sceptre. Thou lovest righteousness, and hatest wickedness: therefore God, thy God, hath anointed thee with the oil of gladness above thy fellows (45:6,7).

Hebrews 1:8,9 make crystal clear that the Father (the First Person of the Godhead) was addressing the Son (the Second Person of the Godhead). The RSV greatly tampered with this Messianic prophecy by removing Christ's Deity from the passage and leaving Him only with a Divine Throne. Even their own rendering of Hebrews 1:8,9 condemns their modernistic treatment of Psalm 45:6,7.

Christ as creator is clearly established in these words,

> Of old hast thou laid the foundation of the earth: and the heavens are the work of thy hands. They shall perish, but thou shalt endure: yea, all of them shall wax old like a garment; as a vesture shalt thou change them, and they shall be changed: But thou art the same, and thy years shall have no end (102:25-27).

The writer of Hebrews 1:10-12 quotes this very passage and applies it to the Mighty Messiah. That Christ is creator is seen in such other great and precious passages as John 1:1-3; Colossians 1:15-17 and Revelation 3:14.

David in Psalm 110 establishes both the Deity of the Messiah as well as His high priesthood. In verse 1 he wrote, "The Lord said unto my Lord, Sit thou at my right hand, until I make thine enemies thy footstool." The two Lords respectively are Jehovah the Father and the one we know as Jesus, the Second Person of the Sacred Three. Jesus used this very effectively in a great and decisive argument for His Deity in Matthew 22:41-46. No infidelic Jew in His audience could handle it then; no one has been able to handle it since. It is an "ungetoverable" argument touching His Deity. Relative to His priesthood David said, "The Lord hath sworn, and will not repent, Thou art a priest for ever after the order of Melchizedek" (110:4). Hebrews 5-10 in the New Testament in general as chapters and Hebrews 7:17 as a particular passage make crystal clear that David was speaking of our great high priest in Christianity—Jesus Christ.

Throughout the Old Testament it was the divine intention for the Second Person of the Timeless Trinity, as brother Roy H. Lanier, Sr., delighted to call the Sublime Three, to come to earth and pitch His tent among men as a man (John 1:14; Galatians 4:4). One of the clearest prophecies pointing to this in the Old Testament is,

> Sacrifice and offering thou didst not desire; mine ears hast thou opened: burnt offering and sin offering hast thou not required. Then said I, Lo, I come: in the volume of the book it is written of me, I delight to do thy will, O my God: yea, thy law is within my heart (40:6-8).

Hebrews 10:5-8 looks back to this very passage. The Hebrew penman has a "body hast thou prepared me" whereas the psalmist has "mine ears hast thou opened" or "digged" as the margin conveys. There is not as much of a problem here as some commentators have intimated. The expression in Psalms means a thorough willingness on the part of the Messiah to do the Father's bidding in His misison to earth. But this demanded His being supplied with a body. The two thoughts are in beautiful harmony, in unique unison; they are not in discord or jarring disharmony.

PREDICTIVE PROPHECIES RELATING TO HIS PERSONAL MINISTRY

Parabolic teaching was part and parcel of our Lord's ministry. There were times when this type of teaching formed the burden of His message such as in Mark 4:34. The psalms predicted such. Psalm 49:4 states, "I will incline mine ear to a parable:..." Psalm 78:2 reiterates a similar sentiment by stating, "I will open my mouth in a parable: I will utter dark sayings of old:..." The eye of the inspired Matthew must have been riveted on one or both of these passages as he penned Matthew 13:35 but possibly on the latter passage in Psalms.

Psalm 69:9 states, "For the zeal of thine house hath eaten me up; and the reproaches of them that reproached thee are fallen upon me." John 2:17 and Romans 15:3 both connect these sentiments with the Saviour's ministry. The former concerns the first cleansing of the temple by the Lion of the tribe of Judah and the Roman passage mirrors the Messiah as He shields His Father by taking on Himself the reproaches aimed at the Father.

Psalm 91:11,12 declare, "For he shall give his angels charge over thee, to keep thee in all thy ways. They shall bear thee up in their hands, lest thou dash thy foot against a stone." Students of our Lord's temptations in Matthew 4 and Luke 4 will recall Satan's employment of these very verses. In response Jesus did not deny that they applied to Him but showed how that another scripture, Deuteronomy 6:16, offered a necessary qualification. Furthermore, a careful reading of what appears in Psalm 91:11,12 and what the devil actually said reveals that the clever deluder left out a key expression—"to keep thee in all thy ways." Quite obviously, it was not in Satanic interest to quote that expression! The verses in Psalm 91:11,12 did not imply at all that angelic protection would abide the Son if He became reckless in His ways and if He departed from the Father's ways. Deuteronomy 6:16 tones and tempers Psalm 91:11,12 also. This Satan either forgot or ignored but Jesus neither forgot nor ignored.

PREDICTIVE PROPHECIES ABOUT HIS DEATH, BURIAL AND RESURRECTION

The death, burial and resurrection of Christ is the heart of the gospel as Paul depicts in 1 Corinthians 15—the great resurrection chapter of Holy Writ. These cardinal themes also occupy the heart of many predictive prophecies relative to the Messiah in the Old Testament such as Isaiah 53 and several verses in Psalms as this section will fully exhibit. The rejection of the Messiah by obstinate Jews and the crucifixion of God's Son which they triggered did not catch the Godhead off guard as pernicious premillennialism currently contends. He came to suffer; He came to die; He came to be buried; He came to be raised from the dead. These precious predictive psalms so attest and do so in crystal clear language.

David wrote,

> I have set the Lord always before me: because he is at my right hand, I shall not be moved. Therefore my heart is glad, and my glory rejoiceth: my flesh also shall rest in hope. For thou wilt not leave my soul in hell (Sheol—ASV); neither wilt thou suffer thine Holy One to see corruption (16:8-10).

Peter on Pentecost makes clear that David spoke not of himself but of his Son—the Mighty Messiah (Acts 2:25-34). Temporary would be the Messiah's death. It would not be long enough for His body to begin decay or decomposition. His stay in the Hadean realm of comfort (called Sheol in the Hebrew Text of Psalms and Hades in the Greek text of Acts 2) would be short. His resurrection was sure, David avers.

138

Psalm 22:1 contains one of the seven sayings of Christ on Calvary. David wrote, "My God, my God, why hast thou forsaken me? why art thou so far from helping me, and from the words of my roaring?" Matthew 27:46 and Mark 15:34 contain the precise fulfillment of this. In Psalm 22:7,8 we note again, "All they that see me laugh me to scorn: they shoot out the lip, they shake the head, saying, He trusted on the Lord that he would deliver him: let him deliver him, seeing he delighted in him." Matthew 27:39-44 is a striking fulfillment of this as description is made vividly of those who milled maliciously around cruel Calvary. Psalm 22:16 affirms that He would be pierced in hands and feet and this is suggestive of a crucifixion (Luke 23:33). In Luke 24:39 Jesus requested the stunned disciples to behold both His hands and feet. Implied are the wounds still evident. So minute is the psalmist that he even describes the provisions for the Lord's garments (divided among the executioners) and the casting of lots for his vesture or seamless (inner) coat (22:18). John 19:23,24 contains the striking and accurate fulfillment.

Apparently, Jesus, in Luke 23:46, had in mind Psalm 31:5 as He commended His spirit into the hands of the Father on high.

Psalm 34:20 predicts that "He keepeth all his bones: not one of them is broken." John 19:36 fulfills this in remarkable fashion.

That the Messiah would be betrayed by a close friend is predicted in Psalm 41:9. Judas Iscariot fulfills this in Matthew 26:47-50.

Some Bible students are of the opinion that Psalm 55:4,5 is a portrayal of the sorrows of Gethsemane. The passage by David states, "My heart is sore pained within me: and the terrors of death are fallen upon me. Fearfulness and trembling are come upon me, and horror hath overwhelmed me." Matthew 26:36-44 record the sorrows of the Saviour in darkened Gethsemane that Thursday night. Even more graphically does Luke 22:39-46.

PREDICTIVE PROPHECIES ABOUT CHRIST AS DAVID'S SON

The Messiah was to be of David's seed; He was to be his Son. "Son of David" in the New Testament is a ready reference to the Messiah (Matthew 22:42ff). The psalmist says in Psalm 89:3,4, "I have made a covenant with my chosen, I have sworn unto David my servant, Thy seed will I establish for ever, and build up thy throne to all generations." In Luke 1:32,33 the dispatched angel from heaven, Gabriel, referred to David's throne that Mary's soon-to-be-born Son would one day occupy. Paul at Antioch in Pisidia referred to Jesus as being the seed of David (Acts 13:22,23).

139

In Psalm 132:11 we read, "The Lord hath sworn in truth unto David; he will not turn from it; Of the fruit of thy body will I set upon thy throne." This must have been the very passage on which Peter had his eye riveted when he spoke the words,

> Therefore being a prophet, and knowing that God had sworn with an oath to him, that of the fruit of his loins, according to the flesh, he would raise up Christ to sit on his throne;... (Acts 2:30).

Doubtlessly, 2 Samuel 7:12ff was also before Peter's inspired mind as he preached the magnificent, marvellous and monumental lesson on that memorable Pentecost in Acts 2—the birthday of God's kingdom—Christ's church—on earth.

PREDICTIVE PROPHECIES RELATIVE TO CHRIST'S AMAZING ASCENSION

Both ancient and modern commentators of the Psalms have thought Psalm 24:7-10 is a precious portrayal of the resurrected Redeemer as He returns to the Palace of the Universe subsequent to His highly successful mission of mercy to our mundane sphere. With resplendent and regal beauty David writes,

> Lift up your heads, O ye gates; and be ye lift up, ye everlasting doors; and the King of glory shall come in. Who is this King of glory? The Lord strong and mighty, the Lord mighty in battle. Lift up your heads, O ye gates; even lift them up, ye everlasting doors; and the King of glory shall come in. Who is this King of glory? The Lord of hosts, he is the King of glory.

The high honor, genuine glory and ardent acclaim all His upon returning to heaven are royally reflected in Ephesians 1:19-23; Philippians 2:9-11 and 1 Peter 3:22. Psalm 24:7-10 could with certainty and scriptural ease be applied to the amazing ascension. I know of no scriptural truth we violate in so doing.

The ascension is portrayed predictively in this expressive statement, "Thou hast ascended on high, thou hast led captivity captive: thou hast received gifts for men; yea, for the rebellious also, that the Lord God might dwell among them" (68:18). Paul's eye definitely is riveted on this very passage as he pens a message dealing with miraculous measures of the Spirit in Ephesians 4:8ff.

PREDICTIVE PROPHECY ABOUT CHRIST AS JEHOVAH'S CHOSEN STONE

Expressed in Psalm 118:22-24 are these words of weight and wisdom,

> The stone which the builders refused is become the head stone of the corner. This is the Lord's doing, it is marvellous in our eyes. This is the day which the Lord hath made; we will rejoice and be glad in it.

That this has reference to the Jewish rejection of Jesus and His ultimately being made the cornerstone is made sure by such new Testament passages as Matthew 21:42; Mark 12:10; Ephesians 2:20 and 1 Peter 2:4,7.

CONCLUSION

After studying all these many, marvelous references to the Mighty Messiah one can appreciate much better our Lord's affirmation in Luke 24:44 that the Psalms spoke of Him. They did so frequently and fervently; they did so beautifully and basically; they did so eloquently and enthusiastically.

POINTS TO PONDER ABOUT THE MESSIANIC PSALMS

1. The psalmists who wrote of Jesus were not modernists; they accepted His Deity and His coming Incarnation.
2. The psalmists who wrote of Jesus were not Jehovah's Witnesses; they accepted Him as God, as Creator and as eternal.
3. The psalmists who wrote of Jesus were not "Jesus only" proponents; they spoke of two Lords—First Person and Second Person of the Timeless Trinity.
4. The psalmists who wrote of Jesus were not materialists; they spoke of His spirit and His body.
5. The psalmists who wrote of Jesus were not theological liberals; they did not deny the miracles of either the Messiah or those to whom He gave supernatural powers.
6. The psalmists who wrote of Jesus were not Roman Catholics; they gave the honor and glory to the Messiah—not Peter—not Mary—not Popes.

DISCUSSION QUESTIONS

1. Why is Luke 24:44 an appropriate way to introduce this chapter?
2. How do Psalm 102:25-27 and Hebrews 1:10-12 prove Christ to have been Creator?
3. Distinguish between incarnation and reincarnation, discuss the truth of the one and the falsity of the other and refute the one that is false.
4. Discuss in detail the incarnation of Christ as portrayed in Psalms.
5. Discuss the apparently different renderings in Psalm 40:6-8 and Hebrews 10:5-8 and show their actual harmony and unity.
6. Read and discuss briefly the selected verses in Psalms that touch our Lord's personal ministry.
7. Read and discuss briefly the selected prophecies relative to Christ's death, burial and resurrection and their fulfillment in the New Testament.
8. Discuss the Psalms that refer to Christ as David's seed or son and the New Testament references to them.
9. What do the Psalms have to say about Christ's ascension and give New Testament references to the same?
10. Read and discuss the Points to Ponder About the Messianic Psalms.

MULTIPLE-CHOICE: Underline correct answer

1. Messiah in Hebrew and Christ in Greek both mean: (A) Anointed; (B) approved; (C) admired; (D) angelic — in English.
2. In Psalm 110 David establishes Christ as both (A) prophet and judge; (B) preacher and teacher; (C) Son of man and Son of God; (D) Deity and high priest after the order of Melchizedek.
3. "The Timeless Trinity" refers to: (A) the Godhead—Father, Son and Holy Spirit; (B) Abraham, Isaac and Jacob as founders of the Israelite people; (C) Shem, Ham and Japheth as founders of new races subsequent to the flood; (D) Peter, James and John—the eminent apostles under Christ.
4. In Acts 2 Peter quotes the very psalm that was penned by: (A) David; (B) Solomon; (C) Moses; (D) Asaph.
5. Hades and Sheol are Biblical terms that refer to: (A) eternal heaven; (B) eternal Gehenna; (C) just the grave; (D) the intermediate state of departed spirits employing both a Greek term and a Hebrew word respectively.

SCRIPTURAL FILL-IN: Only one word is required in each blank.

(1) "Thy _____, O _____, is for _____ and ever: the _____ of thy _____ is a _____

142

sceptre. Thou lovest _____, and hatest _____: therefore _____, thy _____, hath _____ thee
with the _____ of _____ above thy
_____."

(2) "I will _____ my _____ in a _____: I will
_____ dark _____ of _____."

(3) "_____ up your _____, O ye _____; and
be ye _____ up, ye _____ doors; and the
_____ of _____ shall come in. _____ is this
_____ of _____? The Lord _____ and
_____, the _____ mighty in _____.
_____ up your _____, O ye _____; even
_____ them _____, ye everlasting _____;
and the _____ of _____ shall come in.
_____ is this _____ of _____?
The _____ of _____, he is the _____ of
_____."

(4) "The _____ hath _____ in _____ unto
_____; he will not _____ from _____;
Of the _____ of thy _____ will I set upon thy
_____."

(5) "The _____ which the _____ refused is
_____ the _____ stone of the _____.
This ·is the _____ doing, it is _____ in our
_____. This is the _____ which the _____
hath _____; we will _____ and be _____ in
it."

TRUE OR FALSE: Put either a "T" or "F" in the blanks

_____1. Psalm 2 teaches clearly and convincingly that there is but one person and one person only in the Godhead.

_____2. Satan made an eminently correct application of Psalm 91:11,12 in Matthew 4 and Luke 4 in his temptations of the Christ.

_____3. The Jehovah's Witnesses are eminently right in classing Jesus as creature and not as creator and minus any and all Deity.

_____4. The death, burial and resurrection of Christ are all predicted in the Old Testament.

_____5. Reincarnation, as taught by ancient Orientals and modern day occultism, is defended as true by both the Old and New Testaments.

THOUGHT QUESTIONS

1. *Discuss the Deity of Christ as set forth in Psalm 2:7,12.*

2. *Discuss the RSV (Revised Standard Version) and how it handled Psalm 45:6,7 and Hebrews 1:8,9.*

3. *What argument does Jesus present in Matthew 22:41-46 that is actually based on Psalm 110:1?*

4. *Read and discuss Psalm 118:22-24 and the three New Testament passages that mention this very passage.*

5. *Just how does a diligent study of Psalms enhance and exalt our views of the Mighty Messiah? Discuss this in some detail.*

CHAPTER SEVENTEEN

TREMENDOUS TRIBUTES TO GOD'S WORD IN PSALMS

Two earlier chapters in this volume, nine and ten, dealt with Psalm 119 which is the greatest, grandest and most glorious tribute ever penned in elevating, extolling and exalting the precious word of our God on high. We cannot overdo this topic of paying tribute to the Holy Bible. Therefore this chapter will treat that topic also. In the two earlier chapters our study centered in Psalm 119. Material for this current chapter will be drawn from throughout the book of Psalms. Every verse quoted exhibits the awe and respect which the various psalmists held for God's verbally inspired and infallibly revealed word of truth. To see crippling doubts relative to the inspiration and infallibility of God's word one has to go to the writings of men outside the circle of Biblical penmen — never inside that coveted circle!! Religious leaders who breathe forth such crippling doubts relative to the Bible have gone to school to the wrong type of teachers. They need to go to school in general to the forty men who penned the Bible and in particular to the powerful penmen of the precious psalms.

THE POWER AND INFLUENCE OF HIS WORD

In beauty and brilliance the psalmist wrote,

> By the word of the Lord were the heavens made; and all the host of them by the breath of his mouth. He gathereth the waters of the sea together as an heap: he layeth up the depth in storehouses. Let all the earth fear the Lord: let all the in-

habitants of the world stand in awe of him. For he spake, and it was done; he commanded, and it stood fast (33:6-9).

Without doubt or quibble the psalmist has his mind riveted on Genesis 1. "And God said" appears in verses 3,6,9,11,14,20,24,26 and 29 of this tremendous chapter of creative accounts. He spoke the universe into existence. The starry heavens and all their hosts (the heavenly armies) were made by the breath of His mouth. He did the same in bringing into being His footstool—the earth and its great seas into one place. Such exerted power should constrain the whole world to extend God proper fear and to stand in ready awe of Him. Reiterated again in verse 9 is His creative power at work. He spoke and it was! The *done* here is inserted by the translators and somewhat enfeebles the true, literal import of the Hebrew text. At God's command the marvelous universe sprang into prompt, functional and precisely working existence. Shall we believe a NOTHING did this or was it God? The latter is the ONLY sane and sensible response any intelligent mind can give. Only the empty head and heart (*nabal*) of Psalm 14:1 and 53:1 could possibly deny the Almighty's existence!

The protecting power of His word is seen in this royal reflection from the discerning psalmist, "He shall cover thee with his feathers, and under his wings shalt thou trust: his truth shall be thy shield and buckler" (91:4). The famed Pauline armor for the Christian refers to the shield of faith and of course comes by hearing Jehovah's word (Ephesians 6:16; Romans 10:17).

The converting and restoring power of God's word is seen in the attractive affirmation, "The law of the Lord is perfect, converting (restoring—margin) the soul:..." (19:7).

Psalm 108:4 affirms that God's "truth reacheth unto the clouds (skies—margin)." It permeates His whole creation.

Psalm 147:15 forcefully affirms, "He sendeth forth his commandment upon earth: his word runneth very swiftly." Nature hastens to obey His every impulse; how fine if man, the very apex of His earthly creation, would be like-minded. But man is much more apt to procrastinate than be prompt in obeying God's worthy will. Slowness is a curse to humanity in this realm. We need to hasten to put God's word into prompt practice. One of my very favorite verses in Psalm 119 is the positive-negative response of verse 60 which states, "I made haste, and delayed not to keep thy commandments."

THE WORD OF THE LORD IS RIGHT

The great black evangelist, Marshall Keeble, was very fond of the expression, "The Bible is right." Brother Keeble did not invent or originate that precious concept. He obtained it from the great book he loved, the Bible, and from such passages as the following,

For the word of the Lord is right; and all his works are done in truth. He loveth righteousness and judgment: the earth is full of the goodness of the Lord (33:4,5). Thy testimonies are very sure: holiness becometh thine house, O Lord, for ever (93:5). The works of his hands are verity and judgment; all his commandments are sure. They stand fast for ever and ever, and are done in truth and uprightness (111:7,8). Therefore I esteem all thy precepts concerning all things to be right; and I hate every false way (119:128).

In essence the foregoing verses affirm that: (1) the Bible is right; (2) the Bible is truth; (3) the Bible came from Him who loves righteousness and judgment; (4) the Bible came from Him who is the precious personification of goodness—Jehovah God; (5) the Bible is sure in its testimonies; (6) the Bible came from Him who is holy and hence is the HOLY Bible; (7) the Bible is filled with sure—never unsure—commandments; (8) the Bible is filled with commands which are destined to stand eternally; and (9) the Bible is right in all its ways and is an adamant adversary to any and all false ways. Brother Keeble never overstated the case; he said it wisely and well. The Bible is right and we can NEVER be right unless we hear it sincerely and heed it diligently. These are the two great imperatives before men—*hear* God's word and *heed* God's word. This is the one-two line of approach that permeates all of the Bible in general and all of Psalms in particular.

THE WORD OF GOD IS PURE

Many of the current best-sellers are filled with impurities. The dirtier a book is the more apt a sexually abandoned society will buy it in mass sales. The cost is usually NEVER PROHIBITIVE if the book promotes PROMISCUOUS behavior (in reality misbehavior) between men and women or even between those of the same sex—homosexuality or lesbianism.

The Holy Bible is at the other excellent extreme. It is a book that majors in purity. Any impurity such as David's adultery, Reuben's incest or the Corinthian who had stolen his father's wife is condemned—never condoned.

Three stately selections exhibit so eloquently the purity of God's lovely language to man. His words are minus all vice and corruption. They are purity personified. With eloquence and earnestness they state,

147

The words of the Lord are pure words: as silver tried in a furnace of earth, purified seven times (12:6). As for God, his way is perfect: the word of the Lord is tried (refined—margin): he is a buckler to all those that trust in him (18:30). Thy word is very pure: therefore thy servant loveth it (119:140).

God's word is "tried or refined." This is what the Hebrew term means in Psalm 119:140. There is absolutely NOTHING this old sinful world needs more than the purity of God's word. Pollution surrounds us on every hand. Many are concerned with polluted air, polluted dump sites of deadly chemicals, polluted water, polluted food, etc. But few are concerned with polluted minds or hearts that feed on fleshly garbage. Sometime back a group got together in a certain city to discuss pollution. They discussed it over cocktails!! How utterly inconsistent! But few are concerned with polluted Bibles and other religious works of irreverent men who make void God's word by the commandments and doctrines of men. How great is our need for the pure word of God, the unadulterated gospel of God!!

FIDELITY TOWARD GOD'S WORD

God is faithful to His word; His word breathes the firm, fervent faithfulness of Deity. Man's aim should ever be a firm, fundamental fidelity extended to God's word. To aim at less than this is to set our sights far, Far, FAR too low. Fidelity toward God's word permeates all the precious psalms. The following selections simply serve as stately samples of what abound in Psalms,

> Give ear, O my people, to my law: incline your ears to the words of my mouth (78:1). Teach me thy way, O Lord; I will walk in thy truth: unite my heart to fear thy name (86:11). He spake unto them in the cloudy pillar: they kept his testimonies, and the ordinances that he gave them (99:7). He hath remembered his covenant for ever, the word which he commanded to a thousand generations. Which covenant he made with Abraham, and his oath unto Isaac; And confirmed the same unto Jacob for a law, and to Israel for an everlasting covenant:... (105:8-10).

Closely akin to all the foregoing is the Messiah's deep regard for stately submission to God's will as seen in these words of weight and wisdom, "I delight to do thy will, O my God: yea, thy law is within my heart" (40:8). Such Johannine passages as 4:34; 6:38; 2:49; 17:4 and Hebrews 10:5-9 all attest to the Messianic intent to be absolutely faithful to God's word in every aspect.

Inherent in all these foregoing passages are such vital observations as: (1) the great need to give diligent hearing to God's law; (2) the imperative need to be taught the right way of the Lord so that a correct walk may occur in the same; (3) the fidelity with which Jehovah's submissive saints kept His testimonies or ordinances; (4) the faithfulness of God to the great Abrahamic promises given initially to the father of the faithful, sworn again to Isaac and confirmed to Jacob of the third generation of Hebrew founders; and (5) the Messiah's resolute determination to keep perfectly the Father's will for His life on earth and His mission to men. Deity is faithful to the heavenly will; humanity must emulate this precious principle likewise and do so with diligence.

THE MAJESTY DUE HIS WORD

Marvelous, majestic and magnificent are the words of God Almighty. This trio of verses provides praise, manufactures majesty and delivers delight relative to God's wonderful words of love and life. This Davidic declaration occurs in Psalm 56:10, "In God will I praise his word: in the Lord will I praise his word." In a chapter that promises security to the godly, Psalm 112, the psalmist states, "Praise ye the Lord. Blessed is the man that feareth the Lord, that delighteth greatly in his commandments" (112:1). Psalm 138:2 has been one of my favorite verses in Psalms since early youth. Perhaps it is of yours also. It states with breathtaking beauty, "I will worship toward thy holy temple, and praise thy name for thy lovingkindness and for thy truth: for thou hast magnified thy word above all thy name."

Emphasized in these words from Psalms are such crystal clear concepts as: (1) the praise that is proper for God's word; (2) the great delight that a true man of God will see and sense in God's word; and (3) the interesting, intriguing fact that Jehovah has magnified His word even above His name. Jehovah has always had deep jealousy (the right kind) for His name. The third of the Decalogue (Ten Commandments) said, "Thou shalt not take the name of the Lord thy God in vain; for the Lord will not hold him guiltless that taketh his name in vain" (Exodus 20:7; Cf. Deuteronomy 5:11). Yet God's word has been magnified even above His noble name. If God would not allow Physical Israel to take His name in vain, how severe will be the meted-out punishment for those who treat His word recklessly, rebelliously and irreverently. Those prone to add to, take from, alter, modify or substitute relative to God's word should sit up and take careful caution from Psalm 138:2. In the New Testament Jesus said relative to His words, "He that rejecteth me, and receiveth not my words, hath one that judgeth him: the word that I have spoken, the same shall judge him in the last day" (John 12:48).

HOPE IS CENTERED IN HIS WORD

Hope points neither to past nor present; its direction is future. In Romans 8:24,25 Paul writes, "For we are saved by hope: but hope that is seen is not hope: for what a man seeth, why doth he yet hope for? But if we hope for that we see not, then do we with patience wait for it." Titus 1:2 speaks of the hope of eternal life—something yet future. Hope is anticipation; it is expectation; it is desire for an ultimate quest to reach fruition.

Hope is a key word in Psalms. It is found in excess of twenty-five times in the book. Several Hebrew terms are translated simply as hope in our English translations. Here are a few selected verses where hope is centered in God's word,

> And take not the word of truth utterly out of my mouth; for I have hoped in thy judgments (119:43). They that fear thee will be glad when they see me; because I have hoped in thy word (119:74). Thou art my hiding place and my shield: I hope in thy word (119:114). I prevented (anticipated—ASV) the dawning of the morning, and cried: I hoped in thy word (119:147). I wait for the Lord, my soul doth wait, and in his word do I hope (130:5).

With God's word deeply entrenched in our hearts we have hope. With that word removed, not any of us could have a degree of holy hope. Hope and heaven have been joined together by God Almighty. We discover the lovely link in the Bible and hence heavenly hope is centered in God's word and nowhere else.

POINTS TO PONDER ABOUT TRIBUTES TO GOD'S WORD

1. God's word is spiritual dynamite.
2. Since God's word is right no man can be wrong who patterns his life faithfully thereby.
3. To be right in religion means that we hear and heed God's word to the best of our ability.
4. The very personification of purity on earth is the Bible—God's word.
5. No man can be faithful unless he practices fidelity to the word of our God on high.
6. Marvelous majesty inheres the word of our great and glorious God.
7. Heavenly hope is centered in God's Book and this is why no other book is in the class with the peerless volume of the ceaseless centuries.

DISCUSSION QUESTIONS

1. *How does Psalm 33:6-9 serve as an excellent commentary on Genesis 1?*
2. *Just how powerful and influential is God's word?*
3. *Read and discuss briefly the various scriptures that stress the righteousness of God's word.*
4. *Contrast many current best sellers and the Bible as touching impurity and purity.*
5. *Read and discuss briefly the selected passages about the purity of God's word.*
6. *Read and discuss briefly the selected passages that stress fidelity toward God's word.*
7. *Read and discuss the selected passages that touch the majesty due God's word.*
8. *What is said of hope in Romans 8:24,25 and Titus 1:2?*
9. *Read and discuss the selected passages from Psalms that center hope in God's word.*
10. *Read and discuss the Points to Ponder about tributes to God's word.*

MULTIPLE-CHOICE: Underline correct answer

1. *Psalm 119: (A) is the Bible's shortest chapter; (B) is the greatest, grandest and most glorious tribute ever penned of the Bible; (C) makes no mention of God's word from beginning to end; (D) was written by an obvious skeptic who rejected God's word as vervally inspired and completely infallible.*
2. *According to Psalm 14:1 and Psalm 53:1 (A) the fool; (B) the wise man; (C) Satan; (D) every fallen angel—denies the existence of God.*
3. *Marshall Keeble, the great black evangelist, often said: (A) "The Bible is right;" (B) "The Bible is just a human production;" (C) "The Bible is an unsafe book for man to follow;" (D) "The Bible has not yet been proved to be a book inspired of God."*
4. *David's adultery, Reuben's incest and the Corinthian who had stolen his own father's wife are: (A) treated with total indifference in the Bible; (B) condoned in the Bible; (C) condemned in the Bible; (D) set forth as good examples for all to follow.*
5. Relative to His word we may say that God's attitude toward it is that of: (A) faithlessness; (B) faithfulness; (C) hatred; (D) opposition; (E) indifference.

SCRIPTURAL FILL-IN: Only one word is required in each blank.

(1) "By the _____ of the _____ were the _____ made; and _____ the _____ of them

151

by the _____ of his _____."

(2) "I made _____, and _____ not to _____ thy _____."

(3) "_____ I _____ all thy _____ concerning all _____ to be _____; and I _____ every _____ way."

(4) "I will _____ toward thy holy _____, and _____ thy _____ for thy _____ and for thy _____: for thou has _____ thy _____ above all thy _____."

(5) "Thou art my _____ place and my _____; I _____ in thy _____."

TRUE OR FALSE: Put either a "T" or "F" in the blanks

___1. The various psalmists held God's word in awe and reverence.

___2. "And God said" occurs repeatedly in Genesis 1.

___3. Nature is both slow and reluctant to obey God's commandments touching its functions.

___4. Both the Old and New Testaments stress the high regard of Christ for God's word.

___5. It is a sure mark of great respect for God to play down His word constantly.

THOUGHT QUESTIONS

1. How do the various writers of the Bible contrast with religious writers who compose nothing but religious doubts in their literary works?

2. Why is it so utterly ridiculous and absolutely absurd to advocate that a great big NOTHING is responsible for our marvelously and precisely functioning universe?

3. What is a far more reasonable alternative as set forth in the Bible?

4. Discuss the magnifying of God's name and God's word.

5. What are some current ways men fail to magnify God's word?

6. As Christians what can we do to magnify the great word of our glorious God?

7. Just how vital is hope to God's people?

CHAPTER EIGHTEEN

WORSHIP IN THE PSALMS

In preparation for this chapter I went through the entire book of Psalms and took special note of passages that portrayed with preciousness various concepts of worship. More than fifty passages were noted and these will be incorporated and interwoven into some nine segments of thought. This will be a book, chapter and verse division of our book and this will please all students who prefer that inspired men have said over human comments relative to the Bible.

Worship defined is homage paid; it is adoration extended; it is reverence extended; it is the prostration of man as inferior to God as superior. Only Deity is to be worshipped (Matthew 4:10; John 4:23,24; Revelation 19:10; 22:8,9). This readily rules out all created objects whether animate or inanimate, whether heavenly or earthly, whether seen or unseen. The various psalmists from whom quotations will be made in this chapter knew of these imperatives of worship and reflect them in their inspired sentiments. Drink deeply of the contents of this chapter and your own worship of God under the new covenant of Christ will be deepened, enhanced and made far more meaningful.

WORSHIP GOD IN THE BEAUTY OF HOLINESS

God is holy; His throne is holiness; his book is the Holy Bible; he has prepared the holy city for His people in eternity. Therefore, He has every right to expect that His people will be holy and will worship Him in holiness—in the bright and blessed beauty of holiness. David wrote, "Give unto the Lord the glory due unto his name; worship the Lord in the beauty of holiness (29:2). In a strikingly similar sentiment

153

we read in a later psalm, "Give unto the Lord, O ye kindreds of the people, give unto the Lord glory and strength. Give unto the Lord the glory due unto his name; bring an offering, and come into his courts. O Worship the Lord in the beauty of holiness: fear before him, all the earth" (96:7-9). The God who is holy deserves and demands to be worshipped in holiness. His holiness is portrayed in these striking statements, "Exalt ye the Lord our God, and worship at his footstool; for he is holy...Exalt the Lord our God, and worship at his holy hill; for the Lord our God is holy" (99:5,9).

Holiness becomes our God and He desires that it becomes His people and the worship they extend Him. The God of such infinite holiness could not be pleased with unholy, impure and sensual worship such as characterized the pagan religions of antiquity and the modern religions of materialism, emotionalism and sensualism of our day. Better that a man NOT worship God at all than that he worship God with unholiness permeating his whole being in attitude and action.

WORSHIP GOD WITH WHOLENESS OF HEART

Just as we are to love God with wholeness of heart and confess Christ's Deity with wholeness of heart so our worship should flow from a wholehearted, true-hearted approach to God (Matthew 22:37; Acts 8:36,37). Worship in the Psalms is of this wholehearted, true-hearted type. David wrote, "I will praise thee, O Lord my God, with all my heart: and I will glorify thy name for evermore" (86:12). Psalm 111 contains another allusion to wholehearted, true-hearted worship. A one line summary of this short and sweet psalm is, "The psalmist incites to praise God." The opening verse reads, "Praise ye the Lord. I will praise the Lord with my whole heart, in the assembly of the upright, and in the congregation" (111:1). A striking, stately, beautiful and blessed tribute is given David's wholehearted, true-hearted resolution relative to God's house in these valiant verses which read,

> Lord, remember David, and all his afflictions: How he sware unto the Lord, and vowed unto the mighty God of Jacob; Surely I will not come into the tabernacle of my house, nor go up into my bed; I will not give sleep to mine eyes, or slumber to mine eyelids, Until I find out a place for the Lord, an habitation for the mighty God of Jacob (132:1-5).

Were every Christian characterized by wholehearted and true-hearted worship we would see a tremendous increase at ALL our worship periods. No longer would we major in excuses as to why we prefer to practice *absenteeism* over *attendance.* Here is the key to solving poor attendance Sunday night, Wednesday evening and all weekday services of gospel meetings.

WORSHIP GOD IN SONG

Since the psalms were composed to be sung by Israelite worshippers, we would expect many ardent and attractive allusions throughout the Psalms regarding songs and singing. Just a sample of the many is now presented,

I will praise the Lord according to his righteousness: and will sing praise to the name of the Lord most high (7:17). I will sing unto the Lord, because he hath dealt bountifully with me (13:6). Sing unto the Lord, O ye saints of his, and give thanks at the remembrance of his holiness (30:4). And he hath put a new song in my mouth, even praise unto our God: many shall see it, and fear, and shall trust in the Lord (40:3). Sing praises to God, sing praises: sing praises unto our King, sing praises (47:6). I will praise thee, O Lord, among the people: I will sing unto thee among the nations. For thy mercy is great unto the heavens, and thy truth unto the clouds (57:9,10). But I will sing of thy power; yea, I will sing aloud of thy mercy in the morning: for thou hast been my defense and refuge in the day of my trouble. Unto thee, O my strength, will I sing: for God is my defense, and the God of my mercy (59:16,17). All the earth shall worship thee, and shall sing unto thee; they shall sing to thy name (66:4). I will sing of the mercies of the Lord for ever: with my mouth will I make known thy faithfulness to all generations (89:1). O sing unto the Lord a new song: sing unto the Lord, all the earth. Sing unto the Lord, bless his name; shew forth his salvation from day to day (96:1,2). O sing unto the Lord a new song; for he hath done marvellous things: his right hand, and his holy arm, hath gotten him the victory (98:1). O give thanks unto the Lord; call upon his name: make known his deeds among the people. Sing unto him, sing psalms unto him: talk ye of all his wondrous works (105:1,2). O God, my heart is fixed: I will sing and give praise, even with my glory...I will praise thee, O Lord, among the people: and I will sing praises unto thee among the nations (108:1,3). Praise the Lord: for the Lord is good: sing praises unto his name; for it is pleasant (135:3). Praise ye the Lord: for it is good to sing praises unto our God; for it is pleasant; and praise

155

is comely (147:1). Praise ye the Lord. Sing unto the Lord a new song, and his praise in the congregation of saints (149:1).

Were *all* the foregoing facets and sacred sentiments relative to singing prevalent among *all* God's people, never again would we have people ignore the opening song at the beginning, leave before the final song is sung, be irreverent during our songs or feel that singing is just a prelude to the actual beginning of worship. No more would our song services be dull, drab and dead to us. Quite to the contrary, they would be vibrant, moving and lively. But far, Far, FAR too many saints today do not view worship in song as these enthusiastic psalmists did in the ancient past.

WORSHIP GOD JOYFULLY

This is an imperative of worship that *pleases* God and *profits* us. Joy permeated the worship of the various psalmists as the following beautiful and striking sentiments surely attest,

> I will be glad and rejoice in thee: I will sing praise to thy name, O thou most High (9:2). Make a joyful noise unto God, all ye lands (66:1). Sing aloud unto God our strength: make a joyful noise unto the God of Jacob (81:1). O come, let us sing unto the Lord: let us make a joyful noise to the rock of our salvation. Let us come before his presence with thanksgiving, and make a joyful noise unto him with psalms (95:1,2). Make a joyful noise unto the Lord, all ye lands. Serve the Lord with gladness: come before his presence with singing (100:1,2).

The person who worships God joyfully is not bored while so engaged. He is not a constant clock watcher during services. He does not EVER ask, "Do I HAVE to attend ALL services of the church?" No joyful saint wants to miss deliberately any of the services. They are too meaningful to him to use hackneyed or trite excuses for absenting himself as lukewarm members habitually and constantly do. Joyful worshippers among all our membership would mean but slight variation of attendance figures among Sunday morning, Sunday evening, Wednesday evening or ALL services of a gospel meeting. Large percentages of our "do not care" members are trying their best to kill gospel meetings and they have in far, FAR TOO many places!! This is sad; it is immeasurably, inexpressibly sad.

WORSHIP GOD REGULARLY

The psalmists lived under a law that demanded daily sacrifices at the altar by their priests, the weekly remembrance of the sabbath

156

day, the new moons (monthly activities), the annual feast of Passover, the feast of weeks (called Pentecost in the New Testament) and the feast of tabernacles as well as their family devotionals such as are inculcated in Deuteronomy 6:4ff. Regularity of worship over a lifetime is seen in these timely selections from Psalms. Let us read reverently and relish permanently these sacred sentiments, "I will sing unto the Lord as long as I live: I will sing praise to my God while I have my being" (104:33). One of the psalms Israel hymned as they ascended Jerusalem at regular intervals was Psalm 134. Two of its three verses read, "Behold, bless ye the Lord all ye servants of the Lord, which by night stand in the house of the Lord. Lift up your hands in the sanctuary, and bless the Lord" (134:1,2). As long as breath was in the body just that long the psalmist of Psalm 146 declared his persistent resolution to praise his adorable Creator and Lord on high. He stated, "While I live will I praise the Lord: I will sing praises unto my God while I have any being" (146:2).

Regularity of worship among our members now is the life's blood of any local church. The local congregation cannot function in its absence. Irregularity of worship, if practiced by all, will kill a local congregation quicker than almost any other persistent problem. Ask any experienced elder or veteran preacher if this is not the case.

WORSHIP GOD THANKFULLY

Gratitude to God is an intense imperative to all acceptable worship. The psalmists recognized this elementary observation to be valid and wrote accordingly,

I will praise the name of God with a song, and will magnify him with thanksgiving (69:30). Unto thee, O God, do we give thanks, unto thee do we give thanks: for that thy name is near thy wondrous works declare (75:1). It is good thing to give thanks unto the Lord, and to sing praises unto thy name, O most High (92:1). Enter into his gates with thanksgiving, and into his courts with praise: be thankful unto him, and bless his name (100:4). Praise ye the Lord, O give thanks unto the Lord; for he is good: for his mercy endureth for ever (106:1). O give thanks unto the Lord, for he is good: for his mercy endureth for ever. Let the redeemed of the Lord say so, whom he hath redeemed from the hand of the enemy (107:1,2). O give thanks unto the Lord; for he is good: because his mercy endureth for ever...O give thanks unto the Lord: for he is good: for his mercy endureth for ever (118:1,29).

Note all the repetition that inheres these passages. Exhortations for men to be grateful to God, the Generous Giver of every good and perfect gift—James 1:17, will NEVER be repeated TOO much.

In Christian worship gratitude should form a prominent part of our songs and prayers. In preaching and teaching we can reflect gratitude to our Maker on high. Gratitude should always grace our giving to God and will if the precious principles of 2 Corinthians 8 and 9 are closely adhered to at all times. Genuine gratitude should be reflected in communion as we recall the scenes of suffering our Saviour experienced for us on Execution Hill that Friday nearly two thousand years ago.

WORSHIP GOD REVERENTLY

Reverence and awe become every worshipful approach to our Maker. The psalmists were deeply cognizant of this as the import of these scriptures fully attests,

> But as for me, I will come into thy house in the multitude of thy mercy: and in thy fear will I worship toward thy holy temple (5:7). God is greatly to be feared in the assembly of the saints, and to be had in reverence of all them that are about him (89:7). Let them exalt him also in the congregation of the people, and praise him in the assembly of the elders (107:32). Praise ye the Lord. Blessed is the man that feareth the Lord. that delighteth greatly in his commandments (112:1).

Sentiments like the foregoing and applied to Christian worship now need to be stamped indelibly into the hearts of all current Christians. Surely, reverence for God would enhance all our worship periods. Irreverence in worship is NEVER becoming to the children of God. Hebrews 12:28 inculcates that we "serve God acceptably with reverence and godly fear."

WORSHIP GOD PERMANENTLY

This segment of thought is closely akin to regularity of worship but too much cannot be written in its rich regard. Permanence of worship permeates all this valiant set of verses from the precious psalms,

> I will bless the Lord at all times: his praise shall continually be in my mouth (34:1). I will praise thee for ever, because

thou hast done it: and I will wait on thy name: for it is good before thy saints (52:9). From the rising of the sun unto the going down of the same the Lord's name is to be praised (113:3). I will extol thee, my God, O king; and I will bless thy name for ever and ever. Every day will I bless thee; and I will praise thy name for ever and ever (145:1,2).

Such a resolute determination along lines of permanent worship would insure every diligent saint now against his ever casting off God in later life due to developing apathy.

WORSHIP GOD LOVINGLY

This is really the bottom line of all that has been written in this chapter and every quotation from the Psalms. Do we love God? Then worship and serve Him we MUST. The psalmist loved the Lord's house. He wrote, "Lord, I have loved the habitation of thy house, and the place where thine honour dwelleth" (26:8). His own great love for the Lord and his worship prompted the psalmist to wish for a similar sentiment to permeate all others. He wrote, "Oh that men would praise the Lord for his goodness, and for his wonderful works to the children of men!" (107:8). This verse is repeated verbatim in verses 15 and 21 of this chapter. This is significant repetition! Out of a heart that overflowed with love for the lovely Lord the psalmist wrote, "I will greatly praise the Lord with my mouth; yea, I will praise him among the multitude" (109:30).

CONCLUSION

Truly, the book of Psalms, if heard and heeded in its great principles, would enhance the worship of all Christians. There is no way that such could be avoided. If so, HOW?

POINTS TO PONDER ABOUT WORSHIP IN PSALMS

1. Worship involves both attitudes and actions.
2. Worship is to be divinely directed—not humanly centered.
3. Man is at his best when he worships God acceptably.
4. Man will worship some object—either God or that less than God.
5. The kind of worship depicted in this chapter will act as a unifying element in any congregation of God's people.
6. Man will never rise higher than the object he worships.

DISCUSSION QUESTIONS

1. *Define worship.*
2. *Read and discuss briefly the selected passages that stress the worship of God in the hallowed framework of holiness.*
3. *Read and discuss briefly the selected passages that stress wholehearted, true-hearted worship.*
4. *Read and discuss the various selected passages that stress the worship of God in song.*
5. *What do the psalms have to say about worshipping God joyfully?*
6. *What do the psalms have to say about worshipping God regularly?*
7. *What do the psalms have to say about worshipping God thankfully?*
8. *Discuss reverence in worship as depicted in the psalms.*
9. *Read and discuss the selected passages that stress the worshipping of God permanently.*
10. *Read and discuss the Points to Ponder about Worship in Psalms.*

MULTIPLE CHOICE: Underline correct answer

1. *The proper object of worship is: (A) Mary; (B) a parent; (C) Satan; (D) God.*
2. *God is to be worshipped: (A) any way man chooses; (B) according to the dictates of the devil; (C) in the beauty of holiness; (D) in the framework of impurity.*
3. *The psalmist of Psalm 9:1 who wrote, "I will praise thee, O Lord, with my whole heart; I will shew forth all thy marvelous works," was: (A) Solomon; (B) Samuel; (C) Moses; (D) Asaph; (E) David.*
4. *The three great annual feasts among Israelites under the Mosaic Dispensation were: (A) Easter, Christmas and Thanksgiving; (B) Purim, Dedication and New Moon; (C) Passover, Feast of Weeks and Feast of Tabernacles; (D) sabbath day, day of atonement and the first day of each Hebrew new year.*
5. *The Feast of Weeks in the Old Testament is known in the New Testament by the designation of: (A) the Lord's Day; (B) Pentecost; (C) Passover; (D) Lent.*

SCRIPTURAL FILL-IN: Only one word is required in each blank.

(1) "_____ unto the _____ the _____ due unto his _____; _____ the _____ in the _____ of _____."

(2) "_____ ye the _____: for it is _____ to sing _____ unto our _____; for it is _____; and _____ is _____."

160

(3) "_____ a _____ noise unto the _____, all
    ye _____. _____ the _____ with
    _____: _____ before his _____ with
    _____."

(4) "_____ is _____ to be _____ in the
    _____ of the _____, and to be had in
    _____ of _____ them that are about
    _____."

(5) "_____, I have _____ the _____ of thy
    _____, and the _____ where thine _____
    dwelleth."

TRUE OR FALSE: Put either "T" or "F" in the blanks

____1.   It is better to worship wrongfully than not worship God at all.

____2.   It matters but little with God whether men worship Him or not.

____3.   Man—not God—is the primary object to please in worship.

____4.   "We do it because we like it" has caused many an innovation to come into worship.

____5.   The various psalmists had a widely known reputation of absenteeism from public worship under the Mosaic Dispensation as per the sacred record.

____6.   An excellent way to build up the local church is to be slack in attendance and lukewarm in work habits.

THOUGHT QUESTIONS

1. Why should we prefer to read and reflect on what God actually says than on what man says relative to God's word?

2. Why is there a great need today to have far more book, chapter and verse preaching, teaching, lecturing and writing than we currently possess?

3. In your judgment what constitutes worship that is wholehearted and true-hearted?

4. How did David feel about the physical house of the Lord under the Mosaic Dispensation and what lesson should we draw about how we should feel toward the Lord's spiritual house—the church—today?

5. Why should God be worshipped lovingly?

6. What would an intense inculcation of all major points covered in this chapter do for worship among all churches of Christ today?

CHAPTER NINETEEN

PRAYER IN THE PSALMS

No one can read the Psalms very much or very long without being duly and deeply impressed with the piety of the psalmists. A very prominent part of that piety is in their own prayer lives, what they wrote about prayer, their assurance that God had heard and would continue to hear their prayers and the inspirational encouragement they gave their readers to be a people of persistent prayer and of sincere supplications. In the posture of prayer and in the stance of supplications men and women of God approach the heavenly tableland. We are never closer to heaven then when we allow God to speak to us by His wonderful word—the Bible—and when we converse with Him by prayer. These form the twin lines of communication between the faithful on earth and the Father above.

Richer and deeper will be our appreciation for the power of prayer after a study of the great texts in which the various psalmists have expressed so eloquently their stately sentiments relative to precious prayer.

JEHOVAH: THE PRAYER-HEARING GOD

To the psalmists there was a God in heaven and He heard the prayers of His pious people on earth. Prayer to them was a marvelous means to address Him who rules and moves the universe at His bidding. Prayer was not just a means of getting something off one's chest; it was not a psychological device to relieve pent-up emotions that cried for release. Had they believed that prayers rise no higher than ceilings, the current attitude of skeptics and even of many religionists relative to any and all prayer, we may rest assured that none of the great passages on prayer we study in this chapter would have ever seen the light of printed day.

David wrote, "O thou that hearest prayer, unto thee shall all flesh come" (65:2). In another psalm David is sure there is a God in heaven who hears and answers prayers. He penned these sentiments in Psalm 86:6,7, "Give ear, O Lord, unto my prayer; and attend to the voice of my supplications. In the day of my trouble I will call upon thee: for thou wilt answer me." A ready recognition that an ear is ready to hear the cry of the distressed on earth undergirds Psalm 102:1,2 which states, "Hear my prayer, O Lord, and let my cry come unto thee. Hide not thy face from me in the day when I am in trouble; incline thine ear unto me: in the day when I call answer me speedily."

The psalmists verily believed their petitions of need would register in the great All-Hearing Ear on high and that God would answer them promptly and prosperously.

PRAYERFUL PLEAS TO BE HEARD

The psalmists were not proud, dictatorial leaders who told God what to do and what not to do. They were suppliants; they were men of humility; they were men with needs; as inferiors and dependents they approached the superior who could and would mete out just such help as they needed. They were people who needed and desired to be blessed by the very one who could bless. Their prayerful pleas we now note breathe forth these attractive attributes. In one of the very earliest of the psalms David says,

> Give ear to my words, O Lord, consider my meditation. Hearken unto the voice of my cry, my King, and my God: for unto thee will I pray. My voice shalt thou hear in the morning, O Lord; in the morning will I direct my prayer unto thee, and will look up (5:1-3).

Just a few psalms later David expressed, " I have called upon thee, for thou wilt hear me, O God: incline thine ear unto me, and hear my speech" (17:6). In Psalm 54:2 David again pleads, "Hear my prayer, O God: give ear to the words of my mouth." Psalm 55 opens with the plea, "Give ear to my prayer, O God; and hide not thyself from my supplication" (v-1). David reiterates in Psalm 61:1, "Hear my cry, O God: attend unto my prayer." In two of the psalms near the end of the book we read respectively,

164

Out of the depths have I cried unto thee, O Lord. Lord, hear my voice: let thine ears be attentive to the voice of my supplications...Hear my prayer, O Lord, give ear to my supplications: in thy faithfulness answer me, and in thy righteousness (130:1,2; 143:1).

Sincere souls reaching for needed help from a higher source permeate each of these foregoing pleas of prayerful preciousness. To the psalmists prayer was the bridge that brought earthly needs and heavenly help into precious proximity. It WAS that way then; it still IS today. If not, why not?

ASSURANCES THAT PRAYERS HAVE BEEN HEARD

The psalmists viewed God as one willing to be addressed in prayer. They did address Him. Then they wrote as grateful recipients of answered prayers. The following passages so attest as we read,

I cried unto the Lord with my voice, and he heard me out of his holy hill (3:4). The Lord hath heard my supplication; the Lord will receive my prayer (6:9). Blessed be the Lord, because he hath heard the voice of my supplications (28:6). I cried unto God with my voice, even unto God with my voice: and he gave ear unto me (77:1). In my distress I cried unto the Lord, and he heard me (120:1).

They prayed in the beauty of their belief in God. By the wings of faith their spoken petitions on earth soared to the ears of the Lord of Sabaoth or the God of all power and strength. Answers were conveyed back to them in petitions granted. Sublime gratitude then welled up in their touched souls and they were neither slow nor reluctant in expressing such. The praying psalmists were not infidelic and hence were not disbelievers in any and all prayers. They were not fatalists or men who believed that what is to be will be and there is no change possible. They were not deists who allow for God as Creator but disallow Him any and all interest in His current creation. They were not modernists who have so destroyed God that there can be no prayers heard and heeded. They were not modern charismatics who contend that God can only answer prayer and engage in providential care of us by a daily barrage of miracles surrounding us at all times. They prayed to a God they knew existed. They knew He would hear. That is why they prayed! They knew He had heard. That is why they wrote as they did. Answered prayers were their sustaining proof.

PERSISTENCY IN DAILY PRAYER

To the psalmists prayer was just as common to their daily activities as breathing, eating, sleeping, exercising, working, etc. They knew that a day without prayer erodes one's dedication to Deity. They knew that a *week* without daily prayers made one *weak* indeed! Three selected scriptures portray the persistency of their daily prayers. We read,

> As for me, I will call upon God; and the Lord shall save me. Evening, and morning, and at noon, will I pray, and cry aloud: and he shall hear my voice (55:16,17). Bow down thine ear, O Lord, hear me: for I am poor and needy...Be merciful unto me, O Lord: for I cry unto thee daily (86:1,3). O Lord God of my salvation, I have cried day and night before thee: Let my prayer come before thee: incline thine ear unto my cry (88:1,2).

Pious Hebrews had the holy habit of praying thrice daily. Daniel did in Babylonian Exile in Daniel 6 and which habit was well known to his enemies. They used this as the very lever to trick the Medo-Persian monarch, Darius, to sign a decree which prohibited just such prayers for the next thirty days and made violations of such a devilish decree punishable by sure death in the den of vicious lions. David prayed thrice daily. Note that he mentions evening, morning and noon. We would possibly suggest morning, noon and night in our descriptive approach. But recall that the Hebrew people began their new day at evening or sundown and not from midnight to midnight as with us. Hence, David prayed as the new day began, after the night had passed or in the morning and at noon or in the middle of the day. The ascription that heads Psalm 88 does not attribute this chapter to David's pen. Yet its first verse contains an allusion to prayers day and night. Hence, other psalmists, as well as David, believed in daily prayer.

Prayer is the precious privilege of God's children. Surely, we, as Christians, should never desire to allow a day to go by but what we pray or speak to our Father above. The Lord's Supper is a *weekly* practice but prayer can be and should be a *daily* practice in the life of every Christian.

ESSENTIALS OF ACCEPTABLE PRAYER

In Luke 11:1 the disciples requested of Jesus that He teach them how to pray even as John taught his disciples how to pray. Jesus promptly acquiesced and gave them the Model Prayer. Teaching HOW to pray involves the essentials of prayer.

166

Several great passages in Psalms also touch prayer imperatives. A few selected verses will be given which are,

> But know that the Lord hath set apart him that is godly for himself: the Lord will hear when I call unto him (4:3). Hear the right, O Lord, attend unto my cry, give ear unto my prayer, that goeth not out of feigned lips (17:1). I waited patiently for the Lord; and he inclined-unto me, and heard my cry (40:1). He will regard the prayer of the destitute, and not despise their prayer (102:17). For my love they are my adversaries: but I give myself unto prayer (109:4). I love the Lord, because he hath heard my voice and my supplications. Because he hath inclined his ear unto me, therefore will I call upon him as long as I live (116:1,2).

These essentials are set forth in the verses we have just noted: (1) that the godly man can expect to have his prayers heard and heeded on high as long as he prays in harmony with God's will; (2) that the man who is engaged in the cause of right and true justice can expect to have his prayers heard and heeded; (3) that the man who prays with unfeigned lips or lips that speak sincerity and not deceit may expect to have his prayers register on high; (4) that the man who prays with patience, with other things equal, may expect to have his prayers answered; (5) that the destitute man or the one who is humble, poor in spirit, stripped of all self-righteousness and is wholly dependent on God can expect to have his prayers heeded and honored; (6) that the person who gives himself to prayer in unreserved fashion may expect to have his prayers register in God's mind; (7) that the man who loves God may expect to have his prayers answered; and (8) that the man who is persistent in prayer may expect his prayers to avail.

Essentials set forth in the New Testament are that we: (1) address the prayer to the Father (Matthew 6:9); (2) pray in the name of Jesus (John 14:13,14; 1 Timothy 2:5; 1 John 2:1, 2); (3) pray in faith (James 1:6,7); (4) pray in harmony with the Lord's will (Matthew 26:36-42; 1 John 5:14,15); (5) pray selflessly (James 4:1-3); (6) praise God in prayer (Matthew 6:9ff); (7) extend our spirit of thanksgiving for all gifts received (1 Thessalonians 5:17,18); and (8) request pardon even as we forgive those indebted to us (Matthew 6:12-15; Colossians 3:13; Ephesians 4:32).

PRAYERS THE LORD WILL NOT HEAR

Many people seemingly think the Lord will hear and heed any prayer regardless of who does the praying or what is requested by way of petition. Not so. James 4:1-3 tells of praying people whose prayers were not heeded on high. The formerly blind man of John 9 observes that "we know that God heareth not sinners" (v-31). There is a time when a prayer can even be an abomination. Solomon observed, "He that turneth away his ear from hearing the law, even his prayer shall be abomination" (Proverbs 28:9). There are times in which God prohibits our praying for certain types of people. In Jeremiah 7:16; 11:14 and 14:11 Jehovah prohibited Jeremiah from praying for his rebellious contemporaries. The apostle John said there was no profit in our praying for a man guilty of the sin unto death (a sin of which a brother will neither repent nor confess) (1 John 5:16). Sometimes people pray when other duties are more pressing. In essence Ananias told Saul of Tarsus to cease his praying and arise to be baptized (Acts 9:11; 22:16). This was how he was to attain redemption—not by prayerful continuation as still an alien from the Messianic kingdom.

The psalmist suggested a clear-cut time when prayers will neither be heard nor heeded. He stated in plain and pointed language this weighty warning, "If I regard iniquity in my heart, the Lord will not hear me" (66:18). The obviously clear meaning is that a cherishing of sin, a refusal to give it up and an adamant intention to commit it again and again all present at the time of a prayer simply mean that one's prayers will neither be heard nor heeded. For prayer to be heard the very sins that separate us from God must be abhored and there must be present a resolute intention to forsake them. Included would be sinful motives, fleshly thoughts such as sexual fantasies involving others rather than spouse, evil speech and all deeds of impropriety.

GREAT MEN OF PRAYER

The Bible is filled with such. A few of them would be Abraham, Samuel, David, Hezekiah, Josiah, Daniel, Ezekiel, Jesus, John the Baptist, Peter, John, Paul and others far too numerous to mention specifically. The psalmist mentions three great men of prayer in just one verse. We read in Psalm 99:6, "Moses and Aaron among his priests, and Samuel among them that call upon his name; they called upon the Lord, and he answered them." (99:6). In the Hebrew sands of time these three illustrious men—great lawgiver, great first high priest of the Mosaic System and great prophet, priest and judge respectively—left monumental footprints of faithful worship and persistent prayer.

CONCLUSION

A careful and close study of this chapter should enrich and deepen the prayer lives of all of us without question or quibble.

POINTS TO PONDER ABOUT PRAYERS IN THE PSALMS

1. The psalmists prayed because they knew there was an ear open to their petitions.
2. The psalmists prayed because of deeply-felt needs which only their God in heaven on high could supply.
3. The psalmists prayed because they knew that prayer moves the hand of Him who moves the universe.
4. The psalmists prayed because they knew that prayers change things and for the better.
5. The psalmists wrote much about prayer to encourage others to be of like mind.
6. The psalmists were as quick to thank God for an answered need as the initial request that it be granted. In this we need to emulate them much more closely than we do.

DISCUSSION QUESTIONS

1. *List and discuss the twin lines of communication between earth and heaven.*
2. *How did the psalmists NOT view prayer and how DID they view it?*
3. *Read and discuss briefly the selected verses that stress Jehovah as the Prayer-Hearing God on high.*
4. *Read and discuss briefly the selected verses that stress their assurances of prayers which had been heard.*
5. *Read and discuss briefly the selected texts that emphasize persistency in daily prayers.*
6. *Read and discuss briefly the selected texts from Psalms that set forth the essentials of prayer.*
7. *What essentials relative to prayer are set forth in the New Testament?*
8. *Discuss in some detail Psalm 66:18.*
9. *List some great men of prayer who are mentioned in this chapter.*
10. *Read and discuss the Points to Ponder About Prayers in Psalms.*

MULTIPLE-CHOICE: Underline correct answer

1. *The psalmists were: (A) infidels and as such rejected any and all value of prayer; (B) fatalists who believe that what is to be will be and no changes are possible; (C) modernists who deny a God who hears and heeds prayerful petitions. (D) ancient charismatics who contended prayers may be answered* only *by miraculous performances; (E) God-believing men who prayed in faith and had their prayers heard and heeded on high.*

2. *David and Daniel had in common the fact that both: (A) were contemporaries of each other; (B) were kings of God's people; (C) were both high priests in the Levitical system; (D) were devout servants of God who each prayed thrice daily.*

3. *In Luke 11:1 the disciples requested of Jesus that He teach them to: (A) preach; (B) sing; (C) pray; (D) study.*

4. *According to the Bible acceptable prayers are to be addressed to: (A) God the Father; (B) God the Son; (C) God the Holy Spirit; (D) angels; (E) Mary; (F) Abraham.*

5. *The formerly blind man in John 9 declared relative to God and prayer that: (A) God hears all prayers indiscriminately; (B) God hears no prayers; (C) God hears not sinners; (D) his own prayer to God had given him sight for the first time in his life.*

SCRIPTURAL FILL-IN: Only one word is required in each blank.

(1) "_____ my _____, O _____, and let my _____ come unto _____. _____ not thy _____ from me in the _____ when I am in _____; _____ thine _____ unto me: in the _____ when I call _____ me _____."

(2) "_____ my _____, O _____, _____ ear to my _____: in thy _____ answer _____, and in thy _____."

(3) "I _____ the _____, because he hath _____ my _____ and my _____. _____ he hath _____ his _____ unto me, therefore will I _____ upon _____ as _____ as I _____."

(4) "_____, and _____, and at _____, will I _____, and cry _____: and he shall _____ my _____."

(5) "He that _____ away his _____ from _____ the _____, even his _____ shall be _____."

(6) "If I _____ _____ in my _____, the _____ will not _____ me."

TRUE OR FALSE: Put either a "T" or "F" in the blanks

____1. *To the psalmists prayer was ONLY a psychological device to get some pressing problem off their chests.*

____2. *Prayer is a device to be employed only in emergency situations.*

____3. *For the Christian the Lord's Supper is to be a* weekly *practice but prayer should be a* daily *activity.*

____4. *There can never be a prayer prayed that the Lord will count as an abomination.*

____5. *Ananias told Saul of Tarsus to keep on praying until he prayed through and thus had attained redemption by his persistent prayers.*

THOUGHT QUESTIONS

1. *Why is prayer such a grand imperative of true piety?*

2. *What attitudes did the psalmists possess as they begged to have prayerful petitions heard on high?*

3. *Why should EVERY Christian be a DAILY petitioner of God in prayer?*

4. *What are some prayers prayed today the Lord surely will not hear?*

5. *Take each great man of prayer listed in this chapter and see if you can find out one thing for which he prayed and relative to which the Lord answered him.*

CHAPTER TWENTY

TREASURES OF TRUST IN THE PRECIOUS PSALMS

Trust is one of the key, kingly words of each testament. It means to rely upon, place confidence in, lodge credence toward, lean upon and look upon as a refuge. Two of the great passages on trust outside the Psalms are found also in the great poetic section of the Old Testament—Job and Proverbs. In strength of spirit Job declared, "Though he slay me, yet will I trust in him: but I will maintain mine own ways before him" (Job 13:15). A choice and classic statement from Solomon, Wisest of the Ages, says in the beauty of great brilliance, "Trust in the Lord with all thine heart; and lean not unto thine own understanding. In all thy ways acknowledge him, and he shall direct thy paths" (Proverbs 3:5,6). One of the great trust passages in the New Testament is 2 Corinthians 1:9,10 wherein the trusting apostle wrote, "But we had the sentence of death in ourselves, that we should not trust in ourselves, but in God which raiseth the dead: Who delivered us from so great a death, and doth deliver: in whom we trust that he will yet deliver us;..." Paul trusted God totally in three thrilling tenses of divine providence: (1) God *has* delivered us—past providence; (2) God *now* delivers us—present providence; and (3) God *shall* deliver us—future providence.

Psalms is one of the great books in the Bible that majors in precious passages relative to trust. In seven segments of thought we shall take note of more than thiry-five passages from Psalms. Most of them will actually contain the word trust. The *tone* and *tenor* of trust is found in the ones we shall note where the actual word is omitted from reference.

173

THE BEAUTIFUL, BOUNTIFUL BLESSINGS OF TRUST

Psalm 2 is a Messianic psalm. It closes with an admonition to pay holy homage to the Son and pronounces a heavenly benediction on those who place trust in the Mighty Messiah. The psalmist penned, "Kiss the Son, lest he be angry, and ye perish from the way, when his wrath is kindled but a little. Blessed are all they that put their trust in him" (2:12). The converse of the latter statement would be, "Cursed are all they that distrust him." In Psalm 40:4 David declared so beautifully, "Blessed is the man that maketh the Lord his trust, and respecteth not the proud, nor such as turn aside to lies." The conclusion of another psalm states, "O Lord of hosts, blessed is the man that trusteth in thee" (84:12). In a beautiful and sweeping analogy the psalmist expresses these words in one of the songs they used as they approached Jerusalem for worship, "They that trust in the Lord shall be as mount Zion, which cannot be removed, but abideth for ever. As the mountains are round about Jerusalem, so the Lord is round about his people from henceforth even for ever" (125:1,2). Zion was the mountain David fortified and later became a stately synonym for the whole city. It represented stability, solidity, firmness and a place divinely protected. What an attractive analogy or a stately simile for those who trust in God. The second comparison of those who trust in God refers to Jerusalem which was almost surrounded by mountains and high hills. Though built on four hills itself—Zion, Moriah, Bezetha and Acra—yet the city on four hills was surrounded or encompassed by high hills. With this as stately imagery the psalmist makes mention of Jehovah's encompassing His people—the people who trust in Him. In a breath of literary beauty David says in Psalm 143:8, "Cause me to hear thy lovingkindness in the morning; for in thee do I trust: cause me to know the way wherein I should walk; for I lift up my soul unto thee."

How bountifully and beautifully blessed is every fortunate soul who puts his total trust in the God of heaven.

THE LOVELY LINKING OF JOY AND TRUST

It is my firm, unbending conviction that real joy will ever evade the person who never places his total trust in Deity. Three great selections from Psalms exhibit the lovely link of joy (or one of its derivatives such as rejoice and glad) and true, total trust. Note the joy that permeates the great passage on trust in Psalm 5:11,12 and which states, "But let all those that put their trust in thee rejoice: let them ever shout for joy, because thou defendest them: let them also that love thy name be joyful in thee. For thou, Lord, wilt bless the righteous with favour wilt thou compass him as with a shield." Truth and the trust that grows therefrom bequeath a beautiful blessing of joy, happiness, gladness and rejoicing. In another majestic message of trust the psalmist pens, "For our heart shall rejoice in him, because we have trusted in his holy name" (33:21). Joy and gladness ring out in another Davidic psalm. We read in Psalm 64:10, "The righteous shall be glad in the Lord, and shall trust in him; and all the upright in heart shall glory."

Would you know joy now? It is found in Jesus. It is found in the total trust of truth. Happiness of a real nature is found in holiness. Gladness is experienced in God. Satisfaction is found in the Saviour; contentment is available in Christ and Christ only.

TRUST IN HIS PROTECTING, PRESERVING AND SAVING POWERS

Some fifteen selections from Psalms set forth wonderfully well this segment of our study. We shall list them consecutively and then summarize their treasured content. They read,

O Lord my God, in thee do I put my trust: save me from all them that persecute me, and deliver me:... (7:1). My defense is of God, which saveth the upright in heart (7:10). And they that know thy name will put their trust in thee: for thou, Lord, hast not forsaken them that seek thee (9:10). But I have trusted in thy mercy; my heart shall rejoice in thy salvation (13:5). Preserve me, O God: for in thee do I put my trust (16:1). Shew thy marvellous lovingkindness, O thou that savest by thy right hand them which put their trust in thee from those that rise up against them (17:7). For the king trusteth in the Lord, and through the mercy of the most High he shall not be moved (21:7). Our fathers trusted in thee: they trusted, and thou didst deliver them. They cried unto thee, and were delivered: they trusted in thee, and were not confounded (22:4,5). O keep my soul, and deliver me: let me not be ashamed: for I put my trust in thee (25:20). But thou, O God, shalt bring them down into the pit of destruction: bloody and deceitful men shall not live out half their days; but I will trust in thee (55:23). Be merciful unto me, O God, be merciful unto me: for my soul trusteth in thee: yea, in the shadow of thy wings will I make my refuge, until these calamities be overpast (57:1). I will say of the Lord, He is my refuge and my fortress: my God: in him will I trust (91:2). O Israel, trust thou in the Lord: he is their help and their shield..Ye that fear the Lord, trust in the Lord: he is their help and their shield (115:9,11). But mine eyes are unto thee, O God, the Lord: in thee is my trust; leave not my soul destitute (141:8) My goodness, and my fortress: my high tower, and my deliverer: my shield and he in whom I trust; who subdueth my people under me (144:2).

God Almighty is worthy of trust because He: (1) is able to save, deliver and defend those who are persecuted for righteousness' sake, those who are upright in heart; (2) will not forsake those who seek Him; (3) is of deep mercy and will save; (4) is able to preserve; (5) is filled with lovingkindness; (6) is able to keep us from being moved; (7) has never let down our fathers who trusted Him but delivered them; (8) is a powerful keeper of souls; (9) will ultimately put down all His enemies; (10) is an impregnable refuge and fortress in time of trouble; (11) is both a help and a shield to them who love and serve Him; (12) is the one person who will not leave the soul of the righteous destitute; and (13) is our goodness, high tower, deliverer and is able to subdue all enemies. Are not these stately and sufficient reasons why Jehovah God is eminently worthy of our treasured trust?

TRUST IN HIM WHILE ASLEEP

It is proverbial that we can only sleep soundly and refreshingly when safe, secure and well protected. Sleep departs our eyes when in presence of dangers, terrors and harm. Yet such is the nature of our trust in God that we can lie down to pleasant dreams and refreshing repose when we know He is our protection. Such is reminiscent of a child's sublime petition in prayer, "Now I lay me down to sleep; I pray the Lord my soul to keep. And if I should die before I wake; I pray the Lord my soul to take." Add "In Jesus' name" and it is a prayer God's child can and should pray in youth, in sunset years and in all the years in between. The psalmist felt similar sentiments relative to sleep and trust. He wrote, "I laid me down and slept; I awaked; for the Lord sustained me (3:5). "I will both lay me down in peace, and sleep: for thou, Lord, only makest me dwell in safety" (4:8).

During a very perilous period a little child once was able to sleep and remain serene on a ship in a dangerous storm. When later asked how, the answer was signally simple to her. She said, "My father pilots this ship!" As Christians we have the Heavenly Father as pilot of the ship on which we travel through this life. Full and free trust in Him means serenity during the day and peaceful slumber at night. The bottom line of it all is treasured trust in God.

UNRELIABLE OBJECTS OF TRUST

In weaker and less stable moments in Hebrew history fickle, wavering and faithless Israelites placed trust in unreliable objects. At times it would be Egypt to the southwest; at other times it would be Assyria to the northeast; at other times it was in pagan idols, in the number of their own arrogant armies, their weapons, in witchcraft and other occult powers. Certain of the psalms portray unreliable objects of trust. They read,

> Some trust in chariots, and some in horses: but we will remember the name of the Lord our God (20:7). Lo, this is the man that made not God his strength: but trusted in the abundance of his riches, and strengthened himself in his wickedness (52:7). It is better to trust in the Lord than to put confidence in man. It is better to trust in the Lord than to put confidence in princes (118:8,9). Put not your trust in princes, nor in the son of man, in whom there is no help (146:3).

Relative to the last quoted passage a word of explanation is imperative. In the New Testament "Son of man" is used eighty or more times to designate Jesus Christ. It was one of His favorite designations of Himself. He did it to emphasize His humanity—that He was Deity in human flesh. Therefore, it is eminently right that we place our total trust in Jesus Christ as Son of man and as Son of God, twin descriptions of both His humanity and Deity. "Son of man" here in Psalm 146:3 has *no* reference at all to the Second Person of the Godhead; to the contrary it has simple reference to humanity that is filled with hopeless, helpless and hapless weakness in time of real need. Unquestionably, man is impotent as a reliable object of trust; God is potent as a reliable object of truthful trust.

Today, people place trust in humanity, in riches, in human governments, in an arsenal of weapons, etc. But few are placing total trust in Jehovah God. In Him our total trust should be centered. He loves us enough to care; He protects us by His power; He will never be out of the picture due to death, desertion or disloyalty as can be the case so frequently with man and the trust we place in him.

JEHOVAH IS EMINENTLY WORTHY OF LIFELONG TRUST

He is the one in whom we should place our trust in early life; He is the one in whom we should trust in the mature years; He is the one in whom we should trust in the sunset years and till the very time of our

177

final breath. Then trust can continue in Him through the Hadean experience as we await judgment in Abraham's bosom or the realm of comfort and rest and then into eternity in heaven itself. Meditate with much profit these great passages on a lifetime of trust in God. "In thee, O Lord, do I put my trust; let me never be ashamed: deliver me in thy righteousness" (31:1). Never in a lifetime did David wish to lose this trust or become ashamed of his holy God on high. "Trust in him at all times; ye people, pour out your heart before him: God is a refuge for us" (62:8). "In thee, O Lord, do I put my trust: let me never be put to confusion...For thou art my hope, O Lord God: thou art my trust from my youth" (71:1,5). In this stately psalm David traces his course from youth to old age. Trust was the tone and tenor of his life in the spring, summer, autumn and winter of his life cycles on earth— youth, early maturity, later maturity and at life's sunset. "He shall not be afraid of evil tidings: his heart is fixed, trusting in the Lord. His heart is established, he shall not be afraid, until he see his desire upon his enemies" (112:7,8). Our interests whether in early life, later life or the years in between are eminently safe when centered in God Almighty. Trust in Him is a sure way in winning happiness here and attaining the same felicity through life and on into heaven at last. Needless to say, this is the courageous concept of "Trust and Obey," as the great Christian hymn inculcates, that we have in mind in this optimistic observation.

HUMANITY IS ACTIVE IN THIS TRUST

Deity alone is not active with humanity as passive in this momentous matter. Humanity alone is not active with Deity passive. Both God and man are active in this momentous matter of trust, reliance and confidence. Three selections in Psalms make this crystal clear. "Judge me, O Lord; for I have walked in mine integrity: I have trusted also in the Lord: therefore I shall not slide" (26:1). Psalm 37 has been summed up so stately as describing with delight, "The happy state of the godly, and the shortlived prosperity of the wicked." Two of its valiant verses state, "Trust in the Lord, and do good; so shalt thou dwell in the land, and verily thou shalt be fed...Commit thy way unto the Lord; trust also in him; and he shall bring it to pass" (37:3,5). The third and final passage reads, "But it is good for me to draw near to God: I have put my trust in the Lord God, that I may declare all thy works" (73:28). Note the activities of the psalmist in declaring human responsibility in this marvelous matter of true trust. (1) There is the walk of integrity; (2) there is active trust placed in the Lord; (3) there is concentrated effort to avoid sliding; (4) there is the

178

charge to do good; (5) there is the committing of one's way to the Lord; and (6) there is the drawing near unto God on the psalmist's part.

Deity is wonderfully worthy of our total trust; we are ardently active in its formation and courageous continuation.

POINTS TO PONDER ABOUT THE TREASURES OF TRUST

1. It is sublimely wonderful that we have someone like God who is so sure, stable and stedfast in whom we CAN and SHOULD place unwavering trust, unbending confidence and unfailing reliance.
2. Miserable is any man's existence who has no one in whom to place his trust except himself or some other EQUALLY finite, frail and feeble man.
3. Trust in God and human happiness are holy handmaidens.
4. Jesus lived the perfect life of trust and He is our Marvelous Model. Ashley S. Johnson once wrote a book partly about Jesus and entitled it THE LIFE OF TRUST.
5. Victory in death comes after living a life of trust.
6. Total trust in God means complete trust in Jesus Christ and full trust in the Bible as Jehovah's inspired word *to* us and *for* us.

DISCUSSION QUESTIONS

1. *Define trust.*
2. *Discuss the three tenses of providence as expressed so eloquently in the great Pauline pronouncement of 2 Corinthians 1:9,10.*
3. *Read and discuss briefly the selected texts that depict the beautiful, bountiful blessings of true trust.*
4. *Read and discuss briefly the selected texts that link so lovely the tremendous traits of joy and trust.*
5. *Read the fifteen selections from Psalms that stress God's protecting, preserving and saving powers.*
6. *Read and discuss the selected texts that treat of unreliable objects of worship, trust and service.*
7. *Tell why Jehovah is eminently worthy of lifelong trust.*
8. *Discuss trust as a mutual matter which involves both Deity and humanity.*
9. *Read and discuss the scriptures that depict this mutual matter.*
10. *Read and discuss the Points to Ponder relative to the Treasures of Trust.*

MULTIPLE CHOICE: Underline correct answer

1. *"Though he slay me, yet will I trust in him: but I will maintain mine own ways before him"* is a great Bible statement made by: *(A) David in Psalms; (B) Solomon in Proverbs; (C) Paul in Romans; (D) Job in the book of Job.*

2. Psalms 2 is a: *(A) psalm written by Moses about Israelite experiences in the wide wilderness over four decades of time; (B) psalm written by an exile about Israel's experiences in the Babylonian Captivity; (C) Messianic psalm; (D) psalm written by Solomon about his early days as king.*

3. Zion, Moriah, Bezetha and Acra were: *(A) rest stops of Israel in journeying from Egypt to Canaan; (B) four great prophets of the Old Testament; (C) the first four cities conquered by General Joshua and his Israelite army after they crossed swollen Jordan; (D) the four hills or mountains on which Jerusalem was situated.*

4. In the New Testament the expression, *"Son of man,"* is: *(A) always a reference to a mere man; (B) never used to refer to Jesus Christ; (C) how Paul frequently referred to himself; (D) used some eighty times plus to refer to Jesus our Lord and Saviour.*

5. Relative to the psalmists and trust we may say that in aim: *(A) theirs was TOTAL trust in God; (B) theirs was only a PARTIAL trust in God; (C) they possessed NO trust in Jehovah; (D) theirs was a trust ONLY in man which was consistent with Humanism of which they were ardent, avid advocates.*

SCRIPTURAL FILL-IN: Only one word is required in each blank.

(1) "_____ in the _____ with all thine _____; and _____ not unto thine own _____. In all thy _____ _____ him, and he shall _____ thy _____."

(2) "_____ me to _____ thy _____ in the _____; for in thee do I _____: _____ me to _____ the _____ wherein I should _____; for I _____ up my _____ unto thee."

(3) "The _____ shall be _____ in the _____, and shall _____ in him; and all the _____ in _____ shall _____."

(4) "Lo, this is the _____ that made not _____ his _____: but _____ in the _____ of his _____, and _____ himself in his _____."

180

(5) *"In thee, O* _____, *do I* _____ *my* _____: *let
me never be put to* _____...For thou art my* _____,
O _____ *God: thou art my* _____ *from my*
_____.*"*

TRUE OR FALSE: Put either a "T" or "F" in the blanks

___1.   *Jerusalem was a city built on a low lying plain and with no nearby hills
or mountains.*

___2.   *There can be real security of soul and serenity of mind when we
resolutely take God as pilot of our ship.*

___3.   *Man sustains no standing obligation in this momentous matter of trust.*

___4.   *The world of our day has largely lost its trust in God.*

___5.   *Man is safe when he places his chief trust in money.*

THOUGHT QUESTIONS

1.   *Why is trust the foundation for any meaningful relationship whether between man and God or man and man?*

2.   *Tell why joy, real joy is found in Jesus Christ.*

3.   *Tell why God is eminently worthy of trust placed in Him.*

4.   *What is truly significant about trust placed in God while we are asleep?*

5.   *What are some of the very unreliable objects of modern trust now popular
and pleasing?*

CHAPTER TWENTY-ONE

ABUSES OF PSALMS

The Bible is often abused by people who deny its verbal inspiration, its infallibility, its all-sufficiency, its supreme authority, etc. Books of the Bible are abused. Genesis is abused by those enamored with organic evolution, religious modernism, theological liberalism and outright atheism or Humanism, simply the sophisticated form of atheism today. Revelation is abused by the premillennial speculators of the day. Great chapters are frequently abused. These would include Genesis 1; Matthew 24; Acts 2; Revelation 20; etc. Great verses are abused such as Matthew 19:9; Mark 16:16; John 3:5; 3:16; Acts 2:38, etc. The precious book of Psalms has not escaped such arrogant abuses and malicious misuses. Some of its verses have been greatly abused and misused. A volume on Psalms would be definitely deficient were we to omit any and all references to these abuses and misuses. If space allows, I shall take brief note of some nine abuses or misuses that men make of Psalms.

SEEKING TO MAKE OF IT A NEW TESTAMENT BOOK

The Bible easily divides itself into the two major testaments— the Old and the New. In the Old Testament we have thirty-nine books; in the New Testament we have twenty-seven books. Psalms does not belong in the New. That would make twenty-eight for the New; it would reduce the Old Testament number to thiry-eight. Perhaps the chief reason why so many associate it with the New Testament is because many printed New Testaments have included Psalms along with the twenty-seven books of the New Testament. This is usually the only Old Testament book such publishers will append to the New Testament. POPULARITY of Psalms has no doubt led to this practice and not PROPER PLACEMENT of this poetic product. Some no doubt wish Psalms were part and parcel of the New Testament for it would be the Biblical source they would employ eagerly to present a supposed measure of sagging support for mechanical instruments in Christian worship. There is neither proof nor support for such a popular innovation in the New Testament. To this they attest when they vacate the New Testament and seek their proof from Psalms, an Old Testament book.

Psalms is not part and parcel of the New Testament. It belongs to the Old Testament. This is its proper placement in our complete Bibles. Where the whole of our English Bible is given its position is immediately subsequent to Job and just prior to Proverbs. It never follows Revelation in the complete Bible as in New Testaments that include it at the end. Jesus makes crystal clear that Psalms belongs to the Mosaic Covenant. In John 10:34 Jesus inquired, "Is it not written in your law, I said, Ye are gods?" Jesus addressed Jews here. He quoted Psalm 82:6. He classed it as being "your" law. It was something written right then. Not that first syllable of Christ's law was written at that time. Also in Luke 24:44 Jesus divided the Old Testament into the law of Moses, the prophets and the psalms. Psalms' proper placement therefore is in the Old Testament—the poetic portion—and not among the New Testament books or at the end of Revelation.

VIEWING IT AS THE MOST IMPORTANT BOOK IN THE OLD TESTAMENT

It is eminently right to exalt, extoll and elevate all the Bible. It is a mistake to take one book of either testament and declare it to be greater than all its literary colleagues. Some seemingly want to do this with Psalms. Appending it with the New Testament perhaps has contributed to this. Its pristine preciousness and resplendent beauty of language have perhaps been other contributing factors. That it touches practically every chord of the human heart may have caused some to view it as being of higher altitude and superior value to its thirty-eight Old Testament literary colleagues. Jesus placed no greater value upon it than He did the law of Moses and the prophetic writing in Luke 24:44. New Testament penmen often quoted from Psalms but never at the disparagement of all other Old Testament books. All books of the Old Testament are vastly important; the same is true of all New Testament books. The Bible is somewhat like a golden chain that drops down from God in heaven to man on earth. The chain is composed of sixty-six golden links. Each one serves its own purpose; each is of equal value in serving the function God intended. This volume has sought the function God intended. This volume has sought to lift Psalms to a mountain peak of marvel and majesty. But the peak of Psalms is no higher than the peaks that represent its thirty-eight literary colleagues in the Old Testament or its twenty-seven literary colleagues in the New Testament. Each book is part and parcel of God's inspired will. We are under the New but the Old aids us greatly in understanding the new.

JEWISH SUPERSTITIONS RELATIVE TO IT

In his great chapter on Psalms for The Spiritual Sword Lectureship volume of 1977, THE LIVING MESSAGES OF THE BOOKS OF THE OLD TESTAMENT, brother Hugo McCord lists a number of Jewish superstitions linked with certain of the psalms. They believed that reading or praying Psalm 3, when connected with a small amount of olive oil anointing the head or back, would afford prompt relief of a headache or backache. According to brother McCord Psalm 9, if written out on a prescribed type of writing material with a brand new pen and hung about a sick boy's neck would produce healing. Jewish exorcists advised various uses of the Psalms pronounced repeatedly and superstitiously as aiding in the ouster of demons. All such breathe forth the same superstition as the current presence of a horseshoe, a rabbit's foot or a St. Christopher's medal worn about the neck for some type of special blessing. The book of Psalms was written in a framework of *spirituality*—not *superstition*. It was written to help with maladies of the spirit—not ailments of the flesh. It was designed to build up *spiritual* strength—not *physical*. Were this one of the valid uses of Psalms many would hearken to it for *physical healing* properties and would never be drawn by its *spiritual beauties* at all.

SEVEN PSALMS AND MORTAL SINS AMONG ROMAN CATHOLICS

Brother McCord also has a section dealing with Catholic superstitions and Psalms. This is not surprising in the least because much of Catholicism is superstitious in source and scope. During the Middle Ages certain Roman Catholics contended that certain of the Psalms were "penitential" in nature and, if recited, would keep a person from anger (Psalm 6), pride (Psalm 32), gluttony (Psalm 38), luxury (Psalm 51), covetousness (Psalm 102), envy (Psalm 130), and sloth (Psalm 143). Jesus and the apostles taught against all these but never by counseling people just to recite seven so-called penitential psalms and the sins would be overcome with relative ease. They knew better than to accept such NONSENSE. Such would have been a rejection of their use of COMMON SENSE to perceive correctly God's REVEALED (inspired) SENSE!! RECITING scripture will not *prevent* sins; PRACTICING what the scriptures inculcate will! Satan recited a scripture from Psalm 91:11,12 while he was in the very process of trying to persuade Jesus to sin. Reciting the passage did not change his devilish, diabolical nature. Jesus cited scripture and practiced what the scripture inculcated. Therein lay a major difference between Satan and the Saviour. Social drinkers, for instance, will cite scriptures they think are favorable to their pet sin which really condemn their nefarious, dangerous, injurious habit and will proceed to down their "waters of eternal destruction" with Bibles at their very sides. How exceedingly strange and utterly inconsistent!!

Dividing sins into mortal and venial is a totally Catholic concoction. There is NO basis for such in the Bible from Genesis to Revelation. Any sin, all sin will condemn if not repented of and cleansed by the blood of God's Son.

EFFORTS TO PROVE MECHANICAL MUSIC RIGHT FOR CHRISTIAN WORSHIP BY APPEALS TO PSALMS

When pressed for scriptural authority for mechanical instruments in Christian worship, many will immediately head for Psalms. On the very surface this is a clear admission that they cannot find it in the New Testament. Sometimes efforts are made to link Psalm 33:2 with Ephesians 5:19. The former mentions the harp, the psaltery and a ten string instrument. The argument is that Paul commands to sing psalms, hymns and spiritual songs and psalms cannot be sung without mechanical instruments. They can and we do!! A psalm is simply a song and there is no proof Paul restricted the psalms he had in mind with the 150 contained in the Hebrew Psalter of the Old Testament. Also if Psalms determines what is to be in our worship, we would be required to bring in dancing and animal sacrifices. The former is mentioned in Psalm 150 and the latter is mentioned in Psalm 51:19. Thus this argument proves too much and what proves too much proves nothing.

A less common but still an occasional argument is made seeking to link Psalm 49:4 with Matthew 13:35. The former mentions speaking in parables and the speaking of dark sayings upon a harp. Jesus spoke in parables according to the latter passage. The argument is that Jesus would both speak in parables and play on a harp. Jesus indeed did speak in parables but there is NO record of His ever playing on the harp. This is nothing but plain sophistry. It is far more likely that Matthew 13:35 refers to Psalm 78:2 rather than to Psalm 49:4.

An argument frequently advanced is that one cannot psallo without mechanical accompaniments. But if this is true, then the translators of our highly accurate Bibles have misled us in their renderings of Romans 15:9; 1 Corinthians 14:15; Ephesians 5:19 and James 5:14 where the term psallo or a derivative occurs five times. It is found twice in 1 Corinthians 14:15. If mechanical accompaniments inhere psallo, then no longer is the matter optional. Yet most will shy away from this untenable position. Also every worshipper is to psallo and hence each person would have to have his own mechanical instrument. In either case it would be a sin to omit it or a sin if any was without his/her individual instrument. Psallo has had various uses across the centuries such as: (1) STRIKE—when one spits and the saliva STRIKES the ground; (2) PULL—as when a mischievous boy PULLS a girl's hair; (3) PLUCKS—as when one PLUCKS his beard or PLUCKS the carpenter's line; (4) PLUCKS the strings of a harp as in Psalm 33:2,3; (5) to SING without mechanical accompaniment as in Psalms 7:17; 9:2; 13:6 or 18:49 where no man-made instrument is used at all; and (6) to PLUCK figuratively the chords of the heart as Paul inculcates in Ephesians 5:19. Thayer in his scholarly lexicon is definite and decisive when he says that psallo means "in the N. T. to sing a hymn, to celebrate the praise of God in song" (p. 675). Thayer settles it once and for all, definition-wise, as touching the New Testament usage of the term.

Authority for what we do in Christian worship is derived from the New Testament—not Psalms and the Old Testament.

CALVINISTIC ABUSES OF PSALMS

A deeply entrenched doctrine of Calvinism is total hereditary depravity or that children are born in sin. Calvinists frequently appeal to David's statement in Psalm 51:5 and 58:3 for sustaining proof. The former we dealt with in an earlier chapter that covered each verse of Psalm 51. David was born into a world of sin; his mother had sinned before his birth (as have all accountable people save Jesus) and David sinned when he became responsible. But he is confessing sins in this chapter that he committed as a man—perhaps a fifty-year-old man—such as adultery, deception, murder, etc. He was not guilty of these in conception or at birth, quite obviously. The passage in Psalm 58:3 speaks of their GOING astray—not their being BORN astray. They go astray speaking lies but newborn babies do not speak lies at the very moment of birth.

Neither in Psalms nor in all the Bible is there any shred of proof for Calvinism in general or Total Hereditary Depravity in particular.

SATAN'S ABUSE OF PSALMS

In one of the temptations of the Lord in Matthew 4 and Luke 4 Satan sought to persuade the Lord to jump from the temple heights. He quoted Psalm 91:11,12. Jesus exhibited promptly that such a quotation was out of its God-given context and was modified by other passages. Careful examination will show that the devil left out part of the passage he quoted. We must ever be careful lest we take a verse out of its context, misuse it with a wrong exegesis, leave out a very important part of it or jump to a conclusion that it fails to support.

ABUSES AND MISUSES BY SOUL SLEEPERS

Materialists, at times, will claim that Psalms upholds their doctrine that the soul ceases when death occurs. But this cannot be. Two passages refute it. Psalm 16, a Messianic chapter, speaks of Jesus' soul in Sheol (same as Hades in the New Testament) and that the Messiah's body would see no corruption. The soul or spirit of Jesus was conscious in the place of departed spirits. The spirit of the redeemed thief—now penitent—was to be with Jesus in Paradise according to Luke 23:43. Their dead bodies would have had no conscience of each other even if buried side by side which was not even the case. The other scripture is Psalm 116:15. If the souls or spirits of saints cease to exist at death as do the souls or spirits of the vile and wicked as per this error, then saints have no advantages over the evil at death. Not one whit!! But Psalm 116:15 declares there is an advantage. Soul sleeping is not taught in Psalms; it is not taught anywhere in the Bible. To find it taught one has to go to the writings of uninspired materialists who are false teachers of deepest dye.

THE IMPRECATORY PSALMS AND EFFORTS TO JUDGE THEM BY CHRISTIAN STANDARDS

An objection frequently leveled at certain psalms that breathe a spirit of vengeance or a desire for punishment to be inflicted upon enemies has been one of the greatest difficulties faced by commentators of the Psalms. Space will not allow the quoting of all the so-called imprecatory psalms. Here are a few of them that each reader is encouraged to read for himself: 3:7; 5:9,10; 18:34ff; 35:1ff; 58:4ff; 137:9; 139:19ff; 140:8ff; 141:10; 144:1ff; 149:7ff. What observations can be made relative to these? (1) It will not do to deny, as some have done, the inspiration of these psalms. David affirmed, "The Spirit of the Lord spake by me, and his word was in my tongue" (2 Samuel 23:2). Peter affirmed in Acts 1:16 that David spake by the Holy Spirit.

(2) All of the so-called imprecations were against enemies of righteousness. Not that first one was directed against the pure and the pious. (3) Some of these simply registered how different ones would feel when they engaged in these atrocities such as with the Babylonians in their coming destruction as set out in Psalm 137:8,9. (4) Some of these were made by a head of state—David for instance—who was legally obligated to mete out punishment to criminals against the Israelite state. (5) The very fact that God frequently used His people as an instrument to punish evildoers would have encouraged a reflection of some of these sentiments. (6) It is right—not wrong—that evil be punished. This is an undergirding element of our whole system of law. (7) Some of these no doubt reflected the true feelings of men less than perfect and the Bible is not to be defaulted and its inspiration impugned anymore for these than for other imperfections associated with the finite scribes of Holy Writ and the erring people they portrayed. (8) These people lived under a law greatly inferior to Christianity. It is wrong, grossly wrong to judge them by Christianity when they never lived a day under the sunlit truths of Jesus Christ and His religion.

These will not solve all questions about these difficult-to-understand verses but perhaps will aid to some degree.

POINTS TO PONDER RELATIVE TO ABUSES IN PSALMS

1. It is the height of irreverence and disrespect to abuse any passage of Sacred Scripture.

2. The Bible in general and Psalms in particular uphold the sensible—not silly superstitions.

3. Authority for mechanical music in Christian worship must be sought in the New Testament—not the book of Psalms— and if not found in the New Testament, such MUST NOT be used.

4. It is a grievous sin to take a meaning of a word like *psallo* which once applied to a certain thing in the past and force it to apply to a later age long after it had lost that earlier meaning.

5. It is Satanic to pull a passage out of its context and force a usage of it never intended by the Spirit and the initial scribe of it.

6. Some people who have been critical of the so-called imprecatory psalms have not done their homework before they became supercharged critics in this area of faultfinding.

189

DISCUSSION QUESTIONS

1. *In what ways is the Bible frequently abused?*
2. *Give some specific books of the Bible, chapters and verses which have come in for abuse.*
3. *What, seemingly, is the major reason for people's associating psalms with the New Testament?*
4. *Give some of the probable factors that have caused some people to elevate Psalms over all other Old Testament books.*
5. *Discuss certain Jewish superstitions relative to Psalms and refute each one thoroughly.*
6. *Do the same with Catholic superstitions relative to seven selected Psalms and mortal sins.*
7. *Deal thoroughly with what is presented on psallo here.*
8. How did Satan abuse Psalms and give our Lord's reply to it?
9. Deal quite thoroughly with the material touching the so-called imprecatory psalms.
10 Read and discuss the Points to Ponder Relative to Abuses of Psalms.

MULTIPLE CHOICE: Underline correct answer

1. *Psalms, as a book, belongs: (A) to the Old Testament; (B) to the New Testament; (C) to neither testament; (D) to either testament as humanity so chooses.*
2. *"Is it not written in your law, I said, Ye are gods?" is a: (A) statement Jesus quoted from Psalms; (B) statement Paul quoted from Isaiah; (C) statement Peter quoted from Moses and the Pentateuch; (D) statement Luke quoted from Job.*
3. *In Luke 24:44: (A) Jesus; (B) the apostles; (C) the Jewish Sanhedrin; (D) Pilate and Herod Antipas—divided the Old Testament into the law, the prophets and the psalms.*
4. *Mortal and venial sin classifications are: (A) Roman Catholic concoctions; (B) solidly set forth in the Old Testament; (C) solidly and soundly supported by New Testament teaching; (D) definitions thought up by Protestants and then slavishly copied by Roman Catholics.*
5. *Soul sleeping is taught: (A) only in Psalms; (B) only in the Old Testament; (C) only in the New Testament; (D) by materialists who reject the true Bible Doctrine of the Soul.*

SCRIPTURAL FILL-IN: Only one word is required in each blank.

(1) Psalm 82:6 says, "I have _____, Ye are _____; and all of you are _____ of the _____ High."

190

(2) In Luke 24:44, Jesus said, "_____ are the _____ which _____ spake unto you, while _____ was yet with you, that _____ things must be _____, which were _____ in the _____ of _____, and in the _____, and in the _____, _____ me."

(3) Ephesians 5:19 states, "_____ to _____ in _____ and _____ and _____ songs, singing and making _____ in your _____ to the _____."

(4) Psalm 78:2 says, "_____ will _____ my _____ in a _____: I will _____ dark _____ of _____."

(5) Psalm 58:3 states, "The _____ are _____ from the _____: they go _____ as soon as they be _____, speaking _____."

TRUE OR FALSE: Put either a "T" or "F" in the blanks

____1. Some would like to have Psalms IN the New Testament for the support they think it contains for mechanical music in Christian worship.

____2. Simply reciting scripture will prevent certain sins from occurring.

____3. *Authority for what we do in Christian worship may be derived from either Old or New Testaments.

____4. It is quite obvious that none of the so-called imprecatory psalms are really inspired of God Almighty.

____5. Every student has the right to abuse and misuse the Bible as much as self-preference desires.

THOUGHT QUESTIONS

1. Show clearly that Psalms belongs to the Old Testament and not the New Testament canon.

2. What is basically wrong in taking any one book of either testament and exalting its importance over all its literary colleagues?

3. What is basically wrong with having to appeal to Psalms as authority for what we do in Christian worship and especially in reference to singing with mechanical accompaniment?

4. Show how Psalms refutes soul sleeping.

5. Can you think of some abuses of Psalms not covered in this chapter? If so, list and discuss them with other members of the class.

CHAPTER TWENTY-TWO

RELIGIOUS ERRORS REFUTED IN THE PSALMS

There is only one proper position and sound stance for any lover of righteousness and defender of truth to take toward ANY error, toward ALL error—*exposure* and *opposition*. We cannot be FOR truth and FOR error with equal emphasis. In this very regard Psalms is a militant book. Three passages in Psalms so attest. (1) A predictive prophecy of the Messiah stated, "Thou lovest righteousness, and hatest wickedness:..." (45:7). (2) and (3) In Psalm 119, longest chapter in the Bible and a brilliant chapter of defending and extolling God's word, we read in verses 104 and 128 these twin concepts, "Through thy precepts I get understanding: therefore I hate every false way...Therefore I esteem all thy precepts concerning all things to be right; and I hate every false way." Such militant attitudes against error as are reflected in this trio of passages are largely ignored, disbelieved and rejected by the spineless of our day who are FOR everything (except militant truth) and against nothing (except a militant defense of truth). Psalms is not a degree behind other Biblical books in its rousing refutation of entrenched error, of flagrant falsehood.

ATHEISM IS REFUTED

The Lord God is mentioned right at the beginning of Psalms (1:2) and the final word of Psalms in our English rendering is Lord (150:6). Every chapter in between mentions God either directly or indirectly. He is the All-pervading influence throughout the book. In both Psalm 14:1 and 53:1 the psalmist, David in both cases, classed as a fool the man who "hath said in his heart, There is no God." Fool here is translated from a Hebrew term, *nabal,* which means empty person. Empty of both head and heart is the man who would survey all the overwhelming, staggering evidence for God's existence and still deny him. There are a good many fools who are teaching our precious boys and girls in college and university classes these days. They stand before these young, immature and very impressionable youngsters as veteran atheists. They deny God, His Book, His Son and the divine derivation of Christianity. I decided a long, long time ago that no empty-headed and empty-hearted atheistic professor was going to dampen my foundational faith in God or destroy my beautiful belief in Jesus Christ as God's only begotten Son by his blatant brand of ignorant infidelity. And none did! And none have to date! And none are going to if I keep sanity of mind and soundness of heart. Psalm 19 and 139 are two great chapters in this precious book that establish good and great arguments for God's existence.

THE "JESUS ONLY" THEORY IS REFUTED

Among certain Pentecostal Holiness groups there is a large, militant and deeply aggressive element that denies "The Timeless Trinity," as the late and scholarly Roy H. Lanier, Sr., lovingly designated the Sublime Three. Yet Psalms cogently refutes this "Jesus Only" theory again and again. In Psalm 2:2 we have the Lord and His Anointed. The Lord is Jehovah; the Anointed is the Messiah. Messiah is a Hebrew term; Christ is a Greek term; both mean anointed in English. Acts 4:25-27 makes clear that Father and Son are portrayed in this predictive prophecy. Psalm 2:7 makes further mention of this Father-Son relationship by saying, "the Lord (Jehovah) hath said unto me, Thou art my Son (the Messiah or Second Person in the Godhead); this day have I begotten thee." Hebrews 1:5, a potent, precious and powerful passage about Jesus, quotes this very verse from Psalm 2:7. Psalm 2:12 contains the Davidic charge to "Kiss the Son,..." This refers to the homage, honor, adoration and worship of which He was wonderfully worthy to receive. Son, of necessity, implies a Father. Father, of necessity, likewise demands a child and in this case a Son—His only begotten Son. In Psalm 45:6 Jehovah, the First Person of "The Timeless Trinity," addresses the Second Person of the Sublime Three by declaring, "Thy throne, O God, is for ever and ever: the sceptre of thy kingdom is a right sceptre." Hebrews 1:8,9 quotes this very passage and exhibits with crystal clarity that Jesus Christ is the stately object of the predictive prophecy malicious modernism of the twentieth century to the contrary notwithstanding. Two other powerful verses are observed in Psalm 110. Therein we read,

194

The Lord said unto my Lord, Sit thou at my right hand, until I make thine enemies thy footstool...The Lord hath sworn, and will not repent, Thou art a priest for ever after the order of Melchizedek (vs. 1,4).

Matthew 22:41ff and Hebrews 7:17,21 show conclusively that Jesus fulfills these predictive prophecies in Psalm 110:1,4. Note with care the following observations. (1) There are TWO Lords portrayed here—not just one. (2) The first Lord is speaker; the second Lord is the addressee. (3) Usage of pronouns makes crystal clear that the one who did the addressing is a DIFFERENT person than the one addressed. (4) The one who did the addressing is on the throne; the one addressed is to be at His right hand. Being ON the throne and AT the right hand simultaneously imply two persons—not just one. (5) The one who made the oath is Jehovah; the one to whom the oath refers is the addressee—the Christ. (6) The addresser was not to be priest; the addressee was to be the priest.

The book of Psalms proves conclusively that the "Jesus Only" theory is an egregious error, a flagrant falsehood. Passages like Matthew 3:13-17; 28:19 and 2 Corinthians 13:14 speak of three—Father, Son and Holy Spirit. They are not three Gods; they compose the one Godhead or the one Deity. They constitute the One Divine Nature. Each possesses this Deity or Divine Nature.

NO PUNISHMENT IN NEXT WORLD FOR WICKED REFUTED

Hadean punishment for the wicked between death and judgment and Eternal Gehenna, everlasting punishment, are spurned, rejected and ignored themes of our infidelic world. Hell is just the butt of jokes or for profane speaking. It is doubtful there has ever been a generation with as many infidels relative to future punishment for sins as is ours. Yet Psalms refutes this "No Hell" notion that many people now tacitly tolerate or blatantly believe. Psalm 1:6 closes with the observation that "the way of the ungodly shall perish." No promise is extended the wicked of dwelling "in the house of the Lord for ever" as the Shepherd Psalmist of piety envisioned with hallowed and holy hope in Psalm 23:6. Psalm 9:17 is definite, dynamic and decisive in declaring, "The wicked shall be turned into hell, and all the nations that forget God." Does this refer to future punishment? Adam Clarke so thought. He says, "*headlong into hell, down into hell. The original is very emphatic*" (Emphasis his). Albert Barnes thought it referred to future punishment and so stated in his comments on this very passage in Psalms. Unless there is punishment for the wicked beyond death and the reward of eternal redemption for the righteous, there is really no just reason for declaring that the death of saints is precious in the sight of the Lord as Psalm 116:15 does.

CALVINISM REFUTED

The five basic thrusts of cold, cruel and calloused Calvinism are: (1) total hereditary depravity; (2) unconditional election; (3) limited atonement; (4) irresistible grace; and (5) perseverance of all saints regardless of what they do or do not do. Calvinism seeks to support its "born in sin" theology by appeals to such passages as Psalm 51:5 and 58:3. Neither teaches a birth in sin or total hereditary depravity for every baby born into this world. To say that David is saying he was totally depraved at birth places him in utter contradiction of his own affirmation in Psalm 139:14 how that he would praise God because of being fearfully and wonderfully made. How could one be fearfully and wonderfully made and still be a little creature of total hereditary depravity at conception and birth? David, in Psalm 51, was not confessing personal sins at conception or at birth. The context is a confession of his sins as an adulterer, deceiver and murderer which were all involved in the Uriah and Bath-sheba affair. David was born into a world of sin; his parents were sinners before him as indeed all accountable parents are at the births of their children respectively (Romans 3:9,23). But David was not a sinner until he sinned; his parents were not sinners until they sinned. David's parents were not born in sin. Psalm 58:3 is also a Calvinistic sugarstick. It states, "The wicked are estranged from the womb: they go astray as soon as they be born, speaking lies." Barnes, a Calvinistic commentator, thought this passage referred to those that "are apostate and alienated from God from their very birth." But those contemplated in this verse GO astray; they are not BORN astray!! How soon after birth? Not the next day by any means or the first year either!! Not until they are able to speak lies. How many one-day-old infants has any reader ever heard as speakers of lies in between feedings, naps, etc.? This verse does not uphold Adamic or inherited sin by any stretch of the imagination. Of that we can be absolutely positive!!

Another Calvinistic contention connected with Psalms relates to Psalm 37:23,24 and which, in their view, upholds the once-saved-always-saved position. The passage reads, "The steps of a good man are ordered by the Lord: and he delighteth in his way. Though he fall, he shall not be utterly cast down: for the Lord upholdeth him with his hand." What type of man is contemplated here? Not the wicked; not the vile; not the corrupt; not the defiant; not the rebellious. David depicts a GOOD man here. It is true that GOOD is in italics here which means it is a supplied word by the translators. However, it is a *justified* term for the context speaks of a good man. The man depicted here is one in whom the Lord delights. Verse 25 describes the righteous man. Delineated here is a good and righteous man who though he has failures in life yet he is always striving to do God's will. As long as his efforts are of this exemplary type the Lord will be patient and helpful to him. But this passage says nothing of hope to the once righteous man who forsakes his righteousness, becomes a very wicked man and dies in that deplorable condition.

Psalm 78 is a chapter that describes vividly the apostasy of God's children in the wilderness. "Once-saved-always-saved" did not work for apostate Israelites who fell in unbelief by the hundreds of thousands in that barren wilderness and short of Canaan's goal.

The book of Psalms is full of conditions that the God-fearing man must honor. Hence, there is no support for Calvinistic unconditional theories. God's grace is not irresistible either in Psalms or in any other Biblical book. This would destroy man's free moral agency. There is positively no hint in any of the Messianic psalms that the atonement would be limited and not ample for all the race. Calvinism strikes out five times in seeking to find its five-plank theology in Psalms. Not a single one of the five foundational points can be found in this poetic product of the Old Testament.

THE "NO WRATH OF GOD" DOCTRINE IS REFUTED IN PSALMS

Here are four selections from Psalms that speak of God's wrath—the very attribute of His judicial character that many currently reject or deny,

> Thou shalt make them as a fiery oven in the time of thine anger: the Lord shall swallow them up in his wrath, and the fire shall devour them (21:9). The wrath of God came upon them, and slew the fattest of them, and smote down the chosen men of Israel (78:31). Unto whom I sware in my wrath that they should not enter into my rest (95:11). Therefore was the wrath of the Lord kindled against his people, insomuch that he abhorred his own inheritance (106:40).

Lest any think there is no wrath exhibited by God in the New Testament let him remember that both the goodness and the severity of God are mentioned in Romans 11:22, that the terror of the Lord is portrayed in 2 Corinthians 5:11 and the apostolic affirmation in Hebrews 12:29 still reads that "our God is a consuming fire." Brother Thomas B. Warren has said there is more in the Bible about God's wrath than about His goodness. Yet the masses of religionists today do not accept any of this immense amount of Biblical teaching. The Bible Doctrine of God's Wrath is a forgotten and ignored theme of our tolerant times.

THE "ETERNALITY OF MATTER" FALLACY IS THOROUGHLY REFUTED

Psalm 89:11 affirms that the heavens, the earth, the world and its fulness have been FOUNDED. Matter is not eternal! Psalm 95:5 affirms God as MAKER of sea and dry land. Matter is not eternal! "The Lord *made* the heavens" is the affirmation of Psalm 96:5. Matter is not eternal! In Psalms 95:7 and 100:3 we read of God as our MAKER. Matter is not that maker; it is not eternal. Psalm 102:25,26 has God as the one who LAID the earth's foundation, the heavens as being the WORK of His hands and pictures the PERISHING of the earth. Matter is not eternal; it had a beginning and will have an end. All of this fits beautifully and harmoniously into the teaching of the second law of thermodynamics—one of the best understood of all scientific laws. Psalms even says it is wholly unscientific to accept matter as eternal—long a bedrock for silly and senseless organic evolution. These plus many other verses in Psalms picture the universe as having both a beginning and destined to have an end when time is no more. The New Testament teaches the same. (Hebrews 1:11-13; 2 Peter 3:10ff).

IDOLATRY REFUTED

Idols are man-made. Psalm 115:4ff portrays them as made of silver or gold. They have mouths but never speak; they have eyes but never see; they have ears but never hear; they have noses but never smell; they have hands but they cannot handle; they have feet but possess no powers of mobilization. What a stinging indictment of the utter futility of idolatry. A similar indictment against idolatry occurs in Psalm 135:15ff. Yet idolatry WAS a besetting sin and still IS. Anything or anyone that takes God's place in the human heart is an idol whether money, power, prestige, popularity, family, sports, recreation, job, friends, sex, etc.

ABORTION REFUTED

David said,

My substance was not hid from thee, when I was made in secret, and curiously wrought in the lowest parts of the earth. Thine eyes did see my substance, yet being unperfect; and in thy book all my members were written, which in continuance were fashioned, when as yet there was none of them (139:15,16).

David considered himself as human, as the grand object of divine workmanship, as having substance, as possessing members and as being fashioned. All of this would have been in his prenatal period or prior to his birth to Jesse and wife. He was NOT just a blob of flesh or protoplasm; he was NOT something like an appendix or tonsils that could be removed at the optional will of the mother with no subsequent consequences prevailing; he WAS human—just as human before birth as afterwards. Abortion would end YESTERDAY if every womn accepted and practiced Psalm 139:15,16.

DEISM REFUTED

Deism suggests God as initial maker of heaven and earth but now as a totally disinterested spectator to all His creation currently does. Yet Psalm 113:6 affirms that Jehovah humbles "himself to behold the things that are in heaven, and in the earth." Psalm 112:9 says He is a disperser or giver to the poor. God *cares* for what He has made.

POINTS TO PONDER RELATIVE TO RELIGIOUS ERRORS REFUTED IN PSALMS

1. We can only be FOR truth by being AGAINST error.
2. The Psalmists knew truth and how to apply it in refuting error.
3. God is author of truth; Satan is author of error.
4. How we feel about truth is an index to our feelings about God.
5. How we feel about error is a picture of our attitude toward Satan.
6. We have NO obligation to support error in any fashion.

DISCUSSION QUESTIONS

1. What three introductory passages from Psalms were cited which furnish us the tone and tenor of what our stance toward error must be?

2. Show how atheism is refuted in Psalms.

3. Show how the "Jesus Only" theory is refuted in Psalms.

4. How do such New Testament passages as Matthew 3:13-17; 28:19 and 2 Corinthians 13:14 further corroborate the passages in Psalms touching the Sacred Trinity?

5. How does the book of Psalms refute the no-future-punishment error?

6. List the five basic errors of Calvinism and show how Psalms refutes each of them.

7. List and discuss some New Testament passages in which the wrath of God is set forth.

8. Exhibit from Psalms a thorough refutation of the eternality-of-matter error.

9. How is abortion refuted in the Psalms?

10. List and discuss The Points To Ponder relative to errors refuted in Psalms.

MULTIPLE CHOICE: Underline correct answer

1. "Thou lovest righteousness, and hatest wickedness" is a statement in Psalms which finds fulfillment in: (A) the Messiah; (B) the devil; (C) every false teacher of past and present; (D) David.

2. David called the atheist: (A) a wise man; (B) his best friend; (C) a fool; (D) the greatest benefactor a wicked world could have to help make it better.

3. "The Timeless Trinity" is a beautiful designation which refers to: (A) Michael, Gabriel and Urial; (B) Peter, James and John; (C) Abraham, Isaac and Jacob; (D) God, Christ and the Holy Spirit.

4. Relative to the wrath of God the Bible: (A) says but scant little; (B) NEVER mentions the topic; (C) denies vehemently that Jehovah God possesses any wrath; (D) has more to say than about His goodness according to the brilliant Thomas B. Warren.

5. The Bible and the well-known second law of thermodynamics: (A) are in total disarray of each other; (B) both support the contention that matter is eternal; (C) both deny the eternality of matter; (D) say absolutely nothing about whether matter is eternal or had a beginning.

SCRIPTURAL FILL-INS: Only one word is required in each blank.

(1) "_____ thy _____ I get _____: I _____ every _____ way... _____ I _____ all thy _____ concerning all _____ to be _____; and I _____ every _____ way."

(2) "Thou art my _____; this _____ have I _____ thee."

200

(3) "Thy _____, O _____, is for _____ and _____: the _____ of thy _____ is a _____ sceptre."

(4) "The _____ shall be turned into _____, and all the _____ that _____ God."

(5) "The _____ of a good _____ are _____ by the _____: and he _____ in his _____. _____ he _____, he shall not be _____ cast _____: for the _____ upholdeth _____ with his _____."

(6) "My _____ was not _____ from thee, when I was _____ in _____, and curiously _____ in the _____ parts of the _____. Thine _____ did see my _____, yet being _____; and in thy _____ all my _____ were _____, which in _____ were _____, when as yet there was _____ of them."

TRUE OR FALSE: Put either a "T" or "F" in the blanks

____1. Psalms is really a tolerant book of compromise and never hits any error head-on.

____2. The atheist, according to Psalms 14:1 and 53:1, is empty of heart and empty of head, i.e., emptyhearted and emptyheaded.

____3. Messiah in Hebrew and Christ in Greek both mean anointed in English.

____4. Calvinism strikes out five times in seeking support for its entire package of poisonous errors in the Psalms.

____5. Plain old Deism is a doctrine of God supported by the Bible generally and Psalms in particular.

THOUGHT QUESTIONS

1. Why must we be FOR all truth and AGAINST all error?
2. List and discuss some great truths set forth in Psalm 110:1,4.
3. Read and discuss the four selected passages which prove conclusively that religionists are in error who deny God's wrath.
4. List and discuss some of the popular idols of the current era.
5. Why will a thorough acquaintance and a deep belief in Psalms enable us to be far more militant against the errors of the day?

CHAPTER TWENTY-THREE

PSALMS: A BUILDER OF GREAT FAMILIES

The Book of Psalms majors in many of the absolutes of marvelous marriage and happy homelife. These psalms were penned by men of *faith* and *piety*. They breathed forth a tremendous *trust* in God throughout the book. Their *hope* was in the Lord. Here we have a quartet of valiant virtues that are absolutely essential in the firm formation of marriage and the fervent founding of a permanent home. Faith must be the foundation; piety should serve as the floor; trust should form the walls; hope should be the roof. Surrounding it for safety and security should be the fence of worship and service to Jehovah and Jesus.

A BEAUTIFUL BEGINNING AS A MARITAL COUPLE

In marriage ceremonies across the years Johnny Ramsey, brilliant editor of CHRISTIAN BIBLE TEACHER and highly effective preacher of the gospel, has incorporated Psalm 34:3 into his remarks to the groom and bride. The passage says with preciousness, "O magnify the Lord with me, and let us exalt his name together." Quite obviously, the passage is of far wider application than just a husband or wife but is surely inclusive of them in marriage. Surely no one would doubt the precious power in such a regal resolution of the young groom who is a stalwart Christian challenging his beautiful bride to join him in a life of magnifying the Lord and together majoring in the tremendous task of exalting His name together. Surely no one would deny for a moment the attractive appropriateness of a beautiful bride who loves God with all her heart, soul, mind and strength and calls tenderly and persuasively for her Christian groom to magnify the Lord with her and that, as a team of truth seekers, they exalt His name together throughout their marriage. Is this not what Noah and his wife did? Is this not what Abraham and Sarah did? Is this not what Boaz and Ruth did? Is this not what Zacharias and Elisabeth did? Is this not what Joseph and Mary did? Is this not what Aquila and Priscilla did? This is what Ahab and Jezebel should have done and failed to do. It is what Jehoram and Athaliah should have done and failed to do. It is what Herod and Herodias should have done with their FIRST marital mates and then they would have never become involved in an adulterous marriage to each other. It is what Ananias and Sapphira should have done and failed to do.

GOD: THE INTENSE IMPERATIVE IN HOME LIFE

Marriage is not a straightline arrangement with husband at one end and wife at the other end. It should never be just a twosome; it must be a threesome arrangement. A triangle better describes it. God should be at the apex or top angle; husband and wife should be at the base angles. MARRIAGE IS FOR THOSE WHO LOVE GOD AND ONE ANOTHER is how brother Thomas B. Warren expressed it so well in a title of a truly classic volume on marriage. CHRIST IN THE HOME is how I have expressed it in a book title and which is now put out under the Quality label. JESUS CHRIST: THE HOPE OF THE HOME is how I have expressed it in another volume which is put out under the Lambert label.

The triangle also applies in a family sense. God should be at the apex or top angle; righteous parents should be at one of the base angles; submissive children should be at the other base angle.

A trio of scriptures from Psalms describes Jehovah God as the Great Indispensible force of every really successful home. David breathed a prayer in Psalm 86:16 in which he referred to his mother as the Lord's handmaid. The passage reads, "O turn unto me, and have mercy upon me; give thy strength unto thy servant and save the son of thine handmaid." David was reared by a godly mother who was designated as Jehovah's handmaid. Psalm 91 describes the "Happy state of the godly." Verse 9 therein states, "Because thou hast made the Lord, which is my refuge, even the most High, thy habitation;..." If in God we find our refuge and in Him make our home, then He in turn will make our home into a refuge and place for His welcomed presence within our lives. A third passage reads, "O Lord, truly I am thy servant; I am thy servant, and the son of thine handmaid: thou hast loosed my bonds" (116:16). The speaker or writer considered himself as God's servant; he spoke again of his godly mother as being God's handmaid. How fortunate when a child has a mother who belongs to God. What inestimable blessings she bequeathes that child.

THE BASIC UNIT OF SOCIETY

In Psalm 68:5,6 David writes, "A father of the fatherless, and a judge of the widows, is God in his holy habitation. God setteth the solitary in families:..." Those who have lost a father are orphans; those who have lost husbands are widows. God is not unmindful of such bereft people. He sets them in families or "in a house" as the margin states. Recognized here is that the home with a family is the basic unit of society. It is due to such principles as this that we have contended loudly and for a long time for the sympathetic restoration of a home to orphans when they are deprived of such by death, desertion, divorce, etc. This has been a precious part of church benevolence for a long, long time. We are unalterably opposed to that system of anti-ism that classifies congregational benevolence to innocent, helpless children as being liberal and sinful. We believe in restoring that basic unit of society to those who have been deprived of such due to no fault of their own. This is a good, grand and great work that Christians as individuals can do and that congregations collectively can do out of the church treasury.

WISE BEHAVIOR IN THE HOME

Wisdom should be definitely in the ascendancy as marital mates are selected and as marriages are entered with sobriety and solemnity. Surely wisdom must be on the throne in the building of every successful home. David observed in Psalm 101:2, "I will behave myself wisely in a perfect way. O when wilt thou come unto me? I will walk within my house with a perfect heart." This was a noble resolution on the part of David—the great shepherd monarch. Noted are the following observations: (1) In all his ways both at home and abroad he desired to behave himself in the way of wisdom, in the manner of maturity. When the Lord did come and inspect David's motives and manners, his attitudes and actions and his words and ways David desired to receive the Lord's ardent approval. (2) David knew that the Lord inspected every life—that no man and his heart ever escape the notice of the All-Seeing Eye on high. (3) With a perfect (mature, complete) heart he desired to walk before his family. (4) Suggested here is success as husband, as father, as guide and as example. From all the marital collapses and home failures world-wide, it would strongly appear to be the concrete case that very, very few husbands, fathers, wives, mothers and accountable sons and daughters are seeking to walk in their homes with perfect hearts. Violated vows, broken homes and reckless youth all argue otherwise in conclusive fashion!

PROTECTING THE HOME FROM HARMFUL INFLUENCES

David says in Psalm 101:7, "He that worketh deceit shall not dwell within my house: he that telleth lies shall not tarry in my sight." Neither as servant, companion, visitor or family member would the person of deceit be welcome in David's house. Happy family life cannot be found in the presence of trickery, deception and dishonesty. It only takes one deceiver in any home to wreck household harmony and destroy home happiness. It only takes one liar to destroy the truthful foundations upon which a family has built its family relationships.

We should exercise the utmost of care relative to the influences we welcome into our homes. Warm welcomes extended to drunkards, the immoral, the profane and irreverent and known teachers of religious falsehood can bring irreparable injury to a once happy household. Two ladies of my acquaintance faced a similar problem in vastly different ways. One was a strong Christian with a family of little children that she loved better than life. Her father was a drunkard. He lived hundreds of miles away. He sent word that he was coming for a visit. She told him he would be welcome but under NO circumstances was he to bring his liquor with him or consume ANY while in her home. She did not intend for her children to be in company with a drunk granddaddy. He chose not to come. He preferred liquor over his own daughter and her lovely children—his own grandchildren. What an idol he had made of the vicious monster of King Alcohol!! Was she right? Eminently so!! Another lady complained that she and her husband were totally unable to keep their drinking friends from bringing their liquor with them when they made social calls or visits. They needed spine, a new set of friends, a hatred of liquor and the giving up of its presence within their own lives. They did not wish to forbid its being brought into their home. Therein lay the real core of the problem. They did not believe in acting decisively in keeping out King Alcohol.

Happy homes are built on both a positive and a negative—on the good and true and that we welcome and the evil and wrong that we refuse a welcome extended to the same.

206

THE VALUE AND BEAUTY OF A GODLY FAMILY

In Psalm 127 we read,

> Except the Lord build the house, they labour in vain that build
> it: except the Lord keep the city, the watchman waketh but in
> vain...Lo, children are an heritage of the Lord: and the fruit of
> the womb is his reward. As arrows are in the hand of a mighty
> man; so are children of the youth. Happy is the man that hath
> his quiver full of them: they shall not be ashamed, but they shall
> speak with the enemies in the gate (vs. 1,3-5).

The building of a house here may refer to an ordinary dwelling, a temple of worship or most any kind of erecting enterprise of construction
for human habitation. The essential message in both the building erec-
tion and the successful keeping of the city is man's whole dependence
on God. Without that priceless ingredient the builder of the house is
engaged in a vain endeavor and the watchman whose job it is to be a
protecting element or stalwart shield over a city awakes in vain.
Relative to home building think how many couples NEVER have any
room for the Godhead. He was not in their courtship; He was
unwelcome at their marriage ceremony; He has not been welcome in
the building of their home. Theirs are marriages minus God, Christ,
the Bible and the Lord's church. No wonder so many of these falter
and fail. Uniformly, all such are built on sandy foundations—not a
rock foundation.

Relative to the verses at the end of the chapter we see that: (1)
children are God's holy heritage, lovely legacy and beautiful gifts to
parents; (2) children bring a measure of safety and security to a home;
(3) happiness is tied up in the children a gracious God on high has
given parents as precious possessions indeed; and (4) they are worth
their weight in the purest of gold in dealing with enemies at the gate.

Psalm 127 is a great home builder among the Psalms.

THE JOYS OF MOTHERHOOD

Two selections from Psalms stress this segment title. We read in
Psalm 113:9 and 128:3,

> He maketh the barren woman to keep house, and to be a joyful
> mother of children. Praise ye the Lord...Thy wife shall be as a
> fruitful vine by the sides of thine house: thy children like olive
> plants round about thy table.

207

There is the joy of having children and not being deprived of this deeply inherent desire. So many great and godly women of Bible times knew firsthand this deprivation for long periods of time. A lingering look at Sarah, Rachel and Hannah in the Old Testament and Elisabeth in the New Testament all before they were blessed with motherhood in their lives fully reflects how they viewed the barren womb, the childless marriage and their extended inability to bless their husbands with a precious progeny. Such was sufficient to cause praise and Hallelujahs on the lips of such women when they and their husbands were blessed with beautiful children. Each of these couples became a more beautiful, bountiful and blessed family with the addition of a child or children. The second passage reflects the joys of being able to produce the fondly favored fruit of children. Among the Hebrews this was a beautiful blessing of vast value, of inestimable worth. As parents grow old and feeble how rewarding and invigorating that surrounding them are budding, blossoming and blooming children that correspond so beautifully to the attractive analogy of vibrant, healthy and strong olive plants surrounding the table. They will carry on the family name, the family tradition and the family emphasis subsequent to the demise of the aged parents.

THE HOME: GOD'S SCHOOLROOM FOR CHILDREN

In six choice verses from Psalm 78:3-8 we note,

> Which we have heard and known, and our fathers have told us. We will not hide them from their children, shewing to the generation to come the praises of the Lord, and his strength, and his wonderful works that he hath done. For he established a testimony in Jacob, and appointed a law in Israel, which he commanded our fathers, that they should make them known to their children. That the generation to come might know them, even the children which should be born; who should arise and declare them to their children: That they might set their hope in God, and not forget the works of God, but keep his commandments: And might not be as their fathers, a stubborn and rebellious generation; a generation that set not their heart aright, and whose spirit was not stedfast with God.

How exceptionally wise when parents are absolutely and resolutely determined to entrust to their children the truths of God and His law and encourage their imbibing them so that the torch of truth never need touch ground as each coming generation is taught what it should know and practice and then passes it on faithfully and fully to the next

208

generation on the threshold of succession. This passage not only contains needed exhortations about right living but warnings of what price is paid when a generation becomes stubborn, defiant and rebels against the God of all goodness, the Almighty of all authority. The home is an excellent schoolroom wherein just such greatly needed lessons can be taught to impressionable children by parents who know God's will and are sincerely submissive to it.

RIGHTEOUS MARRIAGES AND RIGHTEOUS HOMES

Psalm 145:17 states, "The Lord is righteous in all his ways, and holy in all his works." To have the righteous and holy Jehovah in our homes it is absolutely essential that our homes be characterized by righteousness and holiness. Surely, God will not dwell in adulterous situations or within the fatal framework of fornication whether as live-in liaisons on a permanent basis or occasional one night stances with many partners over a lascivious lifetime. Yet these very situations exist in every case where men and women have formed adulterous remarriages or just simply form a damnable and devilish live-in arrangement without marriage license, marriage ceremony or the permanency of marital commitment. Even among couples who have every right to marry they may be unrighteous and unholy in other realms. The Lord is not going to be present in such situations either. He will never be a party to unrighteousness regardless of its basic nature.

Psalms can go a long, long way in helping our homes to be filled with righteousness (right doing preceded by right thinking and accompanied by right speech patterns) and characterized by harmonious holiness. As a family of Bible believers, why not choose a six-months' period this very year and read, as a family, the entirety of Psalms? Most of the chapters are short enough to read at one devotional setting. A number of times could be devoted to long chapters such as 78, 89, 105, 106, 107 and especially 119—the longest chapter in the book. Such surely would help all of us in family relationships and in our individual obligations toward the Sublime Three.

POINTS TO PONDER ABOUT PSALMS AND BUILDING GREAT FAMILIES

1. The man of God should marry a woman who will aid his ultimately going home to heaven on high in the sweet by and by.
2. The woman of God should marry a man of God who will help her go home to heaven eternally.

3. Righteous parents are far more apt to have righteous children if their righteousness is in both deed and word and not just word alone.

4. The unknown equation in modern marital math is God.

5. Successful marriages contain extra doses of TLC—Tender Loving Care.

6. Marriages flounder because one or both marital mates prefer failure over marital success.

DISCUSSION QUESTIONS

1. *List and discuss the quartet of valiant virtues so essential for marvelous marriages and happy homes.*

2. *List and discuss some Biblical couples—husbands and wives—who magnified and exalted the name of the Lord together.*

3. *List some Biblical couples—husbands and wives—who failed to do this and show how the failure affected their marriage, their lives and their influence for good.*

4. *Read and discuss the trio of scriptures from Psalms which present God as the intense imperative in home life.*

5. *What observations are made relative to David's statement in Psalm 101:2?*

6. *What does the book of Psalms say relative to protecting the home from harmful elements?*

7. *Read and discuss Psalm 127:3-5.*

8. *Read and discuss what is said relative to the joys of motherhood.*

9. *Discuss the home as God's schoolroom for impressionable children.*

10. *Why is righteousness an imperative of happy homelife?*

11. *Read and discuss The Points To Ponder About Psalms And Building Great Families.*

MULTIPLE CHOICE: Underline correct answer

1. *MARRIAGE IS FOR THOSE WHO LOVE GOD AND ONE ANOTHER and CHRIST IN THE HOME are book titles which approve and emphasize: (A) the straightline approach to marriage—man and woman; (B) the threesome approach to marriage—God, man and woman; (C) the totally materialistic approach to marriage minus all religious links; (D) that Christ's law of marriage, divorce and remarriage in Matthew 19:9 is NOT applicable to the world but only in cases where both mates are Christians.*

2. *Psalm 127 describes: (A) David in retreat against Saul; (B) the value and beauty of a godly family; (C) temple worship in the beauty of holiness; (D) the position and destiny of the fool who denies God's existence.*

3. Sarah, Rachel, Hannah and Elisabeth, great and godly women of the Bible, all shared in common the sad fact that they were: (A) barren relative to childbirth for a considerable portion of their early mariages; (B) never married; (C) never mothers at all; (D) all left widows early in their marriages by the premature deaths of their husbands.

4. Psalm 145:17 describes Jehovah as: (A) righteous in His ways and holy in His works; (B) the God of all goodness and severity; (C) the one whose eyes survey the whole universe; (D) the one who gave Israel a great covenant on Horeb.

5. Happy, harmonious and holy marriages are built on: (A) harshness and unkindness; (B) addiction to strong drink and deadly drugs; (C) lasciviousness and sensual forms of entertainment; (D) sobriety, righteousness and godliness.

SCRIPTURAL FILL-IN: Only one word is required in each blank.

(1) "O _____ the _____ with _____, and let us _____ his name _____."

(2) "I will _____ myself _____ in a _____ way. O when wilt thou _____ unto _____? I will _____ within my _____ with a _____ _____."

(3) "_____ the _____ build the _____, they _____ in _____ that build it: _____ the _____ keep the _____, the _____ waketh but in _____."

(4) "Lo, _____ are an _____ of the _____: and the _____ of the _____ is his _____. As _____ are in the _____ of a mighty _____; so are _____ of the _____. _____ is the _____ that hath his _____ full of them: they shall not be _____, but they shall _____ with the _____ in the _____."

(5) "The Lord is _____ in _____ his _____, and _____ in all his _____."

TRUE OR FALSE: Put either a "T" or "F" in the blanks

___1. Psalm 34:3 is a good, great and grand passage to which every marital team should subscribe faithfully, fully and fervently.

___2. It is nobody's business what is done in the privacy of one's own home regardless of how sinful the activities may be.

_____3. It is a God-given right that every husband and wife may and must decide who or what does or does not come into their home by way of guests, entertainment, etc.

_____4. No home can be righteous unless it majors in right-thinking, right-speaking and right-doing.

_____5. Choice of a lifetime mate for marriage has but little to do with one's going home to heaven ultimately.

THOUGHT QUESTIONS

1. Why is the regular and reverent worship and service of God so vital for both husbands and wives, for both parents and children?

2. Discuss marriage as a straightline agreement and then as a threesome arrangement. Which is the proper approach and why?

3. Discuss in detail the home as the basic unit of society.

4. Set forth what the Bible teaches is wise behavior in the home for husbands, fathers, wives, children and any in-law who might also live there.

5. What can be done to protect the home from harmful influences that are ever about us today?

CHAPTER TWENTY-FOUR

PSALMS OF SORROW

Sorrow is as much a part of humanity while on earth as are birth and breath, as are physical death and bodily dissolution. It is no respecter of persons. It comes to good and bad, to rich and poor, to young and old, to the healthy and diseased. It has been said that God had one Son without sin, the Christ, but NO Son without sorrow. Isaiah 53:3 portrays Jesus as "a man of sorrows" and one who would be "acquainted with grief." In early life David was described as a man after God's own heart and yet his life was filled with a multitude of sorrows (1 Samuel 13:14). Many of the psalms he penned had as their rich background the sorrows of his soul. Many souls across the centuries who were burdened with heavy sorrows of soul have gone to Psalms seeking solace and requesting rest from the same. Comfort may always be found and this is one of the main factors which has made Psalms a dearly beloved and sincerely appreciated book among Bible believers. Our STUDIES IN PSALMS would be very deficient were we to ignore this topic and have no specific mention of them and what the psalmists did when sorrows settled upon them.

SORROWS CAUSED BY ENEMIES

David painted this portrait of his sorrows in Psalm 18:4,5, "The sorrows of death compassed me, and the floods of ungodly men made me afraid. The sorrows of hell (cords of Sheol—ASV) compassed me about: the snares of death prevented me." It is now unknown to which period of life David alludes here. It may have been earlier life when Saul hunted him as though he were an incorrigible outlaw, a hardened criminal. David once confessed to Jonathan that only a step separated him and death (1 Samuel 20:3). Whatever the specific dangers they were real and imminently near. His tormentors were ungodly men. The margin has Belial which refers to people of no profit, people who were abandoned, wicked and useless. Facing death surrounded him; the chords of Sheol seemed to have him bound very tightly. Death and its snares rushed upon him as if the rushing torrents of a mighty stream in a flooded stage or of a net or trap springing upon an animal. "Where could I go but to the Lord?" must have welled up in David's sorrowful soul, his crushed heart for verse 6 tells of his taking his burden to the Lord in the cries of deep petitions and was heard on heavenly high.

Psalm 31 is another Davidic psalm as the tried saint again faces calamity at the unholy hands of aroused and adamant antagonists. He wrote out of sorrow of soul,

> Pull me out of the net that they have laid privily for me: for thou art my strength...Have mercy upon me, O Lord, for I am in trouble: mine eye is consumed with grief, yea, my soul and my belly...I was a reproach among all mine enemies, but especially among my neighbors, and a fear to mine acquaintance: they that did see me without fled from me. I am forgotten as a dead man out of mind: I am like a broken vessel. For I have heard the slander of many: fear was on every side: while they took counsel together against me, they devised to take away my life (31:4,9,11-13).

Note the sorrows faced by the psalmist here. (1) His enemies had laid privily the net of destruction for him and minus any forewarning on his part. Humanly, he feared being ensnared in the same. (2) Trouble faced him on every side. (3) Grief consumed his eye, soul and belly; sorrow affected him wholly or entirely. (4) Remotely, his enemies considered him a reproach; nearby his neighbors did the same. (5) Those who knew him feared him. (6) Seeing him was their instant signal to flee his presence. (7) He was forgotten much like a dead man who has passed out of recollection by a surviving generation. (8) He likens himself to a broken or perishing vessel which is rendered worthless. (9) The slander, the unjust accusations and the clever innuendoes against him all came to his ear. (10) Fear stalked him on every side; no one came to be his friend or confidant; no one cared for his soul (Cf. 142:4). (11) His enemies entered into a planned conspiracy that had his life as the center target for their devious designs and poisonous plots. Their malicious machinations were aimed

214

murderously at him. To whom could he go but to the Lord? There he did GO and found solace as the remnant of this psalm depicts with deep delight and jubilant joy. Only the Lord can assuage sorrows caused by cruel and cold enemies to any considerable extent. David learned that and it is one of the good and great lessons we can glean from a patient and persistent perusal of Psalms.

SORROWS CAUSED BY PERSONAL SINS AND SILLINESS

Psalm 38 has been described as a chapter in which "David moves God to take compassion of his pitiful case, confessing his sins to be the cause thereof." A portion of this psalm will be used for the material in this segment and verses in the latter part will be used for the two subsequent segments of study. In a rather lengthy reading David states,

> O Lord, rebuke me not in thy wrath: neither chasten me in thy hot displeasure. For thine arrows stick fast in me, and thy hand presseth me sore. There is no soundness in my flesh because of thine anger; neither is there any rest in my bones because of my sin. For mine iniquities are gone over mine head: as an heavy burden they are too heavy for me. My wounds stink and are corrupt because of my foolishness. I am troubled; I am bowed down greatly; I go mourning all the day long. For my loins are filled with a loathsome disease: and there is no soundness in my flesh. I am feeble and sore broken: I have roared by reason of the disquietness of my heart. Lord, all my desire is before thee; and my groaning is not hid from thee. My heart panteth, my strength faileth me: as for the light of mine eyes, it also is gone from me. My lovers and my friends stand aloof from my sore (stroke—margin); and my kinsmen stand afar off (38:1-11).

These observations are appropriate and in order. (1) David realizes the wrath of God that hovers above him. (2) He pleads for a bestowal of mercy and compassion. (3) The punishment was already being administered. (4) David is conscious of the enormity of his sins but sicknesses and disease add immeasurably to the burdens he bears. (5) Sickness is serious business to him. (6) Sin is silliness personified; it is foolishness finalized to any and all its naive practitioners. (7) He finds no relief for the sins that trouble his mind and the loathsome disease that ravages his whole body. (8) David is confident that the Lord knows his plight and his present position. (9) There is the feeling that death is nearby—not far off at all (Cf. 1 Samuel 20:3). (10) Friends and acquaintances are aloof; they are not nearby comforters and at hand aides. (11) Even his near kinsmen keep their distance after observing the sore or the stroke that hit him.

Sorrow is personified in this piercing portrait. In addition to sorrow anguish, loneliness and heartaches permeate this entire section of Sacred Scripture. David penned it as a veteran son of sorrow, as a person of piercing persecutions and probems.

SORROW, LIKE SIN, WAS EVER BEFORE DAVID

Later in this Psalm of sorrow, chapter 38, David penned the thought, "For I am ready to halt, and my sorrow is continually before me" (38:17). In his great penitential psalm, chapter 51, David said of ascending transgressions linked with Bath-sheba and Uriah the Hittite, "...my sin is ever before me." Sorrow also was his continual lot. It is entirely possible that the sorrow contemplated here was that produced by his sins. To David's mind there was no intermission. The grief and pain were always there. He could not erase or ignore the self-evident fact that he was a sinner—one who had transgressed law.

Is this not the sentiment of every sensitive soul? Sins long pardoned by our obedience and Christ's blood applied still are before us in memory, in lingering consequences faced, in friends lost, in health ruined by foolish habits, etc. A pardoned Paul in the New Testament never forgot the slain Stephen and his leading part therein; there never faded from his memory his persistent persecutions against the infant church (See Acts 7:58; 8:1-3; 22:19,20; 26:9-11; 1 Corinthians 15:9; 1 Timothy 1:13-15).

PENITENT SORROW FOR SIN

The masses of men know sorrow produced as a result of their sins and yet they are never truly sorry for having committed them. About the only sorrow they feel is from having to pay for their sins and crimes. Relative to sin there can be a sorrow of the world or godly sorrow that produces repentance which in turn produces an amended or changed life. Paul speaks of both in 2 Corinthians 7:9-11. The sorrow of the world works death; godly sorrow works repentance which leads toward life. David did not takes the route of worldly sorrow; he chose the route of being really sorry for his sins. We read in Psalm 38:18, "For I will declare mine iniquity; I will be sorry for my sin." David did not rationalize away his sin as too many are prone to do currently. He did not seek to excuse himself by listing an impressive number of extenuating circumstances to make his sins less heinous in nature. He did not seek to hide or cover them improperly. He simply confessed his sin and made known his penitent spirit. By this disposition he could then pray, "Forsake me not, O Lord: O my God, be not far from me. Make haste to help me, O Lord my salvation" (38:21,22). The Lord cannot save the man PROUD in his sins; he can only save the ones who are PENITENT of their sins and meet all his stipulations that are demanded to reach the position of precious pardon. The foregoing is made reverently and in full respect of God's will.

SORROWS IN AFFLICTIONS

Psalm 69 is such a psalm. Lack of space will not permit our quoting it or analyzing it. In the first part David prays from his recognized position as an afflicted saint. In the latter part his prayer of praise to Jehovah leaves his lips and ascends to the Heavenly Father above.

In Psalm 88:9,15 the psalmist speaks plainly of the afflictions he faced. The passages reflect the sentiments of his tortured soul by exclaiming,

> Mine eye mourneth by reason of affliction: Lord, I have called daily upon thee, I have stretched out my hands unto thee...I am afflicted and ready to die from my youth up: while I suffer thy terrors I am distracted.

These observations occur in these verses. (1) Tears flow without interruption due to afflictions experienced. (2) Daily or persistently the pressured psalmist has sought desired relief. (3) Deeply earnest have been his entreaties to heaven on high. (4) The afflictions have been so acute that nearly all life is drained, the psalmist averred. (5) The afflictions have been either since youth or of great duration. (6) The constant terrors inflicted keep the mind of the psalmist in turmoil; there can be no calm attention to clear duties at hand.

Those who have known heavy afflictions can enter with empathy into the very stances of these statements.

SORROWS OF THE EXILE

Psalm 137 is an entire chapter that paints this particular portrait. The psalmist laments,

> By the rivers of Babylon, there we sat down, yea, we wept, when we remembered Zion. We hanged our harps upon the willows in the midst thereof. For there they that carried us away captive required of us a song; and they that wasted us required of us

217

mirth, saying, Sing us one of the songs of Zion. How shall we sing the Lord's song in a strange land? If I forget thee, O Jerusalem, let my right hand forget my cunning. If I do not remember thee, let my tongue cleave to the roof of my mouth; if I prefer not Jerusalem above my chief joy. Remember, O Lord, the children of Edom in the day of Jerusalem; who said, Rase it, rase it, even to the foundation thereof. O daughter of Babylon, who art to be destroyed; happy shall he be, that rewardeth thee as thou hast served us. Happy shall he be, that taketh and dasheth thy little ones against the stones (137:1-9).

This psalm has its setting in the Babylonian Exile. The rivers of Babylon were the Euphrates, the Tigris, the Cheber and some think even canals that connected Euphrates and Tigris may also have been styled as rivers. As the captives sat down by these Babylonian waters they wept unashamedly when memories reflected upon Zion (Jerusalem). A spirit of nostalgia and gloom so settled upon them that playing upon their harps seemed incongruous with current sentiments. Willows grew profusely and their harps were hung upon their branches. Their captors, the very ones who wasted them, demanded of them a song of Zion. It was not fitting, the Jews averred, to sing the Lord's song in a strange land. The Jewish psalmist asked to lose the skill of his right hand or the ability to speak ever again if love for Jerusalem faded from his reflective mind.

Edomites, descendants of Esau and thus cousins to Israelites, had joined the fierce forces of the Babylonian hordes in crying for Jerusalem's full destruction in 586 B.C. "Rase it, rase it" means destroy it totally, to the very base of its foundations. The psalmist requested that such insensitive actions not be allowed to go unpunished.

Babylon is next addressed. The psalmist describes the feelings of satisfaction the enemies of Babylon would experience at Babylon's desired demise. Even joy will be experienced by the enemy (the Medo-Persians) who would slay their very children. The psalmist is not to be faulted for what is clearly a prophetic declaration of Babylon's sure fall and the feelings that such a fall would create in the Medo-Persians who triggered the fall and capitalized on it to such a profitable extent for the new world power yet to be.

THE SORROWS WHEN NO ONE CARES

Psalm 142, according to the inscription, is a Davidic prayer while he was in the cave. This may have been either the cave of Adullam or that in Engedi as he was fleeing the fierce wrath of enraged Saul. In his plight he cried out, "I looked on my right hand, and beheld, but there was no man that would know me: refuge failed me; no man cared for my soul" (142:4). It was a forlorn day to David when all aid evidently evaporated and when no one seemed to care whether he lived or died. Human refuge failed him; no man appeared who cared for his life. Yet he had higher help—a nobler refuge. Hence, in the subsequent verse he stated, "I cried unto thee, O Lord: I said, Thou art my refuge and my portion in the land of the living" (142:5). The lesson is obvious. Men may forsake and forget us; God never has and never will.

POINTS TO PONDER ABOUT PSALMS OF SORROW

1. The twin sister of sorrow is suffering.
2. Suffering to the saint is what refining is to metals—the dross is burned away and the really valuable ore remains. Real character is built in the crucible of suffering.
3. Into every life must fall some rain. Clear skies and bright sunshine cannot be our lot every day of life. That is just not the kind of world in which we live.
4. Sin entered the world first and as its aftermath brought sighing, suffering and sorrow.
5. Every affliction faced will make us BETTER or BITTER.
6. There will never be a time but what God cares for our souls whether men do or do not.

DISCUSSION QUESTIONS

1. *Just how rich a book is Psalms in treating the topic of sorrow?*
2. *Read and discuss the selections from Psalms that touch sorrows caused by enemies.*
3. *Discuss the selected verses and observations that touch sorrows caused by personal sins and sicknesses.*
4. *In what ways was sorrow, like sin, ever before David?*
5. *Discuss penitent sorrow for sin.*
6. *Discuss sorrows in afflictions.*
7. *Read and discuss briefly Psalm 137.*
8. *Why should we not allow blatant atheists and scoffing infidels to get by with their argument based on the imprecatory psalms?*
9. *Discuss the sorrow when no one seemingly cares for our souls.*
10. *Read and discuss the Points to Ponder about Sorrow in the Psalms.*

MULTIPLE CHOICE: Underline correct answer

1. (A) Jesus Christ; (B) David; (C) Job; (D) Paul—is referred to in the Bible as the "man of sorrows."

2. (A) Abraham; (B) Samuel; (C) Daniel; (D) David—is called "the man after God's own heart."

3. Saul's latter attitude toward David was that of: (A) hunter for one considered to be an incorrigible outlaw, a hardened criminal; (B) beloved and respected son-in-law; (C) his personal choice to be the next king; (D) total indifference and an ignoring of him regardless of what David did.

4. "My sin is ever before me" is a statement made by: (A) David; (B) Uriah the Hittite; (C) Bath-sheba; (D) Nathan, the prophet.

5. Psalm 137 treats Israel while in captivity to the: (A) Babylonians; (B) Assyrians; (C) Syrians; (D) Egyptians.

SCRIPTURAL FILL-IN: Only one word is required in each blank.

(1) "For I have heard the _____ of _____: _____ was on _____ side: while they took _____ together _____ me, they _____ to _____ away my _____."

(2) "For I am _____ to _____, and my _____ ____ is _____ before _____."

(3) "For _____ will _____ mine _____; I will be _____ for my _____."

(4) "_____ me _____, O _____: O my _____, be not _____ from _____. Make _____ to _____ me, O Lord my _____."

(5) "_____ the _____ of _____, there we _____ down, yea, we _____, when we _____ Zion."

(6) "I _____ on my right _____, and _____, but there was no _____ that would _____ me: _____ failed _____; no _____ cared for my _____."

TRUE OR FALSE: Put either a "T" or "F" in the blanks

____1. God had only one Son without sin, the Christ, but no Son without sorrow.

____2. Sins continue to pay in CONSEQUENCES long after guilt has been removed by God's pardon.

____3. God will save men regardless of whether they are PROUD of their sins or PENITENT of their sins.

____4. Edom was very sympathetic toward besieged Judah when the Babylonians captured her.

____5. Babylon would never have to pay for her sins.

THOUGHT QUESTIONS

1. Just how widespread is sorrow and list several things that produce sorrow of soul to human personalities?

2. Treat some of the basic differences between the GUILT of sin and the CONSEQUENCES of sin.

3. Distinguish between the sorrow of the world and godly sorrow and give some Biblical examples of each type.

4. Tell of places today where it would be highly inappropriate to sing the songs of Spiritual Israel.

5. In what ways may the Lord's church today show people that we really care for souls?

CHAPTER TWENTY-FIVE

PSALMS: A BOOK OF VICTORIOUS LIVING

Humanity is so constituted that victory is always preferred over defeat. This is positively true in the realm of sports. Not too many avid sports' enthusiasts share the old Grantland Rice ideal that it matters not so much WHO won the game as to HOW it was played. Fired coaches who failed to produce consistent winners can attest to that on a thousand coaching fronts. Military history has stressed victory over defeat as the accepted norm of battlefront success. Only recently have armies been sent forth with a no-win battle strategy back of them and this has been an enigma to many military geniuses. With almost no exceptions we all like to win a victory over a bout of sickness or in the conquering of a disease. All these victories are short-lived at the most and will matter but little in death, judgment and eternity. The Bible speaks of a victory that matters for both time and eternity. John spoke of that when he wrote, "For whatsoever is born of God overcometh the world: and this is the victory that overcometh the world, even our faith. Who is he that overcometh the world, but he that believeth that Jesus is the Son of God?" (1 John 5:4,5). Psalms is a great book on victorious living. Before beginning the writing of this chapter, I gave the entire book a careful reading and noted some thirty passages that stress some nine indispensable ingredients for victorious living in the spiritual realm. This chapter can be a real faith builder for all of us.

THE VICTORIOUS LIFE OF PERSONAL RIGHTEOUSNESS AND GODLINESS

Logically and rightly this should head our list for minus a righteous and godly life no man can be successful in victorious living. That should call for neither question nor quibble. It is just that self-evident. Eight carefully selected passages provide eloquent emphasis to this. These will be noted first and appropriate observations relative to them will follow.

> For I have kept the ways of the Lord, and have not wickedly departed from my God (18:21). Who shall ascend into the hill of the Lord? or who shall stand in his holy place? He that hath clean hands, and a pure heart; who hath not lifted up his soul unto vanity, nor sworn deceitfully. He shall receive the blessing from the Lord, and righteousness from the God of his salvation (24:3-5). But as for me, I will walk in mine integrity: redeem me, and be merciful unto me (26:11). What man is he that desireth life, and loveth many days, that he may see good? Keep thy tongue from evil, and thy lips from speaking guile. Depart from evil, and do good; seek peace, and pursue it. The eyes of the Lord are upon the righteous, and his ears are open unto their cry. The face of the Lord is against them that do evil, to cut off remembrance of them from the earth (34:12-16). Mark the perfect man, and behold the upright: for the end of that man is peace (37:37) I said, I will take heed to my ways, that I sin not with my tongue: I will keep my mouth with a bridle, while the wicked is before me (39:1). A good man sheweth favour, and lendeth: he will guide his affairs with discretion (112:5). Set a watch, O Lord, before my mouth; keep the door of my lips. Incline not my heart to any evil thing, to practice wicked works with men that work iniquity: and let me not eat of their dainties (141:3,4).

These observations are easily discernible from these great gems of truth just presented. (1) Positively, God's ways have been kept; negatively, there has been no wicked departure from Jehovah. (2) The approved man both for now and for eternity is clean of hand, pure of heart, humble in attitude, a keeper of his word and one who receives blessings and righteousness from the God who saves. This passage in Psalm 24 is strikingly similar to Psalm 15. Both are Davidic in composition. (3) Integrity is the chosen walk for the man who wishes to be blessed with redemption and mercy. (4) The lover of life and good days keeps a guard on his words lest he speak evil, departs evil, practices the good, seeks peace, pursues it, is conscious that Jehovah's eyes are upon him and that God's ear is ever open to his prayerful entreaties. He knows how opposed the Lord is to doers of evil. (5) Peace, real peace, comes to the perfect man (the righteous individual), the man who is upright in language and life. (6) The righteous, godly man keeps careful watch over all spoken words. (7) The righteous, godly man is a benefactor to others and conducts his own business with good judgment, with proper prudence. (8) The righteous, godly man realizes the power of prayer in God's aiding him to speak as he should speak, to keep his heart right, to avoid all companionships with workers of evil and not to have fellowship over food with them.

THE VICTORIOUS LIFE OF PATIENCE AND COURAGE

Both of these intense imperatives of the soul are given special prominence in the book of Psalms. A trio of selections from Psalms is now presented with appropriate observations to follow. They are,

> I had fainted, unless I had believed to see the goodness of the Lord in the land of the living. Wait on the Lord: be of good courage, and he shall strengthen thine heart: wait, I say, on the Lord (27:13,14). Be of good courage, and he shall strengthen your heart, all ye that hope in the Lord (31:24). Rest in the Lord, and wait patiently for him: fret not thyself because of him who prospereth in his way, because of the man who bringeth wicked devices to pass. Cease from anger, and forsake wrath: fret not thyself in any wise to do evil (37:7,8).

This quartet of observations occurs. (1) Jehovah is a God of patience. (2) Man is filled with impatience. (3) Those who learn to wait on the Lord within a framework of courage will ultimately be blessed beautifully and rewarded richly. (4) This type of patience and courage will not allow us to fret due to an evil man's apparent prosperity instead of punishment that justice should be inflicting and will keep us from the anger and wrath that might develop when evildoers are not put down as soon as we think they should be. Our vision is calmer and more prudent if the spiritual optic nerve is infused with patient courage and an undying conviction that ultimately right will be rewarded and evil will be exposed and properly punished.

THE VICTORIOUS LIFE OF GRATITUDE

The ingrate will NEVER know victorious living. Only the truly appreciative can attain such. The victorious psalmist wrote, "To the end that my glory may sing praise to thee, and not be silent. O Lord my God, I will give thanks unto thee for ever" (30:12). Psalm 97:12 states, "Rejoice in the Lord, ye righteous; and give thanks at the remembrance of his holiness." Gratitude should be persistent and regular in our lives. Each remembrance of God's holiness and goodness should trigger fresh gratitude in our hearts for God. Gratitude should be both vertical and horizontal—vertical or UP to God; horizontal or OUT to human benefactors. Thank-you is still one of the best bridge builders between us and other people. "I thank thee" should be a daily part of our prayers to Him from whom all good and perfect gifts flow so freely, so generously, so lavishly, so lovingly. He who really THINKS is going to be THANKful.

THE VICTORIOUS BLESSING OF PARDON

A one-line summary of Psalm 32 is the "Blessedness of him whose sins are forgiven." The two initial verses state, "Blessed is he whose transgression is forgiven, whose sin is covered. Blessed is the man unto whom the Lord imputeth not iniquity, and in whose spirit there is no guile" (32:1,2). Here we have precious parallelism. The expression "whose transgression is forgiven" is the same as its synonymous follow-up—"whose sin is covered." There is a wrong way to cover sin. David tried this route at first in the Uriah-Bath-sheba incident by seeking to deceive, to pass off the paternity of the child conceived out of wedlock and in infamous adultery. That failed to work. Such never has, does not now and never will!! Then David resorted to murder and making Bath-sheba his wife before the baby was born. That did not cover his crimson crimes. It only aggravated his atrocious acts; it only compounded his crimson crimes. Finally, he covered his crimson crimes correctly. Then he came to know the precious pardon or the removal of his great guilt. Then he came to know precious peace with God again. Then he came to realize the great blessing that ardently accrues to the one toward whom the Lord does not charge sin or iniquity. For us today God has a first law of pardon. Sins are pardoned upon hearing, faith, repentance, confession of Christ's Deity and baptism (immersion) in water for remission of sins (Romans 10:17; Hebrews 11:6; Luke 13:3; Matthew 10:32; Acts 2:38). His second law of pardon for His erring children requires confession, repentance and prayer (Acts 8:22; James 5:16; 1 John 1:9). People who never know God's pardon of their sins are lonely, burdened and condemned strangers to real victorious living.

THE VICTORIOUS BLESSING OF HEAVENLY HELP

Five selected passages say it so wisely and so well. They are,

The angel of the Lord encampeth round about them that fear him, and delivereth them (34:7). Delight thyself also in the Lord; and he shall give thee the desires of thine heart (37:4). I have

226

been young, and now am old; yet have I not seen the righteous forsaken, nor his seed begging bread (37:25). Blessed is he that considereth the poor: the Lord will deliver him in time of trouble. The Lord will preserve him, and keep him alive; and he shall be blessed upon the earth: and thou wilt not deliver him unto the will of his enemies (41:1,2). O God, thou hast taught me from my youth: and hitherto have I declared thy wondrous works (71:17).

We glean these precious lessons from the foregoing scriptures. (1) The Lord is near to protect and deliver those who fear him. (2) Those who delight in the Lord shall be given the desires of their heart, provided of course, that they harmonize with heaven's will. (3) In a lifetime of close observation from youth through advancing years the psalmist had never seen the righteous forsaken nor their descendants begging bread. Adam Clarke and Albert Barnes, outstanding Bible commentators, both wrote commentaries on the book of Psalms. They were both in advancing years when they penned comments on Psalm 37:25 and they said their long time observation was the same as the pslamist herein noted. (4) Those who are kind and benevolent to others will have in the Lord a preserver, a keeper, a gracious benefactor and a protector against their enemies. (5) The psalmist was grateful that God had been his instructor from youth on up. How vital therefore that youth be taught of and about God. There is NO substitute for this!!

THE VICTORIOUS BLESSING OF BEING IN THE LORD'S HOUSE

The house of the Lord on earth to Old Testament personalities was the temporary tabernacle at first and later the permanent temple. Seven selected passages speak of the pious man's connection with God's house. They are:

But I am like a green olive tree in the house of God: I trust in the mercy of God for ever and ever (52:8). Blessed is the man whom thou choosest, and causest to approach unto thee, that he may dwell in thy courts: we shall be satisfied with the goodness of thy house, even of thy holy temple (65:4). I will go into thy house with burnt offerings: I will pay thee my vows, Which my lips have uttered, and my mouth hath spoken, when I was in trouble (66:13,14). Until I went into the sanctuary of God; then understood I their end (73:17). Blessed are they that dwell in thy house: they will still be praising thee. Blessed is the man whose strength is in thee; in whose heart are the ways of them (84:4,5). The righteous shall flourish like the palm tree: he shall grow like a cedar in Lebanon. Those that be planted in the house of the Lord shall flourish in the courts of our God. They shall still bring forth fruit in old age; they shall be fat and flourishing (92:12-14). I was glad when they said unto me, Let us go into the house of the Lord (122:1).

From these seven stately selections we glean some precious sentiments. (1) Being like a green olive tree in the Lord's house is suggestive of life, safety, prosperity, cultivation of fruitfulness. (2) It is a great blessing to be chosen of the Lord to come near Deity in God's house and experience the Lord's goodness in such a hallowed location. (3) Promises made to worship and serve God while in trouble will be translated faithfully into grateful realities of vows paid and burnt offerings made in God's house. (4) Some things can only be learned by a nearness to God which can never be learned at a distance from Him. (5) There is a beautiful blessing bequeathed to the dwellers in God's house, the ones who praise Him in such a surrounding, the ones who derive strength from the Lord and the ones in whose hearts are the ways of worshipping and serving God in faithful fashion. (6) Devout souls planted in God's house flourish and bear fruit from youth through old age. (7) Gladness should ever be produced when we are invited to go into the Lord's house.

The Lord's house today is the church of Christ and great is our honor to be in the same as worshippers, as servers.

THE VICTORIOUS JOY OF BELONGING TO AND BEING IN THE LORD

God has made man and man will never find his real place until he finds it in the Lord. Three stately selections lend eloquent emphasis to belonging in the Lord, to being in an intimate spiritual relationship with Him. They are:

My meditation of him shall be sweet: I will be glad in the Lord (104:34). Happy is that people, that is in such a case; yea, happy is that people, whose God is the Lord (144:15). Happy is he that hath the God of Jacob for his help, whose hope is in the Lord his God (146:5).

To belong to the Lord is sweetness experienced; it is gladness received; it is happiness achieved; it is hope in concrete prospect.

THE VICTORIOUS BLESSING OF KNOWING
OUR ORIGIN

Many of the psalms speak of God as our Creator and Maker. None does it more beautifully than Psalm 100:3 which states so sublimely, "Know ye that the Lord he is God: it is he that hath made us, and not we ourselves; we are his people, and the sheep of his pasture." This one passage is worth more than all evolutionary pronouncements combined as touching the HOW of our origin. One looks in vain into Darwin, Huxley, Simpson, Flew, Matson, Barnhart, Sagan and all other organic evolutionists for a peer to the psalmist and this one inspired statement in Psalm 100:3. We are creatures of the Sublime (creationist view) and not of slime (the evolutionary view).

THE VICTORIOUS BLESSING OF SAGE AND SOUND
WARNINGS

Like other great books of the Bible Psalms has its weighty warnings also. Psalm 62:10 is a sample of so many more that could be presented but space will not allow. It reads, "Trust not in oppression, and become not vain in robbery: if riches increase, set not your heart upon them." Very solemn warnings in Holy Writ are given to be heeded. Wise is man when he views every warning of Sacred Scripture as a flashing red light!

CONCLUSION

Psalms is truly a book filled with precious principles that help insure victorious living for all eager and willing students.

POINTS TO PONDER ABOUT VICTORIOUS LIVING IN
THE PSALMS

1. Victory comes to the man who lines *up* with God—not *against* Him.
2. There is never any real victory when we surrender to Satan and sin.
3. Victory is not found in giving in to the lusts of the flesh, the eyes and life's pride.
4. Victory is found in a life of sobriety, righteousness and godliness.
5. Victorious living would do much to help the poor mental health in which depression, strain and tension seek to drown people.
6. Heaven at last is the ultimate of our greatest victory.

DISCUSSION QUESTIONS

1. Discuss just how interested humanity is in victory in a number of different realms.

2. Read and discuss briefly the eight selected passages in Psalms that touch victorious living of personal righteousness and godliness.

3. Read and discuss the trio of selected passages in Psalms that treats a victorious life of patience and courage.

4. Read and discuss the two selected passages in Psalms that touch gratitude.

5. Read and discuss the selected passages in Psalms that depict the victorious blessing of pardon.

6. Read and discuss the five selected passages in Psalms that touch and treat the victorious blessing of heavenly help.

7. What is said both in the selected Psalms and the observations relative to victorious blessings of being in the Lord's house?

8. What is God's house today and what should be our attitudes and actions relative to it?

9. Discuss the victorious blessing of knowing our origin.

10. Why do we need warnings in the Bible?

11. Read and discuss The Points To Ponder about victorious living in the Psalms.

MULTIPLE CHOICE: Underline correct answer

1. Relative to victory humanity, almost without exception, is: *(A) eager and enthusiastic to attain it; (B) seldom ever interested in its achievement; (C) totally oblivious to it in any and all fashion; (D) more inclined to prefer defeat in all known realms.*

2. Psalm 15 and 24 have in common their: *(A) Davidic; (B) Mosaic; (C) Pauline; (D) Petrine—composition.*

3. Psalm 32 covers the tremendous topic of: *(A) God's creation; (B) God's pardon; (C) God's wrath upon stubborn Israel in the wilderness; (D) sorrows in Babylonian Exile.*

4. In the Bath-sheba-Uriah incident: *(A) Solomon; (B) Asaph; (C) David; (D) the sons of Korah—sought at first to cover the wrong unacceptably but later did it acceptably.*

5. Under Christianity God has: *(A) a multiplicity of laws that lead to pardon; (B) no law of pardon; (C) left it up to each individual to choose his own preferred law of pardon; (D) two laws of pardon—one for aliens and one for His erring children.*

SCRIPTURAL FILL-IN: Only one word is required in each blank.

(1) "For _____ is _____ of _____ _____ the _____: and this is the _____ that

230

_____ the _____, even our _____. Who is he that _____ the _____ but he that _____ that _____ is the _____ of _____?"

(2) "But as for _____, I will _____ in mine _____: _____ me, and be _____ unto _____."

(3) "_____ on the _____: be of good _____, and he shall _____ thine _____: _____, I _____, on the _____."

(4) "I have been _____, and _____ am _____: yet have I not _____ the _____ _____, nor his _____ begging _____."

(5) "I was _____ when _____ said unto _____, Let _____ go into the _____ of the _____."

TRUE OR FALSE: Put either a "T" or "F" in the blanks

____1. Relative to a victorious life in righteousness and godliness man is totally passive and God alone is active.

____2. Genuine gratitude is an intense imperative to real victorious living.

____3. "Faith only is a most wholesome doctrine and very full of comfort" is God's law of pardon for every alien in the Christian Dispensation.

____4. There is really no essentiality of being taught of and about God in one's youth.

____5. The psalmist who wrote Psalm 100 was a thoroughgoing creationist as touching origins.

THOUGHT QUESTIONS

1. Tell why an unrighteous, ungodly man can never experience any REAL victories in spirituality.

2. Discuss why gratitude is such a lovely trait and ingratitude is such an ugly attribute.

3. Discuss how an alien is pardoned of his sins under Christianity according to the Bible and give scriptures for each condition or commandment.

4. Do the same for an erring child of God under the Christian Dispensation and supply appropriate scriptures.

5. Why do you think there is such an abundance of error taught relative to pardon in our day?

6. Does Psalm 34:7 teach that every person has a "guardian angel" that protects him from any and all danger? Why or why not?

7. Why can evolution as touching origins never lead to any type of victorious living?

CHAPTER TWENTY-SIX

LIVING LESSONS LEARNED FROM PSALMS

Paul makes it crystal clear that one of the prime purposes for studying Old Testament Scripture is to learn lessons helpful to Christians. He wrote, "For whatsoever things were written aforetime were written for our learning, that we through patience and comfort of the scriptures might have hope" (Romans 15:4). It seems appropriate that our final chapter on Psalms should set forth some living lessons learned, some powerful points to ponder the rest of our days on earth as a result of this study. Ten living lessons will be listed and briefly discussed. Brief quotes will be given from the book of Psalms to undergird each point projected.

(1) THERE IS A GOD IN HEAVEN

Brother Otis Gatewood has written a very valuable book that bears this very title. Thirty or more centuries earlier various of the psalmists wrote of the God who resides in high and holy heaven. David classed as fools those who deny there was/is a God in heaven (14:1; 53:1). They knew that "The heavens declare the glory of God; and the firmament sheweth his handywork" (19:1). It is impressive to witness how many of the psalms begin with God in the initial verse and close with Him in the final verse. Psalm 8 does this in marvelous fashion. So does Psalm 46 which begins by affirming, "God is our refuge and strength, a very present help in trouble" (46:1). Twice He is mentioned in verse 11, the final verse of Psalm 46. They knew He existed; they knew His character; they knew He heard and heeded their prayerful petitions; they knew He had a purpose for their lives; they knew that in Him they had a friend even when all earthly brethren or friends forsook them. "There is a

God in heaven" is a golden thread intensely interwoven throughout the fabric of Psalms.

(2) THE PSALMISTS HAD REMARKABLE RESPECT FOR GOD'S WORD

This is seen negatively in what they did not say about God's word. They never said it was humanly-derived or just the word of men. They never said it was a dead letter. They never said it is filled with myths, legends or folklore. They never said it has jarring clashes and upsetting disharmonies. They never said one can prove anything he wanted to by God's word. They never said it was archaic, outmoded or obsolete. They never said we need a new revelation to take the place of what had already been given humanity by the God of heaven. They never said we need something different than what we have as God's word. Negatively, their nobility toward the Bible is attractive and admirable.

Positively, their remarkable respect for God's word stands high and mighty. They said it was pure (12:6; 119:140). They affirmed its amazing accuracy or its being right (33:4; 119:128). They declared the law and the commandments of the Lord to be truth (119:142,151). Their hearts stood in admirable awe of God's word of weight and wisdom (119:161). They knew His word had been true from the beginning (119:160). They loved the commandments of the Lord "above gold; yea, above fine gold" (119:127). They knew God's word to be a lamp for man's feet and a light for his path (119:105).

If all in our day felt towards God's word as did the psalmists of antiquity, we would have none who add to, take from or modify God's word in any way. We would have no creed concocters, no discipline designers and no manual manufacturers. We would have no modern day perverters who are turning out perverted Bibles faster than we can expose them as spurious books. We would have no apathy, indifference or lukewarmness toward the Grand Old Book. We would just have those who delight in God's word as the psalmist delineated in the preface of the book (1:2). Our infidelic world needs desperately to learn how to respect the Bible as the verbally inspired, all sufficient, totally authoritative and fully infallible word of God.

(3) THE BEAUTIFUL HARMONY BETWEEN THE OLD AND NEW TESTAMENTS

Together they form God's Divine Library. They complement each other. The Old Testament is the New Testament concealed; the New Testament is the Old Testament revealed. The precious psalms add a lovely link to the holy harmony of the two major testaments. Jesus knew that and referred to the fundamental fact that the psalms, as well as the Mosaic law and the Hebrew prophets, had spoken of Him (Luke 24:44). He and the apostles frequently quoted from the book of Psalms. He quoted Psalm 82:6 in John 10:34 and called what he quoted "your law." He was addressing a Jewish audience. He quoted Psalm 110:1 in a great argument that touched His being David's Lord (his Deity) as well as being David's Son (Matthew 22:41-46). "My God, my God, why hast thou forsaken me?" is one of the seven sayings of Christ on Calvary and is a quote of Psalm 22:1. The apostles later followed their Lord's example and employed Psalms in their preaching and writings. In Acts 2 Peter quotes from David in Psalm 16. In the prayer that the afflicted apostles prayed in Acts 4:24-30 they quoted from the second psalm. Paul quotes from this same source and says he is quoting the second psalm (Acts 13:33). In speaking of Christ's bestowment of spiritual or supernatural gifts in Ephesians 4 Paul has his inspired eyes riveted on Psalm 68:18. The book of Psalms presents a great sermon on the striking harmony between the Old and New Testaments.

(4) THERE IS PREDICTIVE PROPHECY IN THE OLD TESTAMENT

It has often been stated by knowledgeable Bible students that there are three hundred plus prophecies in the Old Testament that center upon the Mighty Messiah. Many of these are found in the book of Psalms. Some of these have been mentioned in the preceding section. Three or four additional ones are presented now. In the great Upper Room Discourse to the faithful eleven Jesus said in John 15:25, "They hated me without a cause." He had Psalm 35:19 and 69:4 in mind as He phrased these words. Psalm 45:6, at least in a reliable Bible that has not tampered with the Hebrew text in the English rendering as the RSV did, finds fulfillment in Hebrews 1:8,9. Psalm 22:18 suggests what the executioners would do with the Lord's very garment and even His vesture or seamless coat. Fulfillment is recorded by the apostle of love in John 19:23,24. The fulfillment is a minute one. Modernism is grievously and glaringly mistaken in its blatant denial that the Old Testament in general and Psalms in particular are minus any and all predictive prophecies. Of course modernists reject predictive prophecies because they are miraculous or supernatural in origin and nature and modernism rejects any and all miracles lock, stock and barrel. There is an abundance of such and Psalms is not deficient in the least in this regal regard.

(5) PIOUS POVERTY PREFERRED OVER WICKED WEALTH

The entire tenor of Holy Writ underscores this point but no passage does it better, more forcefully or more concisely than Psalm 37:16 wherein we read, "A little that a righteous man hath is better than the riches of many wicked." This is a comparison or really a contrast that the world has never been able to see or willing to accept. It takes a man with a righteous or pious eye to see it and a man with a spiritual heart to accept it. Jesus gives complete confirmation of it in the narrative that touches Lazarus, the righteous beggar, and the banqueting Dives (Latin for riches) in Luke 16:19-31. The rich young ruler, had he been less rich and not so trustful of his vast wealth, might have become a Paul, Peter, Timothy or Titus in the Messianic Kingdom of the first century (Matthew 19:16-22). However, as the final curtain fell on him his back was to the Master and his face was in the definite direction of his great earthly possessions back home—back where his heart really was ALL the time. The magnet of money proved greater than the magnet of the Messiah or the eternal life of which he came initially in quest. Righteousness with a little is far, FAR better than wealth in the framework of wickedness.

(6) GREAT BREVITY OF LIFE

Many Biblical writers touched this sobering theme. Job does in Job 14:1,2 and 16:22. Isaiah writes of it in Isaiah 38:12. James touches this theme in James 4:13-16. David does so graphically in Psalm 39:5 wherein we read, "Behold, thou hast made my days as an hand-breadth; and mine age is as nothing before thee: verily every man at his best state is altogether vanity." This is the spread of the hand when extended. It is one of the shortest of all natural measurements. It is smaller than the length of the foot and much smaller than the cubit or from the elbow to the tip of one's finger. It refers to something very, very short. We are indeed RAPID travelers upon the road from cradle to cemetery. In Psalm 90 Moses spoke of the sobering realization that men are "soon cut off, and we fly away" (90:10). Whatever good we plan to do in honoring God, serving man and saving an imperishable soul must be done soon for temporary is our pilgrimage here. Short indeed is our stay on earth but eternity in heaven or hell is forever. Is fleshly indulgence for short time on earth really worth an eternity of suffering and sighing, of weeping and wailing in hell? The serious mind of sobriety answers with an emphatic and prompt negative.

236

(7) PROPER CONTENT OF ACCEPTABLE PREACHING

Psalms is a great book of preaching gems. The content of all acceptable preaching is underlined and underscored in these words of weight and wisdom, "I have preached righteousness in the great congregation: lo, I have not refrained my lips, O Lord, thou knowest. I have not hid thy righteousness within my heart; I have declared thy faithfulness and thy salvation: I have not concealed thy lovingkindness and thy truth from the great congregation" (40:9,10). Coming immediately after a passage that is decisively Messianic in its noble nature (40:6-8; Cf. Hebrews 10:5-9), it seems eminently safe that verses 9 and 10 are likewise Messianic in scope also. They fit David's Son more than they do David. Barnes and Clarke were of this same persuasion. Every one of these fits the Christ and also the apostles who patterned their preaching after His type of powerful proclamation. Note what is affirmed by way of predictive prophecy and in its precise fulfillment under Jesus Christ and His apostles. (1) Righteousness (right-doing or obeying God's plan for making people righteous) has been preached. (2) It has been preached to the great congregation. In the New Testament fulfillment of this the Jews heard it initially and the Gentiles next. (3) There has been no refraining of lips as touching what ought to have been said. (4) Jehovah knew the perfect type of preaching His Son would do and later did do. (5) God's righteousness had been HERALDED ABROAD—not HIDDEN INTERNALLY. (6) Jehovah's faithfulness had been proclaimed in all its pristine purity. (7) God's plan for saving men has been completely conveyed. (8) The lovingkindness of God has not been hidden; it has been set forth and held high indeed. (9) No truth has been withheld from the great congregation. My friend, here is preaching content in beautiful balance—approached and appropriated both positively and negatively. This is the type of preaching Paul did at Ephesus and other places and with such power and effectiveness (Acts 20:20,26,27,32,35; 1 Corinthians 2:2; 2 Corinthians 4:5).

(8) RIGHTEOUSNESS: THE ROYAL ROUTE TO HIGHER LIVING

Righteousness must be preached as was underscored in the preeceeding section. It also must be lived. Psalm 15:2 affirms that the person who would abide in the Lord's tabernacle and dwell in His holy hill is "He that walketh uprightly, and worketh righteousness, and speaketh the truth in his heart." The remainder of this pithy chapter describes an upright walk and a righteousness that works (15:3-5).

237

There is only one way we can really be righteous and press toward the peaks of higher and higher living and that is by commandment keeping. All God's commands are righteousness (119:172). Righteousness is something we work and do (Acts 10:35; 1 John 2:29; 3:7).

(9) SIN ALWAYS LEADS TO MISERY, HEARTACHE AND DAMNATION

David knew sin has a payday of pain, a stipend of sorrow, a wage of weighty punishment. He wrote of such in Psalm 51. The misery and heartache resulting from sin are treated in Psalm 38. Israelite hearts ached and ached greatly in the sorrows of the exiled people in Babylon. Psalm 137 speaks of this. Damnation for sin is the bottom line of Psalm 9:17.

(10) GOD IS MAN'S COMFORT IN SORROWS

Like a golden thread this runs throughout the Book of Psalms. It is seen especially near the end of chapters when the psalmist pours out his problems and stresses his sorrows only to conclude that God was his stalwart stay and holy helper. An example of this is observed in the final verse of Psalm 54 which reads, "For he hath delivered me out of all trouble: and mine eye hath seen his desire upon mine enemies" (v-7). In 2 Corinthians 1:3 Paul referred to God as "the Father of mercies, and the God of all comfort."

A CLOSING PRAYER

Heavenly Father, we thank Thee for the multitude of Thy mercies and the loyalty of Thy love exhibited to us. We thank Thee for Thy inspired, infallible, authoritative and all-sufficient word in general and the beautiful book of Psalms in particular. We thank Thee for the information it supplies, the comfort it confers, the warnings unfolded therein and the spiritual strength it provides. We thank Thee that it has been our esteemed privilege to engage in this study. Bless us all that we might profit greatly from this study. In the name of Christ, we pray, Amen.

POINTS TO PONDER RELATIVE TO LIVING LESSONS FROM PSALMS

1. One righteous man allied to God really has nothing of real danger to fear from any and all sources of enmity or wrong.
2. Prayer can move the hand of Him who moves the universe.

3. Atheism, agnosticism and modernism are all refuted thoroughly in the beautiful book of precious Psalms.
4. There is a bright and beautiful balance to the book of Psalms. It is not all positive; it is not all negative.
5. Phraseology from Psalms can add many scriptural sentiments to our prayer vocabulary.
6. Psalms is a book for all seasons—for the spring of youth, for the summer and autumn of active adulthood and for the winter of advanced age as the end of life approaches with the loosing of the silver cord and the breaking of the golden bowl (Cf. Ecclesiastes 12:1-7).

DISCUSSION QUESTIONS

1. *What did the Psalmists have to say about there being a God in heaven?*
2. *List and discuss some of the things the psalmists NEVER said relative to God's word.*
3. *On the positive side of the ledger what did the psalmists say that reflected real reverence and deep regard for God's word?*
4. *Discuss what is said about the holy harmony between the Old and New Testaments.*
5. *How did Jesus use the Old Testament in His teaching while engaged in His personal ministry?*
6. *How did the apostolic preachers of the New Testament use the book of Psalms in their preaching and writing?*
7. *Look up, read and discuss what Job, Isaiah, James and Moses wrote relative to the brevity of life.*
8. *What does the book of Psalms say relative to the proper content of acceptable preaching?*
9. *Give the nine observations that are listed and discuss these in some detail.*
10. *Read and discuss the Points To Ponder On Living Lessons Learned From Psalms.*

MULTIPLE-CHOICE: Underline correct answer

1. *Those who love the Bible and are totally loyal to it believe that it is: (A) God's verbally inspired, all-sufficient, fully authoritative and enitrely infallible word; (B) filled with myths, legends and folklore; (C) filled with jarring clashes and upsetting disharmonies; (D) nothing but a human record of man's futile search for an elusive object he calls God.*
2. *"My God, my God, why hast thou forsaken me?" is: (A) not found in the Bible; (B) found only in the Old Testament; (C) found only in the New Testament; (D) found in both the Old and New Testaments.*

3. The RSV: (A) had great respect for Psalm 45:6; (B) omitted all of Psalm 45:6 from its rendering; (C) has Psalm 45:6 to read basically the same as the KJV and the ASV renderings have of it; (D) has Psalm 45:6 in perfect harmony with Hebrews 1:8,9; (E) tampered seriously and fatally with Psalm 45:6.

4. The bottom line of Psalm 9:17 is: (A) total annihilation of all humans at death; (B) universal salvation ultimately for all; (C) no punishment for the wicked in yonder's world; (D) the fact that hell is real for all the wicked.

5. (A) David; (B) Moses; (C) Solomon; (D) Hezekiah—wrote of the sorrows linked with sin, its punishment and consequences in Psalm 51.

SCRIPTURAL FILL-IN: Only one word is required in each blank.

(1) "The _____ declare the _____ of _____; and the _____ sheweth his _____."

(2) "They _____ me _____ a _____."

(3) "A _____ that a _____ man hath is _____ than the _____ of many _____."

(4) "He that _____ _____, and _____ _____, and _____ the _____ in his _____."

(5) "For _____ hath _____ me out of all _____; and mine _____ hath _____ his _____ upon mine _____."

TRUE OR FALSE: Put either a "T" or "F" in the blanks

_____1. Paul stated there was little or no value in a study of Old Testament Scripture.

_____2. One would be hard pressed indeed to find as much as one predictive prophecy in the Old Testament pertaining to Jesus Christ.

_____3. Righteousness is the right doing of God's plan which makes of us a people of righteousness.

_____4. Commandment keeping of God's law has not one single, solitary thing to do with one's attainment of righteousness.

_____5. No true comfort and lasting consolation can be found in Satan and sin.

THOUGHT QUESTIONS

1. How does Romans 15:4 tie in with a study of Psalms?

2. *How does modernism feel about predictive prophecy in the Old Testament and why do modernists feel this way?*

3. *How do the rich young ruler and the rich man of Luke 16:19-31 exhibit the clear dangers of riches in their lives?*

4. *Why is sin always an ally of misery, heartache and damnation?*

5. *Read 2 Corinthians 1:3 and discuss God Almighty as "the Father of mercies, and the God of all comfort."*